CU00843164

MULTINATIONAL NAVAL COOPERATION AND FOREIGN POLICY INTO THE 21ST CENTURY

INTERNATIONAL NAVAL COOPERATION

Multinational Naval Cooperation and Foreign Policy into the 21st Century

Edited by
FRED W. CRICKARD
PAUL T. MITCHELL and
KATHERINE ORR
Centre for Foreign Policy Studies, Dalhousie University

Ashgate

Aldershot • Brookfield USA • Singapore • Sydney

© Fred W. Crickard, Paul T. Mitchell, Katherine Orr 1998

All rights reserved. No part of this publication may be reproduced, stored in a retrieval system, or transmitted in any form or by any means, electronic, mechanical, photocopying, recording, or otherwise without the prior permission of the publisher.

Published by
Ashgate Publishing Limited
Gower House
Croft Road
Aldershot
Hants GU11 3HR
England

Ashgate Publishing Company
Old Post Road
Brookfield
Vermont 05036
USA

British Library Cataloguing in Publication Data
Multinational naval cooperation and foreign policy into the
    21st century
    1.International cooperation - Congresses 2.Naval strategy -
    International cooperation - Congresses 3.Sea power -
    International cooperation - Congresses
    I.Crickard, Fred W. II.Mitchell, Paul T. III.Orr, Katherine
    327.1'7

Library of Congress Cataloging-in-Publication Data
Multinational naval cooperation and foreign policy into the 21st
    century / edited by Fred W. Crickard, Paul T. Mitchell, and
    Katherine Orr.
        p.   cm.
    Papers from a conference held in Halifax, N.S., in May 1996.
    Includes bibliographical references and index.
    ISBN 1-85521-997-2
    1. Navies–International cooperation–Congresses. 2. Sea-power-
    -Congresses. 3. Security, International–Congresses. I. Crickard,
    F.W. II. Mitchell, Paul T. III. Orr, Katherine.
    VA40.M85   1998
    359'.03–dc21   97-50012
                                                                        CIP
ISBN 1 85521 997 2

Printed in Great Britain by The Ipswich Book Company, Suffolk

Contents

List of Figures

List of Maps

List of Tables

List of Contributors

Dr. Lewis M. Alexander is Professor Emeritus of Marine Affairs at the University of Rhode Island. He founded the Department of Marine Affairs at the University, as well as the Law of the Sea Institute which is now located in Hawaii. He was a member of the US delegation to the Third UN Law of the Sea Conference, and served for a number of years as the Geographer of the US State Department. He has been called upon several times as an expert on international maritime boundaries, and has written extensively on this and other law of the sea issues. Some of Dr. Alexander's publications include: (ed.) *The Law of the Sea: United Nations and Ocean Management*, University of Rhode Island, Law of the Sea Institute, 1971; (ed.) *International Maritime Boundaries*, with John Charney, Martinus Nijhoff, 1993. He is a member of the Editorial Boards of *Marine Policy*, *Ocean Management*, *Ocean Development* and *International Law Journal*.

Dr. Jan S. Breemer is Associate Professor of National Security Affairs at the Naval Postgraduate School in Monterey, California. He has published frequently on maritime security issues, including his recent contribution, "European Naval Power after the Cold War: Some not so Common Interests and Risks" in *European Naval Power after the Cold War* (Kluwer Law International, 1996).

Daniel Y. Coulter joined the United States Department of the Navy in 1991 and in the five years since has engaged in a wide variety of projects involving maritime trade issues. In the summer of 1995 he was awarded a sabbatical to do research on commercial maritime affairs in London. He has presented and published extensively on maritime affairs. His latest presentation, titled "World Merchant Shipping and Multinationalism Triumphant", was delivered to the Transportation Research Board of the National Research Council in Washington, DC in January 1996. His latest article, "South China Sea Fisheries", was published in *Contemporary Southeast Asia* in April 1996. In addition, his article, "Sea Power in the

21st Century: Asymmetrical to Economic Power", will be published in the US Naval Institute's *Proceedings*.

Rear-Admiral Fred W. Crickard (Ret'd) is a retired career naval officer with the Royal Canadian Navy for 37 years. Since 1987 he has been on the Faculty of Dalhousie University as a full time Research Associate and Senior Research Fellow with the Centre for Foreign Policy Studies. He organizes conferences, publishes and teaches on maritime security and oceans policy. He is the founding editor of the Centre's *Maritime Security Working Papers*, the Naval Officers' Association of Canada's *Niobe Papers* and co-editor of the book *A Nation's Navy: In Quest of a Canadian Naval Identity* (McGill/Queen's University Press, 1996).

Admiral Sir James Eberle (Ret'd) served in the Royal Navy 1944 to 1983, and was the Director of the Royal Institute for International Affairs from 1984 to 1991, where he led a major expansion of the Institute's activities. Since retiring from this position in 1991, he has maintained strong international connections, writes and broadcasts widely. He is a leading member of the UK-Japan 2000 Group, and serves on the Anglo-German Konigswinter Steering Committee. He is a Euratom representative on the Council for Security and Cooperation in the Asia-Pacific (CSCAP). He holds the honorary appointment for the Royal Household of the Vice Admiral of the United Kingdom.

Alan Goldman is the Chief Executive of Lloyd's Information Services of London, and has 20 years experience in the shipping industry and in analyzing international trade. Mr. Goldman is directly involved in the planning and performance of consultancy work and product development undertaken by both the company's Information Services Division and Consultancy Group, SEA Group. He has managed a wide variety of consultancy projects involving marketing, performance improvement, strategic development and operational analysis for Government organisations, carriers, ports, shippers and shipyards. Recent consultancy projects have been completed for the EU, a private sector port privatisation project, and several market and trade analyses for Government clients.

Ambassador John Halstead served in the Canadian navy 1943-46. He joined the Department of External Affairs in 1946 and served in various assignments in Ottawa, London, Tokyo, the United Nations (New York) and Paris including Ambassador to NATO 1980-82. He retired from diplomatic service in 1982 and has since taught at a number of institutions of higher learning including the School of Foreign Service, Georgetown University in Washington 1983-89, Norman Patterson School of International Affairs, Carleton University 1990, and Skelton-Clark Fellow, Department of Political Studies, Queen's University 1994-96. Also a member of the editorial board of *NATO's Sixteen Nations*. Author of numerous monographs on international affairs, including "Atlantic Community or Continental Drift?", in *Journal of European Integration*, 1993.

Peter T. Haydon is a former career officer with the Royal Canadian Navy who retired in 1988 (with the rank of Commander) to take up a second career as an academic. He is a Research Fellow and Defence Analyst with the Centre for Foreign Policy Studies at Dalhousie University specializing in naval and maritime security issues. He is a widely-published author and a frequent media commentator on Canadian and international defence and maritime security matters. He writes and lectures on Canadian naval policy and operations during the early Cold War period (1946-64). His first book, *The 1962 Cuban Missile Crisis: Canadian Involvement Reconsidered*, was published in September 1993. He is also a Senior Research Fellow with the Canadian Institute of Strategic Studies, Director of Maritime Affairs for the Naval Officers' Association of Canada and an active member of several other professional associations including the Navy League of Canada.

Dr. Hal P. Klepak was educated in Canada, the UK, and Cuba, obtaining his Ph.D. in Latin American studies from the University of London. He began service with the Department of National Defence as a strategic analyst in 1969 working on the Latin American desk. In 1976 he was invited to teach at College Militaire Royale de Saint-Jean after which he went to NATO to study the impact of Spanish entry into the alliance. In 1980, he returned to teach at CMR, being posted to the Royal Military College of Canada in 1994 as professor of Latin American military and diplomatic history. He holds a joint appointment there and as Director of Security Programmes at FOCAL, the Canadian Foundation for the Americas. He publishes widely on international security affairs, especially regional conflicts, Canadian defence policy and Latin American security.

Dr. Seo-Hang Lee is Research Professor and Director-General for Security and Unification Studies at the Institute of Foreign Affairs and National Security, Ministry of Foreign Affairs, Korea. Educated at Seoul National and Kent State University in the early 1970s and 1980s, respectively, he has been a Killam Post-Doctoral Fellow at Dalhousie Law School, Canada. He was also a visiting Fellow at the Pacific Forum/CSIS in 1992. Dr. Lee has published and edited more than 30 monographs and books on oceans politics and on arms control issues. His recent publications include: "Approaches to Regional Security and Arms Control on Northeast Asia", "Security of SLOCs in the Western Pacific", "Naval Power as an Instrument of Foreign Policy: A Case of Korea", and "Arms Control on the Korean Peninsula: Korea's Approach".

Dr. Paul T. Mitchell is a Post-Doctoral Fellow with the Centre for Foreign Policy Studies, Dalhousie University, and adjunct faculty at the Pearson Peacekeeping Institute. In addition, he also serves as foreign affairs editor for *Gravitas*. His Ph.D. examined the bureaucratic interests in the development of the USN's "Maritime Strategy". He has served as an advisor to the Canadian government on several projects including naval confidence-building measures in Southeast Asia. He has written several articles on naval strategy in *The Journal of Strategic Studies* and *Vanguard*. His research interests include naval strategy, conventional arms proliferation and international relations theory.

Dr. Michael A. Morris is a Professor of Political Science at Clemson University, where he teaches courses in international and comparative politics. During his recent sabbatical leave, he was a Fulbright Professor in Chile and a Mellon Fellow at the National Foreign Language Center at the Johns Hopkins University. He has authored four books on marine and naval affairs in addition to edited books, monographs and articles.

Katherine Orr is Assistant Director of the Centre for Foreign Policy Studies at Dalhousie University. She holds an MA in Political Science (international relations) and has research interests in peacekeeping, democratization and marine affairs. Previous positions have included an internship with the Naval Officers' Association of Canada, Project Officer with Canadian Physicians for Aid and Relief - Malawi (southern Africa), and election monitoring in Malawi and Bosnia.

Dr. Rahul Roy-Chaudhury is a Research Officer at the Institute for Defence Studies and Analyses (IDSA) in New Delhi, India. He was educated in India and Britain, and received the M.Litt. degree in International Relations from Oxford University in 1991. He has written extensively on naval and maritime security issues in the Indian Ocean. His first book, *Sea Power and Indian Security* (Brassey's, [UK] Ltd., London), was published last year. He has also written a number of research articles for academic and defence journals in India and abroad. These include *The Asian Strategic Review*, *Strategic Analysis*, *The Indian Defence Review*, *Maritime International*, *The Journal of Indian Ocean Studies*, *Vayu 2000 Aerospace Review* (all published in India) and *Contemporary South Asia* (UK).

Phillip Saunders is Assistant Professor of Law at Dalhousie University, specializing in marine and environmental law. In addition he serves as Assistant Professor with the School for Resource and Environmental Studies, Dalhousie University. Previous positions include Senior Policy Advisor, International Centre for Ocean Development (ICOD), Field Representative with the Canadian Cooperation Office, Fiji and Field Representative for ICOD, South Pacific. He is a widely-published author on environmental and development aspects of oceans law and policy, and is frequently consulted by various agencies on these issues.

General John J. Sheehan, United States Marine Corps, Supreme Allied Commander, Atlantic (SACLANT), Commander-in-Chief US Atlantic Command, (USACOM), has served in various command positions, ranging from company commander to brigade commander, in both the Atlantic and Pacific theatres of operation. General Sheehan's combat tours include duty in Vietnam and *Desert Shield/Desert Storm*. His staff positions include duties as regimental division, and service headquarters staff officer as well as joint duty with the US Army, the office of the Secretary of Defense, and the US Atlantic Command. Prior to assuming his current duties as Supreme Allied Commander, Atlantic and Commander-in-Chief, US Atlantic Command, General Sheehan served as Director of Operations, J-3 Joint Staff, Washington, DC.

Dr. Bilveer Singh is a Senior Lecturer, Department of Political Science, National University of Singapore. He is currently the Coordinator for Research and Publications at the Singapore Institute of International Affairs.

He is also the Member for the Singapore National Committee for the CSCAP, Council for Security Cooperation Asia-Pacific. A Singaporean, he has published widely on regional security issues with regard to Southeast Asia. His latest book is titled *East Timor, Indonesia and the World: Myths and Realities* (1995) and his latest article is titled " Sino-Southeast Asian Relations in the Post-Deng Era", *The Korean Journal of Defense Analysis*, Vol. 7, No. 2, Winter 1995. He is also the Editorial Consultant and Editorial Advisor to *Asian Defense and Diplomacy* and *Asian Airlines and Aerospace*.

Stuart L. Slade is a Senior Analyst of Naval Systems with Forecast International, Connecticut, USA. He is responsible for the authorship of the Forecast International reference books on Warships and on Anti-Submarine Warfare and the management of the Electronic Systems Analysis Group. His publications include joint authorship of *Navies in the Nuclear Age* (Conway Press), and a series of articles on many aspects of naval electronics and weapons technology published in such journals as *Navint* and *Naval Forces*.

Dr. Joel J. Sokolsky is a Professor and Chair in the Department of Political and Economic Science at the Royal Military College of Canada. He is also an adjunct professor at Queen's University and a Senior Research Fellow at Queen's Centre for International Relations. Dr. Sokolsky has been the author, co-author and co-editor of a number of books, including *Sea Power in the Nuclear Age: The United States Navy and NATO, 1949-1980, The Fraternity of the Blue Uniform* and most recently, *NATO's Eastern Dilemmas*. He has been the recipient of several scholarships and awards including two NATO fellowships. During the 1995-96 academic year he was at Duke University as a Canadian-US Fulbright Fellow.

Dr. Milan Vego served 12 years as an officer in the Yugoslav Navy. He resigned from the service in the rank of lieutenant commander and has resided in the United States since 1976. He earned his B.A. and M.A. in Modern History from the Belgrade University and his Ph.D. in European History from the George Washington University in 1981. He has published over 170 articles in professional journals; the book *Soviet Navy Today* in 1986, *Austro-Hungarian Sea Power 1904-1914* and *Naval Strategy in Narrow Seas*. He was Adjunct Professor of East European History and

Government, Defense Intelligence College, DIA, Washington D.C. He is currently with the Joint Military Operations Department at the US Naval War College.

Mr. Hugh Williamson is a 1984 graduate of Dalhousie University in Law and Business Administration. He is currently a Visiting Professor at the World Maritime University, Malmo, Sweden and an Adjunct Professor in Marine Affairs at Dalhousie University in Halifax, Nova Scotia. From 1988 to 1990 he was a lecturer in the Law of the Sea and environmental law at the University of Papua New Guinea and a consultant to the South Pacific Forum Fisheries Agency. From 1990 to 1992 he was coordinator Oceans Resources Management Programme, FFA/University of the South Pacific. He resides in Halifax and is a serving officer in the Naval Reserve of the Canadian Forces.

Preface

GENERAL JOHN J. SHEEHAN, USMC

One of the primary missions of NATO's Allied Command, Atlantic since its establishment in 1952, has been to "safeguard freedom of the seas and economic lifelines". During the four decades of the Cold War, that mission was relatively straight-forward. It was limited to NATO's Atlantic Ocean area of responsibility, and performed exclusively by the Alliance's combined naval and air assets. In the complex post-Cold War world, those parameters no longer make much sense. Global economic interdependence, combined with the dynamics of international trade make NATO's geographic boundaries as relevant as the equator. Today, over four trillion dollars a year in maritime commerce is moving on an "isotropic surface" between ports in Asia, Europe, North and South America and the Middle East. Few merchant fleets are nationally owned. Most shipping is conducted under "flags of convenience", with individual ships owned, operated and insured by different companies from so many nations that they have become "floating multinational corporations".

To discuss this new security environment, its maritime security implications and the opportunities and challenges for enhanced multinational naval cooperation in the future, Dalhousie University's Centre for Foreign Policy Studies and NATO's Allied Command, Atlantic co-hosted a three-day symposium on naval cooperation.

With the assistance of Canada's Maritime Command, the United States Atlantic Fleet and the US Navy's Doctrine Command, we assembled a distinguished group of speakers from around the world in Halifax, Nova Scotia in May, 1996 to discuss how the new global and interdependent economic security environment has fundamentally changed the way we view security, and each other as potential partners.

This book represents most of the key papers and discussions from that conference. It will assist anyone interested in re-examining their views on the changing definition of security, the role of multinational maritime forces in promoting global economic and political stability and obstacles to future cooperation. It also explores many of the opportunities and challenges—political, cultural, budgetary and technological—associated with forming maritime "coalitions of the willing".

Whether or not you agree with the observations and conclusions contained herein, this book provides an excellent basis for further study and debate on maritime security issues in the 21st Century.

General John J. Sheehan
Supreme Allied Commander, Atlantic
Commander in Chief, US Atlantic Command
Norfolk, Virginia

Acknowledgements

In addition to the individual chapter authors, a large number of organizations and individuals have made significant contributions to the production of this book. The Supreme Allied Commander, Atlantic (NATO), Maritime Command (Canada), the United States Atlantic Fleet and US Naval Doctrine Command, were the generous sponsors of the Halifax Maritime Symposium hosted by Dalhousie University in May 1996, which served as the intellectual basis for this book. Their support is much appreciated. We would also like to thank the following Centre for Foreign Policy Faculty and Fellows for their assistance: Timothy M. Shaw, Director of the Centre for Foreign Policy Studies, for supporting both the Symposium and this book project; Fred Deveaux, who worked on the original Symposium Report, and the concept for this collection; Peter Haydon, who in addition to co-authoring a chapter, gave editorial advice with sections of the book; Ann Griffiths also provided editorial assistance; and Glen Herbert provided word-processing support. We are most grateful to our technical editor, Gregory Witol, who did an excellent job of preparing the final copy, and catching our mistakes. His technical expertise was invaluable. The editors alone are responsible for the content, including any errors of fact or omission.

Finally, it is with regret that we note the death of Ambassador John Halstead in Ottawa in February 1998. A career diplomat and educator, he epitomized the best qualities of wise statesmanship. His envoi to this book speaks volumes on the vision, idealism and pragmatism of the man. John Halstead was himself a "leading mark for the 21st century".

List of Abbreviations

2-D	Two Dimensional
3-D	Three Dimensional
ACE	Allied Command Europe
AEW	Airborne Early Warning
AIP	Air Independent Propulsion
ANZUS	Australia, New Zealand, United States Defence Pact
ARF	ASEAN Regional Forum
ASEAN	Association of South East Asian Nations
ASW	Anti-Submarine Warfare
bcf	billion cubic feet
BSP	Basic Security Plan
B-52	Strategic Bomber
BIOT	British Indian Ocean Territory
C^4I	Command, Control, Communications, Computers and Intelligence
C^4I^2	Command, Control, Communications, Computers, Intelligence and Information
CANUS	Canada-United States
CBM	Confidence-Building Measure
CCAMLR	Convention for the Conservation of Antarctic Marine Living Resources
CEC	Cooperative Engagement Capability
CG 47	*Ticonderoga*-Class Cruiser
CINCSOUTH	Commander-in-Chief, Allied Forces, South
CJTF	Combined Joint Task Force
COMAIRSOUTH	Commander, Allied Air Forces Southern Europe
COMNAVSOUTH	Commander, Southern European Naval Force
CONUS	Continental United States
CSCAP	Council for Security Cooperation in the Asia-Pacific
CSIS	Centre for Strategic and International Studies

CUSPRG	Canada-United States Regional Planning Group
DDG 51	*Arleigh Burke*-Class Destroyer
DoD	Department of Defence (United States)
DWFN	Distant Water Fishing Nation
dwt	Dead Weight Tons
E-2C	Hawkeye Airborne Early Warning Aircraft
EEZ	Exclusive Economic Zone
ESDI	European Security and Defence Identity
EU	European Union
EUROFOR	European Force (Army)
EUROMAR	European Maritime Force
EXTAC	Experimental Tactic
F-14	Tomcat Fighter Jet
FAWEU	Forces Answerable to the WEU
FFA	Forum Fisheries Agency (South Pacific)
FFG-7	*Oliver Hazard Perry*-Class frigate
FIC	Forum Island Countries (South Pacific)
FMLN	Farabundo Marti Liberation Front (El Salvador)
FOC	Flags of Convenience
FOCAL	Canadian Foundation for the Americas
FPDA	Five Power Defence Arrangement (Australia, Malaysia, New Zealand, Singapore, Great Britain)
FRY	Former Republic of Yugoslavia
FSLN	Sandanista Front for National Liberation (Nicaragua)
G7	Group of Seven Industrialized Nations
GCC	Gulf Cooperation Council
GDP	Gross Domestic Product
GIUK	Greenland-Iceland-United Kingdom
GNP	Gross National Product
HF/DF	High Frequency Direction Finding
IAEA	International Atomic Energy Agency
ICOD	International Centre for Ocean Development
ICS-3	A type of fully integrated communications suite
IDSA	Institute for Defence Studies and Analysis (India)
IFOR	NATO Implementation Force (Bosnia)
IMO	International Maritime Organization
INCSEA	Incidents at Sea Agreement
IOC	Indian Ocean Commission

IOR-ARC	Indian Ocean Rim Association for Regional Cooperation
IORAG	Indian Ocean Rim Academic Group
IORBF	Indian Ocean Rim Business Forum
IOZOP	Indian Ocean as a Zone of Peace
IPKF	Indian Peace-Keeping Force
IPO	Initial Public Offering
ISL	Institute for Shipping Economies and Logistics
IWRC	International Convention for the Regulation of Whaling
JPN	Japanese Flag Fleet
JSTARS	Battlefield Surveillance Platforms
JWPC	Joint War Plans Committee (United States)
LOSC	Law of the Sea Convention
LPD-17	*Wasp*-Class Amphibious Transport Dock
LTTE	Liberation Tigers of Tamil Eelam
MARPOL	Maritime Pollution Convention
MCC	Military Committee of Cooperation (Canada-US)
MCM	Mine Counter-Measures
MCS	Monitoring Control and Surveillance
MERCOSUR	South American Common Market (Argentina, Paraguay, Uruguay, Brazil)
MEZ	Miliary Exclusion Zone
MIO	Maritime Interdiction Operation
MLRS	Multiple Launch Rocket System
MNCO	Multinational Naval Cooperation
MNMF	Multinational Naval Maritime Forces
MPA	Maritime Patrol Aircraft
MSDF	Maritime Self Defence Force (Japan)
MTC	Minimum Terms and Conditions
NAFTA	North American Free Trade Agreement
NATO	North Atlantic Treaty Organization
NCC	Naval Command Course
NEO	Non-Combatant Evacuation Operation
NETF	NATO Expanded Task Force
NGO	Non-Governmental Organization
NGPV	New Generation Patrol Vessel
nm	Nautical Mile
NORAD	North America Air Defence Agreement

NTF	NATO Task Force
NTG	NATO Task Group
OAS	Organization of American States
ONUCA	United Nations Observor Mission in Central America
OPEC	Organization of Petroleum Exporting Countries
OPV	Offshore Patrol Vessel
OSCE	Organization for Security and Cooperation in Europe
P-3	Orion Maritime Patrol Aircraft
PCB	Polychlorinate Biphenyl
PEO	Peace-Enforcement Operation
PfP	Partnership for Peace
PJBD	Permanent Joint Board on Defence (Canada-US)
PKK	Kurdistan Workers Party
PKO	Peacekeeping Operation
RCN	Royal Canadian Navy
REMARSSAR	Regional Maritime Surveillance and Safety Regime
RIMPAC	US-Led Pacific Rim Exercise Series
RN	Royal Navy
ROE	Rules of Engagement
Ro/Ro	Roll-on/Roll-off Ships
RSS	Regional Security System (Eastern Caribbean)
SAARC	South Asian Association for Regional Cooperation
SACEUR	Supreme Allied Commander Europe
SACLANT	Supreme Allied Commander Atlantic
SAR	Search and Rescue
SFOR	NATO Stablization Force (Bosnia)
SICOFAA	System of Cooperation Among American Air Forces
SIGINT	Signals Intelligence
SLOC	Sea Lines of Communication
SNF	Standing Naval Force
SNFL	Standing Naval Force Atlantic
SOPAC	South Pacific Applied Geoscience Commission
SOSUS	Underwater Sound Surveillance System
SPC	South Pacific Commission
SPF	South Pacific Forum

SPOCC	South Pacific Organizations Coordinating Committee
SPREP	South Pacific Regional Environment Programme
SSB	Ballistic Missile Firing Submarine
SSBN	Nuclear-Powered Ballistic Missile-Firing Submarine
STANAVFORLANT	Standing Naval Force Atlantic
STANAVFORMED	Standing Naval Force Mediterranean
SUBICEX	Submarine Under-Ice Exercise
tcf	trillion cubic feet
TMD	Theatre Missile Defence
UAE	United Arab Emirates
UN	United Nations
UNCED	United Nations Conference on Environment and Development
UNCLOS III	The United Nations Convention on the Law of the Sea
UNITAS	US-Led Inter-American Naval Exercise Series
UNPROFOR	United Nations Protection Force (Bosnia)
UNSCR	United Nations Security Council Resolution
USACOM	United States Atlantic Command
USCGS	United States Coast Guard Ship
USN	United States Navy
USNWC	United States Naval War College
USP	University of the South Pacific
VISA	Voluntary Intermodal Shipping Agreement
VLCC	Very Large Crude Carrier
VSA	Vessel Sharing Agreement
WEU	Western European Union
WMD	Weapons of Mass Destruction
WPNS	Western Pacific Naval Symposium
ZPCSA	Zone of Peace and Cooperation in the South Atlantic

Introduction

FRED W. CRICKARD AND PAUL T. MITCHELL

In December 1991, in the wake of the Gulf War, a conference on *Multinational Naval Cooperation in a Changing World* was held at the Royal Naval College in Greenwich, England. Since then much has changed, not only in the nature of "second generation peacekeeping", but in the purpose of seapower in the management of change in the post-Cold War era. In May 1996, building on the Greenwich conference, NATO's Supreme Allied Commander Atlantic and Dalhousie University's Centre for Foreign Policy Studies invited over 200 participants from 32 countries, including Chiefs of Naval Operations and their staffs, diplomats and foreign service officers, naval and military officers, senior bureaucrats, marine industry executives and academics to Halifax, Nova Scotia to examine multinational naval cooperation and its relation to foreign policy into the next century. For three days, the Halifax symposium compared and assessed regional approaches to the use of seapower across the full spectrum of maritime operations, from fisheries disputes to limited wars. The symposium succeeded in identifying several important security and oceans management issues facing major maritime states, as well as medium powers and coastal and island states.

This book follows the layout of the symposium and contains chapters based on some of the principal addresses and discussion papers for each region, as well as supplementary contributions. It begins with a treatment of some global themes affecting the use of seapower into the 21st century, such as new meanings of maritime security, the changing nature of the high seas, global trade routes and the importance of shipping, the United States and multilateral naval cooperation in the post-Cold War world, and technology in an emerging era of "small wars". Seven maritime regions around the globe are examined in the Asia-Pacific, the Euro-Atlantic and the Americas. The book concludes with some thoughts on the growing utility of navies as instruments of foreign policy as we approach the next century.

The heart of the book lies in the examination of global trends in the regional context. For several reasons, especially for ease of comparative

1

analysis, most of the chapters on the regions contain a general examination of the key issues affecting or likely to affect maritime security in the broadest sense of the term. Within this framework, the authors address specific issues, such as: who are the key players; what are the challenges to regional maritime security; how will economic and trade factors impact on regional security; in what way will the 1982 UN Convention on the Law of the Sea affect regional maritime security; what are the regional naval trends and what are the factors most likely to affect naval cooperation between the regional navies and outside naval powers? Each of the chapters in the sections on the Asia-Pacific, the Euro-Atlantic and the Americas address these questions directly or indirectly.

The themes derived from this approach provide a strategic assessment into the 21st century, explore the roles of navies in the non-military as well as the military dimensions of maritime security, and look at comparative approaches to the politics of multinational naval cooperation, navies in oceans management, navies and seaborne trade, technology and military strategy and evolving doctrine and practice in multinational naval cooperation.

International Order and Multinational Naval Cooperation

At the close of the Cold War, most Western navies faced fundamental challenges to their existence. Long structured to face the Soviet Union on the high seas, the sudden disappearance of their principal foe left many navies scrambling for a mission. The USN struggled long to define its role in a post-Cold War era, producing first *The Way Ahead* in 1991,[1] but it was not until the appearance of *From the Sea* in 1992, in the wake of the Gulf War, that there was a recognition from the premier naval service that business would have to change in a fundamental way.[2]

In many cases, change has been forced on global navies. Save in specific regions, most of the world's established navies have faced a period of retrenchment. The USN has declined from a fleet strength of slightly under 600 ships, the goal of the Reagan administration, to just under 350. The British and French navies too have seen significant reductions in their fleet strength since the end of the Cold War. Smaller navies, particularly those of NATO, have faced similar cuts.

However, from the experience of coalition naval operations in the 1991-92 Gulf War, it became apparent to the United States that with declining naval resources and the seeming explosion of contingencies on a global basis, cooperation with other navies, especially those outside the familiar group of NATO nations and other allies, would become more important.

> The Gulf War's allied coalition may be a harbinger of future security arrangements that will complement longstanding treaties, such as NATO. We must heighten our emphasis on combined operations and training with national forces of many regions—both to facilitate cooperation and coordination with them and to maintain our own expertise in likely operating environments.[3]

This trend was reinforced by the ongoing efforts of the Partnership for Peace (PfP) initiative where the navies of former adversaries were undertaking the often painful process of learning to operate with their new NATO partners. Initially, NATO was reluctant to release its tactical publications *in toto* to assist this process, however, in December 1992, the USN offered to NATO's Maritime Tactical Working Party an expurgated version of the Allied Tactical Manoeuvering and Signals manual. The document was released as *EXTAC 768* (experimental tactics) which gave the NATO *imprimatur* without official endorsement. Since then, the USN has worked to develop common doctrine to support combined naval operations with non-NATO countries in various regions of the world.[4]

The urgency to improve cooperation at sea (particularly given the protracted process of doctrinal development experienced within NATO) has only been part of this process. Along with foundational issues of doctrine, we have seen the extension of the "Incidents at Sea" concept between former Cold War adversaries to the exploration of its utility in the Middle East as well as the Western Pacific. New opportunities for inter-communication amongst fleets have also begun to emerge as well as an increase in regularly scheduled multinational exercises.

These developments are occurring in spite of the pessimism of many analysts as to the likelihood and promise of security cooperation in international relations. In many ways, the international environment is favourable to widespread naval cooperation as a contingent outcome of a uni-polar distribution of power. Samuel Huntington wrote in *Proceedings:*

> The basis of the new doctrine is recognition of the obvious fact that international power is now distributed not among a number of basically naval powers but rather between one nation and its allies which dominate the land masses of the globe and another nation and its allies which mono-

polize the world's oceans. This bi-polarity of power around a land-sea dichotomy is the fundamental fact which makes the Mahanite concept inapplicable today. For the implicit and generally unwritten assumption as to the existence of a multi-sea power world was the foundation stone for Mahan's strategic doctrine.[5]

Writing in 1954, Huntington was premature in his assessment of seapower's lack of relevance in an East/West confrontation. The Soviet Navy soon rose to challenge Western maritime supremacy and its submarine fleet posed a threat to the Western sea lines of communication that pre-dated Admiral S.G. Gorshkov's aspirations for a Navy second to none. Certainly, the USN did not accept that seapower had declined in its utility. Huntington's assertion represents an important cautionary tale on the ephemeral nature of strategic reality. What seemed to be true in 1954 was soon overtaken by events and had to wait nearly forty years before it again seemed relevant. What is interesting about Huntington's thought was how forward looking it is for the present era. The shift from blue water to littoral operations that Huntington describes parallels the shift from *The Maritime Strategy* in 1986 to *From the Sea*.[6] As he noted more than forty years prior, "For decades the eyes of the Navy have been turned outward to the ocean and the blue water; now the Navy must reverse itself and look inland where its new objectives lie".[7]

Still, the post-Cold War world bears little resemblance to the bi-polar structure which Huntington described. Today, the world is dominated by a single maritime power with limited control over (and selective interest in) the outcome of events. Further, since 1954, new transnational challenges defying national boundaries have emerged, suggesting to some the decline of the traditional state system. For the present, however, states remain the best actors capable of directly addressing international security concerns, including those of a non-military nature, such as terrorism, resource depletion, illegal activity and environmental degradation.

Thus, while the absence of a bi-polar power structure or an ocean going "peer competitor" to the US Navy distinguishes the present international environment from that of the Cold War, as Huntington suggested, naval action is likely to occur in the coastal and littoral regions rather than on the high seas. It is possible that in the next century some navies, such as the Chinese or Russian, may grow in strength, though their ability to assert sea control will be highly localized. It is much more likely that American dominance will be challenged by factors internal to the United States. As the USN shrinks in size,[8] its ability to respond quickly with sufficient forces will decline, making the participation of local fleets in regional waters all the more important. For the present, however, the USN will remain the only navy capable of conducting sustained high intensity operations on a global scale. Other navies may be able to contribute to missions around the globe in greater or lesser amounts, however, none will be able to provide the core capability that the USN can. Nevertheless, while most nations outside of NATO, and even some within it may be hard-pressed to contribute ground forces, let alone substantial naval forces, even small powers have been able to send frigates and patrol craft to regional operations in support of peace or collective security. Where battalions are often unavailable, a ship may suffice to indicate commitment and concern.

While a Mahanian "clash of the battle fleets" fought over control of the sea may be highly unlikely in the near future, navies will continue to perform useful functions on, over and under the oceans. The present era's global focus and the proliferation of transnational challenges, many of them located in maritime areas, ensure that states will continue to place considerable value in naval power. In 1954, Huntington noted that the only regional sea where naval power could be usefully applied was the Mediterranean. Today, the area of potential operations is effectively global. The growing dependence of states on oil has enhanced the importance of the flow of oil from the Arabian peninsula through the Straits of Hormuz and Malacca. Differential economic growth rates, political turmoil, or natural disasters may spur entire populations to seek better lives across the Carribean, Baltic, Mediterranean and Southeast Asian seas. Expanded jurisdictions stemming from the UN Convention on the Law of the Sea may generate disputes between nations at sea over resources and boundaries. Finally, criminal activities from piracy to drug and weapons smuggling will all have important naval and maritime dimensions. As Commodore Sam Bateman points out, while these issues can be seen negatively in terms of sources of conflict between nations, they can also potentially serve as positive reference points, providing impetus for cooperation.[9]

Global Factors

Much of this book is on the politics and management of multinational naval operations in the world's ocean areas and seas. Global factors affecting the regional politics of seapower and vice versa are described in the first five chapters. James Eberle's overview sets the scene. In it, he outlines the new dimensions of security—economic interdependence, the growth of economies in Asia, population growth and movement, and the role of military force in the evolving strategic environment. The changing nature of military power in international relations—the utility of force to deter and contain rather than to "win"—is echoed by other authors. Jan Breemer notes the declining ability of the nation-state to apply force other than acting through coalitions. This is reinforced by Joel Sokolsky in his chapter on the United States and multilateral naval cooperation in the post-Cold War era. The US will continue to intervene in regional issues, disputes and conflicts when it perceives its interests to be at stake. While unilateralism remains an option for the US—the only power in the world to which this applies—it will continue to choose partners, particularly from the states in the region involved. Smaller powers, on the other hand, will need the direct or indirect approval and support of the US to deter or contain major regional conflicts, except in less tense confrontations in the shape of policing, humanitarian assistance or classical peacekeeping, where it may be possible for coalitions of smaller powers to act in concert. However, US engagement may come at the price of "acceptance of US command in the field and policy objectives at the negotiating table".

Turning to seapower in the post-Cold War era, most authors explicitly or implicitly assume that the principal role of navies now lies in support of activities on land. Jan Breemer notes that this calls for a major reorientation for traditional ocean-going navies. The so-called "coastal navies" are already in the business of controlling access to the land. Just as international relations are becoming more interdependent and less nationally determined, so naval operations are becoming increasingly multinational across the spectrum of oceans affairs, from fisheries protection to limited wars. The greater the intensity of the situation, the more important it is that navies learn to operate together. While the likelihood of a world war is remote, Stuart Slade is right in assuming the era of "small wars" will continue into the 21st century. He describes how the revolution in information technologies or C^4I^2 (Command, Control, Communications, Computers, Intelligence and Information), which is driving the interoperability of multinational naval operations, has direct applicability in the tactical and operational control, as well as the strategic command, of the diffuse and localized military activities on the ground so characteristic of these "small wars". Paradoxically, naval C^4I^2 systems designed for high intensity, three dimensional "blue water" warfare may be an even more important catalyst in the control and coordination of littoral operations ashore.

While current thinking on seapower is moving towards the use of navies in support of combined and joint operations on land, the objective being to deter, contain, halt and stabilize conflict, two purely maritime fields must continue to demand the attention of politicians, diplomats, naval commanders and planners. These are oceans management and shipping. Lewis Alexander, Daniel Coulter and Alan Goldman set the scene for these aspects of seapower which are elaborated in the chapters on the regions. Lewis Alexander argues the case for a high seas management regime, particularly in the areas of marine resource conservation and the protection of the marine environment. Freedom of navigation and overflight, and marine scientific research should be interfered with as little as possible, but curbs must be placed on "the freedom to fish and the implied freedom to pollute". Multinational naval cooperation offers a means of high seas enforcement under the jurisdiction of the UN or regional competent international agencies. The case for and growing practice of multinational and bilateral naval and coast guard operations in the control of oceanic approaches and coastal zones is evident in all the regions examined in this book.

Classically, navies have always followed the flag, but as Coulter and Goldman point out, seaborne trade is global and multinational, and the gap between flag and ownership is wide and expanding. On the other hand, the security of trade routes, particularly through straits and focal areas, is essential to the global economy. With the exception of military sealift, the historic notion of the protection of trade no longer means the naval protection of shipping, but has come to mean the protection of trade routes to ensure the safe and timely arrival of goods, especially energy supplies. This cannot be left to the United States alone. Medium powers and coastal states must play their part, including the provision of naval forces when necessary.

Aside from the ongoing efforts of the USN's Doctrine Command, there are likely to be few initiatives which aim for a global system of cooperation. Regionally distinct challenges will continue to shape the character of cooperation in particular directions. Habits of multinational maritime cooperation vary widely in different regions, while nontraditional challenges to maritime security, such as maritime boundaries, fisheries conservation, pollution, crime and illegal immigration are common to all. The interest of the United States in any given region will likely prove to be a catalytic factor in the extent and nature of cooperation between navies as well. Traditional balance of power considerations between states in each region and extra-regional maritime powers will remain the major external determinants of naval force structures and levels. In any case, rather than becoming a monolithic whole, naval cooperation will likely take diverse forms and characteristics. The findings of the symposium's regional groups which are reflected in the chapters on the maritime regions amply demonstrate the diverse approaches to naval cooperation around the globe today.

The Asia-Pacific

As always, the question of what defines a maritime region comes up. For example, as Rahul Roy-Chaudhury points out, while the Indian Ocean is geographically demarcated, politically, economically and socially, it defies delineation. Similarly, many analysts speak of Northeast Asia (comprising China, the Koreas, Russia and Japan) and Southeast Asia (comprising China, the ASEAN states, Taiwan and Cambodia) as being distinct areas. However, from any economic, political and security perspective, it is difficult to separate the two regions. The lines of communication running from the Strait of Malacca to the Sea of Japan are perhaps some of the most significant in the world today. In this book, regions are based primarily on geographic ocean areas, and geopolitical and economic factors in which a number of littoral or island states and, in some cases, states outside the region, share mutual interests. In the case of the Asia-Pacific area, the Western Pacific, the Indian Ocean and the South Pacific have been selected.

In the Western Pacific, the key factors are the remarkable economic growth in most of the states in East Asia, and the growing importance of offshore living and non-living marine resources. This brings with it maritime security challenges to seaborne trade, offshore oil and gas, and maritime claims, in addition to longstanding quarrels between states. The United States maintains a high level of interest in the security of Northeast Asia. At the same time, the security architecture that the United States created in the area during the Cold War is being replaced by a matrix of bilateral and multilateral relationships between states in the region, as well as with the United States.

With 47 regional states, it is unrealistic to consider the Indian Ocean as a cohesive entity. Transit shipping routes for commodity traffic, as well as energy supplies with egress points in the Straits of Hormuz and Malacca, underscore its strategic significance. The United States has a vital interest in the Persian Gulf which will endure well into the next century. In addition, the Indian Ocean, like the other oceans examined in this book, has a plethora of interstate disputes based on traditional enmities—e.g., India and Pakistan—maritime boundaries and non-military challenges, such as terrorism, piracy, arms smuggling, fisheries disputes and refugee flows.

The South Pacific, although not a globally strategic area, provides a good case of multilateral relations in the management of marine resources conferred upon small island states by the 1982 UN Convention on the Law of the Sea. It is a successful example of regional maritime cooperation in fishing resource management brought about by circumstances unique to the South Pacific. In this regard, the importance of international development aid and military assistance programs from the wealthy states in the region —Australia and New Zealand—is crucial.

In each of the broad ocean basins surveyed in the Asia-Pacific area, the authors provide examples of the evolving applications of seapower as an instrument of international politics, and functionally in the fields of oceans management and the security of seaborne trading routes. At the strategic and operational levels, one sees a trend towards coalition strategies and multinational naval cooperation brought about principally by enlarged maritime estates and the accelerating cost of technology, particularly information technologies and advanced weapons systems.

The Western Pacific

In the geopolitical sense, the Western Pacific, from the Straits of Malacca to the Sea of Japan, is the most internationally sensitive region in the Asia-Pacific area. China, Russia and Japan are the most powerful states, and the United States is the principal external power. With the end of the Cold War, traditional power politics have become active. As Seo-Hang Lee points out, while intra-regional economic interdependence has increased significantly, territorial disputes, growing non-conventional security issues and internal change, particularly in China and North Korea, make the Northwest Pacific a high risk area. The United States will continue to play a pivotal role in maintaining stability there.

While it is true that the regional navies—the Japanese Maritime Self-Defense Force, the Chinese Navy, and those of the ASEAN states, Taiwan and the two Koreas—are expanding and modernizing, thereby complicating the maritime security outlook, Seo-Hang Lee argues that they can play an important role in building trust and confidence through maritime cooperation on a number of missions, such as search and rescue, building a regional maritime surveillance and safety regime, and the development of common naval doctrine. Given the prevailing strategic uncertainty and growing regional naval power, the current situation in the Western Pacific raises the need for maritime cooperation. The hope is that naval cooperation could be a means to achieve closer collaboration on political, economic and security matters.

Bilveer Singh, in writing on strategic issues facing Southeast Asia, reinforces Lee's conclusions on the geopolitical importance of the East Asian maritime corridor. Despite positive developments, including the warming of relations between former antagonists in the region—e.g., China and Vietnam—the end of the Cold War has developed a kind of power vacuum and competition for dominance, along with the rise of traditional territorial disputes. The Northwest Pacific is predominantly maritime and of growing importance to powers both inside and outside the region. The challenges to maritime security are geostrategic and global because of increasing shipping in commodities and energy supplies, maritime claims to offshore islands, such as the Spratlys in the South China Sea, and non-traditional threats, including piracy, illegal refugees and marine pollution.

The future of naval power in the region will be shaped primarily by traditional balance of power considerations, with particular regard to Chinese foreign policy. Naval modernization has begun already in Southeast Asia because of the fact that the countries in the region can afford it and fleet replacement is long overdue, particularly in light of the new rights and obligations of coastal and archipelagic states under the 1982 UN Convention on the Law of the Sea. The fleet posture of all the regional navies, from the Chinese Navy to those of the Southeast Asian states, will move from coastal to "blue water" capability, including (in due course) fleet logistic trains, naval airpower and submarines.

The future of the naval cooperation in situations other than non-traditional areas will depend on national assessments of threats from neighbours—large and small. In the case of non-traditional challenges, the ASEAN Regional Forum has some potential for multilateral cooperation at the political/diplomatic level. Operationally, a start at developing common doctrine and practice in multinational naval cooperation is in train through the Western Pacific Naval Symposium. The prospects for naval interoperability for maritime crisis response, peacekeeping or peace enforcement are modest. The most promising avenue to train for these eventualities is by building on US or Western-led exercise series, such as the RIMPAC exercises, the STARFISH (Five Power Defence Arrangement) series, or the Australian-hosted KAKADU Fleet Concentration Periods.

The Indian Ocean

Rahul Roy-Chaudhury points out that the chief feature of the Indian Ocean is its geographic diversity, while its geopolitical significance lies in the strategic importance of the shipping lanes which cross it. About 80 per cent of maritime trade in the Indian Ocean is extra-regional, compared with 34 per cent in the Pacific. Of this trade, the security and reliability of oil supplies from the Persian Gulf is the most important strategic factor. With the disappearance of the threat from the Soviet Navy in 1989, it is the main reason for a continuing US naval presence in the Indian Ocean. This is not to say that there are no regional security challenges. Like other ocean areas analyzed in this book, interstate conflict remains a possibility, the security of small island states like Sri Lanka and the Maldives is not assured, maritime boundary disputes are nascent in the Persian Gulf, the Bay of Bengal and the Southwest Indian Ocean, arms smuggling, narco-terrorism and marine pollution persist, and humanitarian assistance and disaster relief remain a concern for the Indian Ocean states. Given the scope of challenges to maritime security, the naval force structures of the major littoral states, such as India, Pakistan and Australia, aim at extending the reach and endurance of their maritime forces.

Although regional cooperation in the Indian Ocean on political and economic matters is evolving slowly, there is no over-arching security organization because of the absence of an agreed "threat" and no historical experience of Indian Ocean-wide defence alliances or arrangements. Naval cooperation continues to be largely bilateral to deal with non-traditional threats, with the exception of the STARFISH and KAKADU joint training exercises mentioned earlier. However, since the early 1990s, bilateral naval or coast guard exercises have increased, as have the exchange of port visits. Another promising development is the guidelines for regional maritime cooperation developed by the unofficial Council for Security Cooperation in the Asia-Pacific, which encourages cooperation in marine safety, order and security, maritime surveillance and the protection and preservation of marine resources and the oceans environment. As Rahul Roy-Chaudhury states, "the development and growth of a web of bilateral naval relationships could, however, evolve into a loosely-defined multilateral set of activities".

Nevertheless, multinational naval cooperation in the Indian Ocean barely exists, is without tradition or historical experience, and notwithstanding a common interest in the security of trade and energy, the benefits of

seapower as a cooperative tool of foreign policy are overshadowed by traditional enmities and fear of competitive advantages between many Indian
Ocean states.

The South Pacific

The last maritime region examined in the Asia-Pacific area is the South
Pacific, which looks beyond naval cooperation to broader maritime cooperation between small island states. The chapter also addresses, at a general
level, the relevance of cooperation, and the prospects of confrontation over
navigation rights in archipelagic states. Since the end of the Cold War, the
South Pacific has receded in strategic importance, but has come to the fore
in oceans management and maritime enforcement as a consequence of the
UN Convention on the Law of the Sea.

In their chapter, Philip Saunders and Hugh Williamson point out
that an important characteristic of the South Pacific has been the extent of
regional cooperation. In the past 25 years, six regional agencies have
developed, the premier one being the South Pacific Forum—the senior
"political" regional organization made up of 22 states and territories,
ranging from Australia to Pitcairn Island. In contrast to, for example, the
Indian Ocean, regional political, economic, environmental and scientific
agencies preceded multinational naval cooperation. The main motivation has
been to control the activities of Distant Water Fishing Nations (DWFN) in
exploiting the region's tuna resources. The South Pacific is a special case
in which the islands have banded together to exert greater leverage and
influence, using the international law of the sea and, until the end of the
Cold War, the Soviet fishing fleet presence, as the basis for the control and
management of marine resources. These cooperative efforts have been built
mainly on legal and diplomatic initiatives, but include operational cooperation in monitoring, surveillance and control activities, thanks largely to
proactive policies of Australia and New Zealand. Whether the South Pacific
"model" can be sustained in the face of increasing internal demographic
tensions and changing international relations, as well as global conditions
is another matter.

The Euro-Atlantic

In contrast to the situation in the Asia-Pacific region, the geopolitics of the
Euro-Atlantic area look landward. The prevailing maritime character of the

Indian Ocean, the Western Pacific and the South Pacific has no parallel in the North Atlantic Ocean, or the Mediterranean and Baltic Seas. European and most Mediterranean and Middle Eastern states are connected by land, while those in East Asia, South Asia and the Pacific are joined by the sea. To be sure, trade routes and the flow of energy supplies connecting Asia with Europe and North America are sensitive in both regions. The preservation and protection of marine resources and the environment, and the maintenance of good order on the seas is equally important. Insofar as multinational naval cooperation is concerned, the major difference between Asia and Europe lies in their over-arching security organizations. In Asia, these are non-existent or slowly developing, whereas in Europe, there are many, although all are being tested by the changing world order and new meanings of security.

The United States will maintain its interest in Europe, particularly in the Mediterranean and the Middle East. Russia remains an uncertainty. NATO continues to be the only integrated military command in the world, although preventive diplomacy and crisis management is becoming an open house affair through arrangements like Partnership for Peace (PfP) and the Combined Joint Task Force concept. The NATO-led international force in the Balkans is a test case. As pointed out by Jan Breemer and John Halstead, military coalitions have become necessary to prevent wars, or contain them should they occur, rather than to "win". Wars in Europe and the Middle East tend to break out on land from territorial or ethnic disputes, and spill over onto the sea. Including its roles in oceans management and the security of trade routes, seapower more than ever is an instrument of politics in international relations. This is nowhere better illustrated than by Milan Vego and Jan Breemer in their chapters on multinational naval cooperation in the enclosed seas and waterways on Europe's southern and northern flanks.

The Middle East and the Mediterranean

As Milan Vego notes, the region is the western end of the trade route for global shipping between Asia and Europe, and crucial to the flow of oil and, hence, the economies of Europe and North America. Regional issues affecting maritime security are mostly land-based; i.e., territorial disputes, religion and terrorism, population growth and movement, water shortages, weapons of mass destruction and the arms trade, and gradual economic decline. Although most maritime threats are part of larger territorial conflicts, such as the 1990-91 Gulf War and the wars in the former Republic of Yugoslavia, there are some distinctly maritime activities, including the freedom of navigation and the safe conduct of shipping in the Mediterranean, the Red Sea and the Persian Gulf, unresolved maritime boundary disputes in the Aegean and Western Mediterranean Seas, and oceans management issues, such as marine pollution, terrorism, arms smuggling, refugee flows and humanitarian assistance.

Turning first to the politics of multinational naval cooperation in the oceans management field, maritime cooperation (apart from NATO countries) is at a primitive state of development in the Mediterranean, the Red Sea and the Persian Gulf. In fact, many states in the region remain sceptical about the "Western" orientation of the UN Convention on the Law of the Sea. At the other extreme, the authorization, planning and conduct of peacekeeping and peace enforcement operations is an alphabet soup of political and security organizations. As Vego points out, only NATO, with the US solidly in the lead, can muster the security consensus and the military capability to carry out high risk preventive diplomacy and peace operations. The Western European Union still has to prove itself, while the UN, the European Union and the Organization for Security and Co-operation in Europe are only suitable for policing and humanitarian assistance, as well as classical peacekeeping.

The Baltic

Jan Breemer's chapter begins with an assessment of the role and functions of navies since the end of the Cold War. He points out that the new focus of naval seapower is land-oriented. Already underway in the USN and the Royal Navy, Breemer contends that "... the centre of gravity for naval operations in an era in which traditional naval strategy has essentially come to an end, must be *on and over the land*". He comments on the changing "political" nature of war. More than ever, navies are political instruments with the need for political support and subject to public scrutiny. Moreover, due to escalatory costs and the changing nature of conflict, "the ability to use force will be the monopoly of coalitions".

Applying these principles to the Baltic Sea and the Nordic states in particular, with their historic traditions of non-provocative defence and cooperative internationalism, multinational naval cooperation, coalescing around oceans management missions—policing tasks, safety of life at sea, humanitarian relief etc.—is not only a practical thing to do, but can foster regional security. If Russia and PfP countries are invited to participate in such low-key maritime operations, the purpose of confidence-building is well served. A "Standing Maritime Force Baltic" is less provocative than a NATO force, as well as providing a Northern European counterweight to a Franco-German dominated WEU. This is an imaginative example of the potential of multinational naval cooperation as a political instrument of 21st century multilateralism.

The Americas

The United States remains, as it has throughout this century, the dominant power in the Western Hemisphere. The one geopolitical feature, common to all states in the Americas, is the asymmetrical nature of their security relationship with the United States. The defence interests vital to the United States are the security of its northern and southern flanks, with Canada, the Caribbean and the Central American states occupying the inner ring, and South America further afield.

The Canadian response to US predominance has been through multilateralism in foreign policy and emphasis on the fundamental rule of law—a similar response in some ways to the island states of the South Pacific. In this regard, since the Second World War, the Canadian Navy has served the interests of the United States (and Canada) in North American defence, and those of Canada overseas in the spirit of multilateralism. In the case of Latin America, the United States has dominated historically and economically, bringing with it, at the governmental and populist levels, suspicion and resentment. Yet, paradoxically, good bilateral and multilateral relations in naval cooperation exist within the Inter-American security system and the growing US-led UNITAS naval exercise series with Inter-American navies. This too has a parallel in the Canadian experience in which the least successful relationship has been at the higher policy level, while very good relations are the norm at the operational, navy-to-navy level, as illustrated in the 1962 Cuban Missile Crisis.

North America

Of all the states in the Western Hemisphere, Canada remains the most important to the United States with regard to the defence of the continental US. During the Cold War, Canada was also fundamental to the security of Central Deterrence. Today, as John Halstead points out, there are, in fact, two maritime security regions in the world—the Euro-Atlantic and the Asia-Pacific—with North America providing the point of intersection between the two. As Robert Wood, the Dean of the US Naval War College, has described it, North America is the global fulcrum between them. Just as Canada was integral to Central Deterrence during the Cold War, so it remains, by virtue of geography, part of the global strategic balance today.

Canada has been described as "a regional power without a region". If this means that Canada has no immediate neighbour whose assertiveness or weakness poses a military threat or vacuum to the Canadian state, then the country is fortunate. In this sense, if Canada is in a "strategic back-water", the objective of Canadian security policy should be to keep it that way. As Peter Haydon and Paul Mitchell point out: "For the Canadians, the problem is still how to manage a security relationship with the Americans in such a way that Canadian sovereignty is respected. And for the Americans, the issue is one of securing Canadian cooperation in those undertakings where North America solidarity is needed".

In their chapter on Canada-US naval cooperation, they describe how bilateral naval cooperation has been brought to a fine art between the two navies since the end of the Second World War. The naval relationship has taken place and grown regardless of differences in foreign policy between the two countries on particular issues. Institutional beliefs in both navies spring from a long lineage of Anglo-American concepts of sea-power. In the Canadian case, geography and the necessity for strategic reach is manifested in a "blue water" maritime force posture which has served the country well in the bilateral defence of North America and the execution of multilateral foreign policy objectives. The authors conclude that the bilateral naval relationship shaped during the Cold War can also work in favour of Canadian foreign policy in the Arctic, the Atlantic, Latin America and the Asia-Pacific into the 21st century.

Latin America and the Caribbean

Seapower is part of the historical experience of most Latin American and Caribbean states from the 19th century wars of independence to the present, as seen by the dominant role it played in Cuba, Nicaragua, the Falklands/Malvinas, Grenada and Haiti. In their chapter, Hal Klepak and Michael Morris describe how the US-led Inter-American security system was politically driven to secure the "southern flank". As a peace-enforcement organization, it remained largely impotent, with the US or extra-regional powers acting unilaterally or under United Nations auspices, as was the case in Cuba (1962), the Falklands/Malvinas (1982) or Haiti (1991).

This may be changing. Since the end of the Cold War, several South American states, notably Argentina, have deployed naval forces in support of UN sanctioned operations in Central America, Haiti and the Persian Gulf War. In addition, confidence and trust building measures between former adversarial states, such as Chile and Argentina, and Argentina and Brazil, are making progress. However, it is in the area of oceans management where the need for multinational naval cooperation is greatest. The authors point out in their analysis of trends in the South Pacific, the South Atlantic and the Caribbean Basin, that prospects are good in peacekeeping and peace enforcement operations (in and out-of-area), as well as in disaster relief and search and rescue, and fair in other activities, including environmental protection, illegal immigration and anti-drug operations. However, differences over maritime boundaries and coastal state jurisdiction continue to be the most sensitive impediment to naval cooperation on oceans management challenges. In these so-called "Operations-Other-Than-War", the US would encourage or stand aside from efforts at regional multinational naval cooperation. However, when it comes to higher level conflict and putting teeth into a revitalized Inter-American security system—particularly in blow-ups in the Caribbean and Central America—the US will tend to act unilaterally, albeit preferably, under a symbolic coalition or even a UN pennant.

Conclusion

Multinational naval cooperation has become a global phenomenon. Virtually every navy in the world is affected by it to some degree. However, as this book shows, it is a concept powerfully conditioned by regional security, economic, social and cultural factors. Although the United States will be influential politically and operationally in when, where and how multinational naval operations are conducted, they are not a template to be applied universally. Above all, as mentioned throughout this work, navies are quintessentially political instruments, as well as military ones. John Halstead has expressed it:

> As deterrence becomes the key to the preservation of peace, and enforcement its restoration, particularly in an era of growing instability, the power projection potential of navies should come into its own. ....the

changes we are witnessing in the international system dictate that navies return to their roots as instruments to influence the outcome of events on land.

While Mahan may be laid to rest, the utility of naval forces as instruments of foreign policy will remain as important as ever, and a significant contribution to global order.

Notes

1. H. Lawrence Garrett III, Adm. Frank Kelso and Gen. A.M. Gray, "The Way Ahead", *Proceedings* May 1991.
2. United States Navy, *From the Sea: Preparing the Naval Service for the 21st Century* (Washington DC, Sept. 1992).
3. Garrett, *et al.*, "The Way Ahead", 39.
4. *EXTAC 768* (later re-numbered 1000) was not restricted to PfP navies and was distributed at the 1993 International Seapower Symposium, a biennial gathering of the world's navies hosted by the USN. The document was favourably received and those in attendance urged greater effort on the development of unclassified and fully releaseable tactical level doctrine for safe/effective *ad hoc* coalition operations, as well as operational level doctrine to address the wider issues of cooperation at sea. As such, the then Chief of Naval Operations, Admiral Frank Kelso tasked Naval Doctrine Command, under the umbrella of the Maritime Tactical Working Party, to "develop common doctrine to support combined naval operations with non-NATO countries in littoral regions" and "ensure consistency with USN doctrine and between various regions of the world". The result has been a series of EXTAC documents together with a Doctrine Command "capstone" publication to tie them all together, *Multinational Maritime Operations* (Norfolk, Va: Naval Doctrine Command, Sept. 1996).
5. Samuel P. Huntington, "National Policy and the Transoceanic Navy", *Proceedings* 80:5/615, May 1954, 488.
6. James D. Watkins, "The Maritime Strategy", *Proceedings* 112 (Jan. 1986 Supplement).
7. Huntington, "National Policy and the Transoceanic Navy", 491.
8. The USN has shrunk from a high water mark of fourteen carriers in 1989 to eleven in 1997. Its combat fleet has declined from 465 to 317 vessels.
9. Sam Bateman, "Maritime Cooperation and Dialogue", in Dick Sherwood (ed.), *Maritime Power in the South China Seas: Capabilities and Rationale* (Canberra: Australian Defence Studies Centre, 1994), 148.

PART I
GLOBAL FACTORS

The Globe

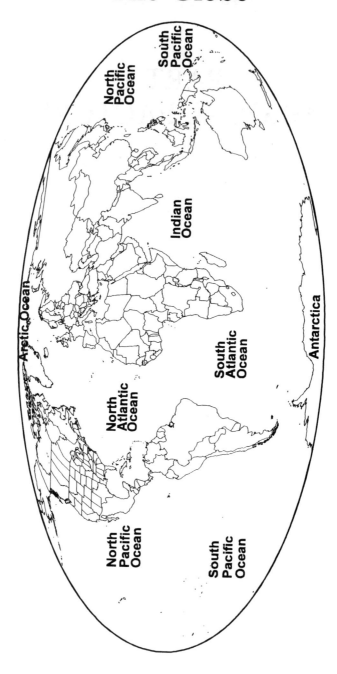

1 Global Maritime Security: What Does it Mean?

ADMIRAL SIR JAMES EBERLE

The decade of the 1980s saw a period of the deepest and most rapid change that perhaps the civilised world has ever known. Following the end of the Cold War, there were many who expressed high hopes for a new era of peaceful change, for a "new world order". With the collapse of Soviet communism, there were high expectations of a new "liberal order" in which confrontation and conflict between East and West would be replaced by a new spirit of cooperation and compromise. Inevitably there would still be tensions between cooperation and competition; the latter being the driving force of progress, and also between the call for consensus and the need for early decisive action, for consensus building is neither easy nor rapid. On the other hand, there were those of a more historical bent who saw the evolution of the international system as a continuing struggle between the supporters of the status quo and those who represented a new order which challenged old orthodoxies. Such challenges inevitably led to conflict along fault lines that were sometimes predictable, and sometimes not. Sam Huntington, in his well known article in *Foreign Affairs*, has forecasted that the future conflict will lie along lines drawn between our several civilizations. Others have turned to methodologies, based on the "drivers" of political economy, social and technological change, to make predictions that will assist in making rational judgments about the impact of global developments upon our security. However, it has to be admitted that the world of today looks more like the "historical view" than that of the "liberal view".

The Growth of Uncertainty

Although the winds of change in almost all parts of the world now seem to be blowing towards Western ideas of pluralist democracy and market-based economics, there can be no early prospect of certainty as to the "end game", the finality, of a future stable international order.

I recall an incident in 1956, when a task force of the US 6th Fleet was operating off the Egyptian coast, just prior to the amphibious landing at Suez by British and French forces aimed at recovering control over the canal. The 6th Fleet Commander had been warned by Washington of the impending events and ordered to bring his force to the highest state of readiness. He acknowledged this dispatch in true naval fashion. "We are ready to fight", he signalled back, "but which side are we on?" Today, anyone concerned with global security, and conscious that we may be in the course of a "Revolution in Military Affairs", might well feel similarly. *"We are ready for change, but in which direction should we now steer?"* However, not only do we not know where we want to get to, we are also in substantial doubt as to the values that we need to retain in order that we can make the journey to wherever it is in good order. In naval parlance, we don't know how to achieve the traditional aim of "the safe and timely arrival of the convoy at its planned destination."

Shifts in Economic Power

It is hardly surprising, therefore, that the 1990s has become the decade of uncertainty. Not the least of these uncertainties is the degree to which the centre of gravity of global economic activity will continue to move away from Europe and the Atlantic area towards the Asia-Pacific region, where China is now emerging to take her place as an actor on the international stage, with influence more commensurate with her size and history. We are, for instance, now seeing the emergence of an Asian middle class. It is estimated that within about the next ten years, there will be more people in Asia than in either Europe or North America with a disposable income equal to or above that of either the average American or European. By the year 2000, 40 per cent of all new purchasing power is estimated to be coming from Asia. However, the growing strength of other areas of regional economic cooperation, such as NAFTA and the EU, reinforced by the coming age of information technology, also represent a challenge to the emergence of any cosmic shift in the balance of global economic power.

Such economic uncertainty has to be weighed against the problems of global population growth. A 1994 report by 58 of the world's leading scientific academies expressed the situation thus:

> It took hundreds of thousands of years for our species to reach a popu-
> lation level of 10 million, some ten thousand years ago. This number

grew to 100 million people about 2,000 years ago, and to 2.5 billion by 1950. Within less than the span of a single lifetime, it has doubled to 5.5 billion in 1993.... Models predict 8.5 billion by 2025, with a possible stabilisation at between 12 and 15 billion by the middle of the next century. Ninety per cent is expected to take place in developing countries.[1]

Change and the State

Next, I would point to the changing nature of the nation state, the very building bloc of the structure of international order and of the United Nations. This is occurring, at least in part, in reaction to the growing multiethnic nature of nearly all of our societies. It is becoming increasingly difficult to define "The Nation". Are the British a nation? Or are the English, the Scots and the Welsh separate nations? If the English are a nation, then do the many Muslims in England consider themselves part of our nation? The answer from many would be "no", for they wish to retain their own religious and cultural identity. Yet they are part of our State. The nation and state are no longer co-terminal. The concept of the role of the state is also changing, a process that lies at the heart of the great debate about the future shape, form and size of the European Union.

Historically, the principal roles of the Government of a nation state have been the protection of its territorial integrity and its political independence, since it has been these factors that have underpinned an individual citizen's sense of security. Today, however, for the citizens of most countries it is not the fear of military invasion that is seen to threaten their way of life; but rather the challenges of social and technological change, the threat of unemployment, the fear of pollution, of AIDS, of drug dependency, and even the prospects of homelessness and starvation. The solution to these challenges are not found in the use of military force. And where the threats to territorial integrity do occur, it is increasingly the international community, through the United Nations, that is called to action. Today, national governments are more concerned with the protection of their perceived "national interests". The idea of "national interest" is not easy to define, nor is it one that readily commands consensus.

New Geostrategic Issues Affecting Global Maritime Security

For a maritime nation, the protection of trade has always been amongst the highest priorities for its naval forces. Seaborne trade has been the lifeblood of the international economic system and the source of its wealth. But sea-borne trade is no longer the lifeblood of the global economy. Its value represents but a small proportion of the level of monetary and capital flows that now pass round the world 24 hours a day almost instantaneously. International finance and know-how is now the lifeblood of the global market place.

Nevertheless, seaborne trade is still a vital part of the global market not least in the energy field. Seaborne trade is now amongst the most international of all sectors of our economies. Ships are built in one country, financed in another, insured in a third, registered in a fourth and are frequently operated by multinational corporations. They carry goods produced by international consortia for global markets. Not only does this greatly reduce the vulnerability of individual nations to military action at sea, but it also helps to establish the legitimacy of action by the international community to counter such threats.

The current debate about a "Revolution in Military Affairs" is important. It should not, however, be conducted in isolation from the revolution that is also going on in the field of political affairs, in which change in the definition of "security" and in public attitudes to the use of force are significant elements. Maritime power cannot be isolated from the changes that we now see in the international system. The first of these is the growing impact of world wide interdependence; not only the rapidly expanding economic interdependence between states, as we move towards the global market, but also the growing interdependence between political, economic and security issues. It was Mr. Gorbachev who first publicly enunciated the proposition that no country could achieve security at the price of the insecurity of another. It was Mr. Nakasone who at the G7 meeting at Williamsburg, Virginia pronounced the now widely accepted view that global security is highly dependent on the achievement of stability in the field of the global economy.

The debate over the revolution in military affairs has tended to fixate on technology. In considering the nature of military security, it is important that we be aware of the dangers of replacing strategic thought and analysis with slogans. The concept of a "quick and decisive military victory", whilst conveying clear military advantage in certain circumstances, does not necessarily provide the underpinning upon which stable political change can be built. Our forces achieved memorable, decisive and overwhelming victory in evicting Iraqi forces from Kuwait. But who won the political contest? Sadaam Hussein is still there, defying the United Nations, oppressing the Kurds in the North and the Shia in the South.

As sophisticated weaponry becomes equally available to both sides in an armed conflict, including terrorists, the dominant factor on the battlefield is, as it almost always has been, the fighting qualities of the soldier on the ground, and the tactical innovation and flair of those in command. To give emphasis to the role of the "man on the ground", and to the importance of the training of our people, is not just to make a "people matter" point. It is to point to the much wider conceptual point about the future nature of military operations that is made by Professor Jan Breemer in *Maritime Forces in Global Security*.[2] The "jointness" of operations is now an overriding necessity for military success, not just a desirable aim. In the professor's own words, "As the rules of the game have changed, so has the meaning of inter-service co-operation. War is no longer a matter of the services taking turns, leading in one game and following the next. The game itself has become joint".[3]

The ending of the Cold War, the collapse of Soviet communism, and the resulting position of the United States as the only superpower, has shifted the centre of maritime operations away from the open oceans towards the world's littoral seas. Legitimacy, flexibility and sustainability, which are inherent in the exercise of maritime power, now provide the underpinning of all peace support operations. Whilst in the longer term, the possibility of war at the higher level cannot be ruled out—indeed to dismiss its possibility is merely to encourage its emergence—there is a pressing requirement for changes in existing force structures that were fundamentally designed for the deterrence of war against the Soviet Union.

It has in recent times been a reasonable assumption that forces designed to meet the requirements of war at the higher level could be used effectively to meet the requirements of low level operations. It is no longer evident that this remains a reasonable assumption. This brings into play very important decisions about the future balance of resources which should be devoted to the most likely low level scenarios, in competition with those that must still be provided for the less likely event of the threat of global conflict. What is clear is that the latter forces are becoming increasingly and prohibitively expensive. This will present America's friends and allies a major problem. Are they prepared to devote the resources to maintaining interoperability with US forces at the highest level; and if not what are the political consequences?

Managing Uncertainty and Change

The armed services have always been, and rightly been, conservative in their approach to change. For their responsibility is for the lives and livelihood of their people. In this decade, the Soviet Navy no longer presents an immediate and global threat to peace. The values of our navies in peace operations, including preventive diplomacy, in maritime coercion (which Sir James Cable calls "Gunboat Diplomacy") and in war, have all been well demonstrated. We have recently brought into the code of international law the UN Convention on the Law of the Sea. We have reached agreement on the difficult issue of straddling fish stocks. It is therefore perhaps tempting to look to the next few years as a period for maritime consolidation. But in today's fast-changing world, it is not enough for us to better manage the world as we know it, we must become "managers as the agents of change".[4] As part of this process of change, we may have to examine the very purposes for which armed force can be used, and its effectiveness as a political instrument.

Maritime Security and Foreign Policies

So where does all this take us? What is the meaning of global maritime security and what is its relationship with foreign policy?

Order on the High Seas

The need for law and order has long been recognised. Order requires regulation; and regulation requires enforcement by a legal and legitimised regime. Good law supported by effective enforcement leads to good order. Bad law or ineffective enforcement is likely to lead to disorder.

Despite the dominance today of personal air travel, the oceans of the world are still a "great highway", across which people and trade can freely flow. This is an international "public good" for the global economy —and it must be protected as such. If legitimacy is to be recognised, we need to recognise the discontinuity which now exists between the increasingly international nature of maritime trade and the sturdily nationalistic nature of the means of enforcement; of "order at sea", which is vital to our continuing prosperity. It is, I believe, not enough to say "Yes—but let us leave that to the United States, the one global superpower. We littoral states have enough to do looking after our own Exclusive Economic Zones".

What does this say about legitimacy then, if another maritime power were to challenge the unilateral US dominance of the high seas?

The UN Convention on the Law of the Sea, in addressing the post Second World War problems of a growing threat to freedom of navigation and overflight by creeping national jurisdiction, has dealt primarily with the rights and duties of coastal states. However, by incorporating the 1958 Convention on the High Seas, it seeks, particularly in the area of environmental protection, to provide a stable framework for promoting law and order at sea; one that provides a proper balance between the interests of smaller coastal states and those of the major maritime powers.

Enforcement on the High Seas

However, the principle of "Mare Liberum", (the freedom of the high seas) does leave open some future issues concerning this regime and its enforcement. There may be a future need to define a new concept of the "lawful use" of the high seas, a high seas that is much diminished in size by the establishment of the 200 mile EEZ. Such a concept would be broadly analogous to that of "innocent passage" through the territorial sea. It would attempt to define a difference between legitimate maritime activities of a "normal" and "defensive" nature on the high seas and those that might be considered harmful to the international community and prejudicial to the concept of the non-use of armed force, or its threat, as set out in the UN Charter.

In 1983, the UN General Assembly called for a review to analyze "the possible implications of naval arms for international security, for the freedom of the high seas, and for the exploitation of maritime resources". The subsequent report to the Secretary General recommended a further study to consider the theme "Security in the maritime environment". Providing we hold on to the fundamental principles of the freedom of navigation and of overflight on the high seas, I do not believe that we should fear the outcome of such a study. Indeed perhaps it is time that we began to think together about these things. For the future prosperity of mankind, the creation of the sort of world that we would want for our children and grandchildren to live in during the next century, can only be founded on confidence in a stable international political, economic and social order and the rule of law.

The maintenance of such a stable order within an essentially global ocean community, (for as General Sheehan told us 70 per cent of the world's population lives within 100 miles of the sea), is strongly, and I would argue increasingly, influenced by maritime affairs. The maintenance of a free, fair and open structure for seaborne trade, and the freedom of safe navigation, is a vital component of a stable international economic order. Issues of international economic and trade policy are, today, at the very heart of what we still call foreign policy. Here lies the fundamental link between the chapters of this book on maritime security and foreign policy.

Conclusion

In conclusion, what are the "leading marks" that we might give to the naval planner to guide him in the future? Let me suggest a few:

- Although the immediate likelihood of general war is remote, we must not ignore its future possibility. To do so would be to encourage it.
- We should not forsake the concept of deterrence, be it conventional or nuclear. It works.
- In war, surprise is likely to remain the norm, not the exception.
- The continuance of navy-to-navy co-operation and the further development and practice of common doctrine and procedures are vital to the effective wielding of global maritime power.
- The retention of interoperability at an affordable cost to major friendly navies will be as important to successful US global maritime leadership.
- There is an ancient Scandinavian saying that "The land divides—the sea unites". Let this be the guiding principle upon which global maritime security is built.

Notes

1.   "The Growing World Population", *Population and Development Review* 20:1 (March 1994): 233-238.
2.   Jan S. Breemer, "Home From the Sea: Have We Entered a New Era of Maritime Strategic Thinking?" in Ann L. Griffiths and Peter T. Haydon (eds), *Maritime Forces in Global Security* (Halifax, Nova Scotia: Dalhousie University, Centre for Foreign Policy Studies, 1995).
3.   *Ibid.*, 34.

4. A recent top level management study, commissioned by a group of major international companies expressed this idea in the following way:

> It is no longer acceptable for leadership to be preoccupied with maintaining the status quo. Senior managers are ideally forced to alter established beliefs and values in advance of generally recognised requirements for change.

2 The Changing Nature of the High Seas

LEWIS M. ALEXANDER

The high seas are defined as those parts of the world ocean beyond the limits of national jurisdiction. In the past, such limits were set by the breadth of the coastal state's territorial sea—three, six, or in a few cases 12 miles[1] from shore.[2] Only in the past several decades have the limits of national maritime jurisdiction been expanded almost exponentially to a generally recognized, 12-mile territorial sea, and a 200-mile exclusive economic zone (EEZ).[3] The extent of high seas has thus been considerably reduced, with most of the reduction taking place in areas potentially rich in living and non-living marine resources.

Since the high seas are not subject to the sovereignty of any state, they have long been considered free to the use of all countries. Freedom of navigation, and in recent decades also of overflight, freedom of fishing, freedom to lay submarine cables and pipelines—these and other freedoms recognized by the general principles of international law—have traditionally been the components of the overall "free seas" regime. But beyond the classic freedoms of the high seas are other freedoms—to pollute, overfish, weapons test and engage in other activities which potentially threaten the "health" of the oceans. In response to these actions, and to possible negative interactions of one freedom on another, the concept of a more "managed" high seas regime is gradually evolving. It is the intent of this chapter to examine the changing nature of high seas freedoms, and to consider the impacts of a managed ocean regime on the uses of the marine environment.

The Evolution of High Seas Freedoms

The contest between "free" (*mare liberum*) and "closed" (*mare clausum*) seas has been a long and complex one. By the end of the thirteenth century, it had been established in Norwegian law that foreigners were not entitled to sail north of Bergen without a royal license. In 1380, Norway passed under the Danish crown, and until the end of the sixteenth century

Denmark maintained a close trade and fishing monopoly with its northern territories (which also included Iceland and the Faeroe Islands), and blocked other countries from utilizing the waters north of the Iceland-Faeroes-Shetlands-Bergen line.

In addition to closed-sea policy issues, there were struggles between local and foreign fishermen, particularly in waters in and adjacent to the North Sea. By the late sixteenth and early seventeenth centuries, the Dutch had developed a viable fishing fleet, particularly for herring, and Dutch vessels moved closer to other countries' coasts. By 1600, Denmark had abandoned its *mare clausum* regime north of the British Isles and proclaimed, instead, an exclusive fisheries zone 16 to 24 miles in breadth off its northern possessions.

In 1605, Hugo Grotius (Huig van Groot), a young Dutch lawyer, wrote *De Jure Praedae*, the twelfth chapter of which was published four years later as *Mare Liberum*. Grotius held that the sea could not be subjected to private ownership (involving fishing and navigation rights), except in the case of gulfs and straits where customary international laws were not violated. He also suggested ownership for enclosed parts of the sea, providing they were not large in comparison with the lands surrounding them. In addition to fishing restrictions, the Dutch at that time were concerned with Portuguese pretensions to sovereignty in East Indian waters, since Holland had already embarked on colonial expansion there.

The British countered with a publication by John Selden in 1619, entitled *Mare Clausum*, which held that the seas of the world were indeed capable of ownership, and since the resources of the seas were by no means inexhaustible, states had a right to protect their interests by restricting the use of certain areas. Although Britain and Holland had several subsequent confrontations over coastal fishing rights, Britain, with its own expanding commerce and navigation, gradually resumed its traditional free seas policies.

> In the closing years of the seventeenth century and the earlier part of the next, there were many signs that the era of claiming an exclusive sovereignty over extensive regions of the sea was passing away; and that ... the policy of fixing exact boundaries for special purposes, either by international treaties or national laws, was taking place.[4]

The question then became one of determining where such boundaries would be delimitated.

During the eighteenth, nineteenth, and early twentieth centuries, the issue of national claims to offshore jurisdiction went through various iterations. The high seas were considered as being beyond these jurisdictional limits. In defining the limits of offshore jurisdiction, one deals not only with the question of the breadth of the territorial sea, but also with the procedure for delimiting the baseline along the coast from which the breadth of the territorial sea is measured, and the status of limited-purpose zones beyond territorial limits as, for example, the contiguous zone.[5] In 1945, a new dimension was added to the maritime sovereignty complex when President Truman issued a Proclamation asserting US jurisdiction and control over the natural resources of the continental shelf contiguous to the US coasts. Although the Proclamation averred that the character of high seas of the waters above the continental shelf is in no way affected by the claim to the shelf resources, a concurrent Proclamation held that the United States "regards it as proper to establish conservation zones in ... areas of the high seas contiguous to the coasts of the United States". It was not difficult for other governments to read the fisheries proclamation as an opening wedge in the struggle for extensive fisheries zones beyond territorial limits.[6]

As the needs of marine science, technology, economics, security, and other concerns became increasingly complex, particularly after the start of the twentieth century, lawyers, diplomats, and others began pressing for some form of global action to compile a uniform system of rules and regulations regarding the jurisdiction and use of the world ocean. In 1930, delegates from 48 countries met at The Hague for a conference sponsored by the League of Nations. One of the major topics discussed was the territorial sea and the baselines from which its breadth was measured, but no agreement on these topics emerged from the conference.

Following the Second World War, the International Law Commission, established by the United Nations, undertook to prepare a draft convention on the law of the sea, based on international practice, legal findings and the opinions of experts in the field. The Commission laboured for seven years, culminating in a 1956 Report covering virtually all aspects of the ocean environment. The work of the Law Commission provided a basis for the 1958 Geneva Conference on the Law of the Sea, which was attended by delegates from 86 states. Four Conventions were adopted by the Conference,[7] all of which eventually came into force.[8]

In Article 1 of the 1958 Convention on the High Seas, the term "high seas" is defined as "all parts of the sea that are not included in the territorial sea or in the internal waters of a State". Article 2 notes "The high seas being open to all nations, no State may validly purport to subject any part of them to its sovereignty". The same article lists the freedoms of the high seas as freedom of navigation and overflight, fishing, the laying of submarine cables and pipelines and "others which are recognized by the general principles of international law". The United States and several other countries contended that this last category included freedom of marine scientific research on the high seas. The Convention on the High Seas came into force on 30 September, 1962.

The two topics on which agreement at the 1958 Conference was impossible were, first, a standard maximum breadth of the territorial sea; and, second, a standard breadth for an extra-territorial exclusive fisheries zone. Added to this were concerns held by both the United States and the Soviet Union regarding freedom of passage through international straits.[9] As a consequence, a Second Law of the Sea Conference was convened in Geneva in 1960. After six weeks of deliberations, the Conference ended without agreement on the subject matters.

Pressures for convening a Third Law of the Sea Conference came essentially from two sources. One pressure was the continuing problems the United States, the Soviet Union and several other maritime states had with the navigational provisions of the 1958 LOS Convention. Added to this was the impact of the 1957 address made by Malta's Ambassador Arvid Pardo to the United Nations General Assembly, wherein he characterized the resources of the deep seabed and subsoil beyond the limits of national jurisdiction as the "Common Heritage of Mankind"; he reasoned that a portion of the profits from exploiting these resources should go to the poor countries of the world. Eventually, these two forces combined to produce a call by the United States for a Third Law of the Sea Conference. The first session of the Conference convened in Caracas, Venezuela in 1973; subsequent bi-annual sessions were held in New York and Geneva for a period of nine years. The final text of the Convention was signed at Montego Bay, Jamaica in July, 1982.[10] The Convention, consisting of 320 Articles and nine Annexes, came into force in November, 1994.[11]

In the 1982 Law of the Sea Convention (LOSC) Article 86 defined the high seas as "all parts of the sea that are not in the exclusive economic zone, in the territorial sea or in the internal waters of a State, or in the archipelagic waters of an archipelagic State".[12] The freedoms of the high seas comprise *inter alia* the freedoms of navigation and overflight, freedom to lay submarine cables and pipelines, subject to Part VI,[13] freedom to construct artificial islands and other installations, again subject to Part VI, freedom of fishing, subject to the conditions laid down in Section 2,[14] and freedom of scientific research, subject to Parts VI and XIII.[15] Thus, the 1958 freedoms were retained, and new ones added, but subject to certain reservations in order to render the articles of the Convention as consistent as possible with one another. The Convention states that the high seas are to be reserved for "peaceful purposes," although nowhere in the Convention text is there a definition of what constitutes non-peaceful purposes.

The Convention also covers the regime of the "Area", that is, "the sea-bed and ocean floor and subsoil thereof beyond the limits of national jurisdiction". To manage the exploration and exploitation of the resources of this Area, the Convention provides for an International Sea-Bed Authority, whose designated structure and powers avoided consensus by the Conference delegates for nearly two decades.[16] It should be noted that the landward limits of the "Area" were, initially, the outer limits of the legally defined continental shelf. Eventually, these outer limits were set at 200 miles, except in cases where the outer edge of the continental margin is beyond the 200-mile limit, in which case the coastal state seabed jurisdiction extends beyond the 200-mile limit, thereby encroaching on the landward limits of the "Area".[17]

On the high seas, warships and government ships used only on governmental, non-commercial service, shall have complete immunity from the jurisdiction of any state other than the flag state. There are prohibitions against the transport of slaves, the illicit traffic in narcotic drugs or psychotropic substances, and unauthorized broadcasting from the high seas.[18] There are also several articles on the suppression of piracy. But the high seas articles, as with other articles in the 1982 Convention, tend to stay well away from matters dealing with the Laws of War.

The Geographic Extent of the High Seas

The high seas, as defined in LOSC, would cover about 70 per cent of the world ocean, assuming all coastal states claimed a 200-mile EEZ. But national offshore claims vary. Some states claim only an exclusive fishing zone between their territorial sea and 200 miles, or the median line of an opposite state.[19] Other states assert a 200-mile territorial sea, with no EEZ at all.[20] Still other states have no claim whatsoever beyond narrow territorial sea limits.[21] A majority of offshore claims are for a 12-mile territorial sea, with an EEZ extending up to 188 miles beyond it. But it should be noted that many coastal states cannot extend their EEZ to anywhere near 200 miles because of the presence of one or more opposite states' exclusive economic zone.[22] In all of these cases, the high seas freedoms of navigation and overflight are retained for the EEZ.

One troubling issue is that of islands. Any island or rock,[23] naturally formed, which is surrounded by water and above water at high tide is entitled to its own territorial sea. Often its territorial sea does not extend to a maximum of 12 miles because of the proximity of other islands, or of the mainland's territorial waters. But even with its own territorial sea, an island or rock may not be eligible for an EEZ. Article 121 of LOSC reads, "Rocks which cannot sustain human habitation or economic life of their own shall have no exclusive economic zone or continental shelf". A naturally formed island, located in mid-ocean, if it meets the necessary criteria, could generate a 200-mile belt of jurisdiction, measuring some 125,000 square nautical miles—an area roughly equal to that of California.

There are other definitional problems. What is the status of the Southern Ocean, surrounding Antarctica, since there is strong international opposition to nations claiming sovereignty, extending poleward from the Antarctic coast? Do the high seas rules apply in enclaves of high seas surrounded by the EEZs of neighbouring states, as in the case of the "Donut Hole" in the Bering Sea between the 200-mile economic zones of Russia and the United States?[24] The United States and some of its allies argued during the Third LOS Conference that the waters of the EEZ should have the status of high seas, with certain coastal state rights, such as those pertaining to fishing, marine scientific research and certain other issues, being left for resolution in the future. But this US position was not adopted at the Conference.

The High Seas Freedoms

Freedom of Navigation and Overflight

The principal impediment to freedom of navigation on the high seas involves ships with hazardous cargoes. There are potential dangers that all or a part of such cargoes may be released, either as a result of accidents or of deliberate discharges. Hazardous cargoes are generally classed into three categories: oil, radioactive materials and other hazardous cargoes, particularly chemicals.[25] Obviously, the severity of impacts due to a release of hazardous cargoes varies considerably from a high seas discharge of crude oil to a release of plutonium,

> ...One of the worst radioactive elements known. A minuscule amount will cause fatal cancer, and if a transport accident occurred, plutonium would be released to the environment and would remain a deadly contaminant for tens of thousands of years.[26]

Two basic problems associated with the transport of hazardous cargoes on the high seas concern standard setting and enforcement. Article 211 of LOSC requires states to adopt laws and regulations for the prevention, reduction and control of pollution from vessels flying their flags or those of their registry. Article 91 notes a state "shall fix conditions for the grant of its nationality" to ships flying its flag, and adds that there must exist a "genuine link" between the state and the ship flying its flag. A precise definition of "genuine link", as used here, has never been internationally accepted.

The problems of hazardous cargoes exist, and often to a greater degree within a state's territorial waters and EEZ than on the high seas. An issue that might eventually affect all parts of the sea is ocean incineration—the burning of highly noxious wastes, such as polychlorinated biphenyls (PCBs). Such incineration, if it becomes commercially and politically feasible, will probably take place well away from inhabited areas.

So far as freedom of overflight on the high seas is concerned, there are two potential types of restrictions. One is the presence of Air Defence Identification Zones which may extend beyond EEZ limits. An aircraft approaching national airspace with the intention of entering such space may be required to identify itself. However, if no entry is intended, identification is not necessary. Second, in the event of actual or imminent hostilities, a state may find it necessary to take self-defence measures that could affect overflight of a portion of the high seas.

Marine Scientific Research

The freedom of marine scientific research on the high seas is unrestricted, except for two conditions. Article 246(6) reads that in cases where a state's continental shelf continues beyond 200 miles, the state cannot withhold consent to foreign research activities relating to its shelf, except in the case of areas specifically designated by the state "in which exploitation or detailed exploratory operation are occurring or will occur within a reasonable period of time".

A second condition involves the "Area" beyond the limits of national jurisdiction, where Article 143 calls upon states engaging in scientific research in the Area to "promote international co-operation in the Area" by undertaking certain responsibilities "for the benefit of developing technologically less-developed States". An interesting aspect of deep seabed exploitation is the existence of organisms taken from deep ocean vent areas (both outside and within the limits of national jurisdiction) known as hypo-thermophiles, or archaea. These microbes "exist and thrive at extremely high temperatures, far beyond those at which other living matter ceases to function".[27] Their anticipated value lies in their potential use for various industrial processes, including "waste treatment, food processing, oil well services and the paper industry".[28]

The United States Navy has a strong interest in marine scientific research, both within and beyond the limits of national jurisdiction, parti-cularly with respect to anti-submarine warfare. One issue relating to naval research vessels, navy-owned but civilian-operated research ships,[29] and other research platforms is the use of expendable marine instruments for data collection. These instruments that accumulate each year in the tens of thousands, have a limited use life; eventually they sink to the bottom, lit-tering the ocean floor.[30] Although they might be considered in violation of LOSC's anti-pollution provisions, warships and government-owned vessels on non-commercial service are immune from such restrictions.

Military Uses

The 1982 LOS Convention, as noted earlier, describes the high seas as "reserved for peaceful purposes". As a partial reinforcement of this state-ment, the 1971 Seabed Arms Control Treaty[31] prohibits the deployment of nuclear weapons and other weapons of mass destruction beyond the 12-mile limits throughout the world ocean.

Warships and aircraft are free to operate throughout the high seas except for certain reservations. One such reservation is due to regional restrictions contained in international agreements in force. For example, the 1961 Antarctic Treaty, which covers the area south of 60 degrees S. Lat. states (Article 1), "Antarctica shall be used for peaceful purposes only. There shall be prohibited ... the carrying out of military manoeuvres, as well as the testing of any type of military weapons".

A similar reservation applies in the 1985 South Pacific Nuclear Free Zone Treaty (Roratonga Treaty), which prohibits within the zone nuclear testing, the land-based deployment of nuclear testing weapons, bases for nuclear-armed ships and aircraft, the storage of nuclear weapons and the dumping or storage of nuclear wastes at sea. The treaty zone includes areas from the western shores of Australia to the western coast of Latin America, north to the equator and south to Antarctica. The treaty does not, however, affect the transit through the area of nuclear-powered vessels or of vessels carrying nuclear weapons.

Another source of restriction on the operations of military vessels on the high seas concerns potential exclusion zones in time of international crises. Such zones, if used in the interests of either defence or offense, may exclude the passage of both military and civilian vessels. Exclusion zones have tended to be delimited within 200 miles of the coast, but exceptions have occurred. For example, during the 1982 Falklands (Malvinas) conflict, the British announced a military exclusion zone (MEZ) extending to 200 miles from a point in the Falkland Islands in which "Any ship and aircraft, whether military or civil, which is found within this zone ... will be regarded as operating in support of the illegal occupation and will therefore be regarded as hostile".[32] The Argentines responded with a proclamation of a "South Atlantic War Zone", a considerably expanded area which led to the sinking of the VLCC *Hercules* by Argentine aircraft, some 500 miles from the Falkland Islands.[33]

Protection and Preservation of the Marine Environment

Preservation of the marine environment, in the form of marine sanctuaries or other unspoiled areas, is not an issue involving the high seas more than 200 miles from land. Protection of the high seas environment, that is, the prevention, reduction and control of pollution, is associated mainly with two problems—vessel-source pollution and the dumping of wastes. The procedures for coping with these problems are dealt with only in general terms in LOSC.

Article 192 holds that states "have an obligation to protect and preserve the marine environment". Article 194, entitled "Measures to prevent, reduce and control pollution of the marine environment" enumerates sources of marine pollution in all juridical parts of the world ocean, and calls on states to take measures "consistent with this Convention" to address the marine pollution problem.

Regarding vessel-source pollution, Article 211 holds that "States, acting through the competent international organization or general diplomatic conference, shall establish international rules and standards" to cope with problems of pollution from vessels. The "international organization" here is IMO, the International Maritime Organization, that, over the years, has adopted and put into force various conventions involving protection against pollution, vessel safety and liability for damages from various incidents. Perhaps the most important of these conventions is the 1973/78 MARPOL, which requires segregated ballast tanks on all new tankers over 70,000 dwt, the installation of reception facilities at ports where tankers and non-tankers have to discharge oil residues and the inclusion of refined oil, as well as "black" oil, as substances covered by the regulations.

One further convention affecting coastal states' rights is the 1969 International Convention Relating to Intervention on the High Seas in Cases of Oil Pollution Casualties, which empowers states to take such action as they feel necessary on the high seas (now also the EEZ) to prevent, mitigate, or eliminate grave and imminent danger to their coastline from oil following upon a maritime casualty.

There are other IMO conventions relating to such issues as vessel construction, vessel safety and the establishment of a world-wide network of Traffic Separation Schemes, Deep Water Routes and Areas to be Avoided. Since 1983, the year that MARPOL came into force, there have been no concerted efforts at IMO or elsewhere to attempt a complete revision of existing conventions (such as requiring double-hulled tankers), but there have also been few incidents of widespread vessel-source pollution of the high seas.

Turning to ocean dumping, the signal convention is the 1972 London Dumping Convention (later renamed the London Convention), which defines dumping as the deliberate disposal of wastes from ships and aircraft, and divides such wastes into three categories. The first category consists of substances listed in Annex I (the "black list") and includes such items as cadmium, mercury, oil, plastics and high-level radioactive wastes. The dumping of such substances is prohibited by the convention. A second category consists of less-noxious substances as listed in Annex II (the "gray list") and comprises, among others, such products as copper, zinc, lead, cyanides, arsenic and "low-level" radioactive wastes. Dumping of these requires a special permit from the national government. A general permit is also needed for the dumping of all other wastes, not included in the first two Annexes.

The responsibility for defining "high-level radioactive wastes" rests with the International Atomic Energy Agency (IAEA), which has evolved a set of definitions and recommendations. There has been some seabed disposal of low-level nuclear wastes, but as yet there are no specific plans for seabed disposal of high-level nuclear wastes, although much has been written on this subject.

Conservation and Management of Living Resources

Conserving and managing the living resources of the high seas is a complex task because of the variety of species involved, the absence of jurisdictional controls, and the frequent lack of political will on the part of flag states and of fishermen themselves to cooperate in restrictive measures. The basic categories of high seas living resources are: marine mammals, including whales, dolphins and seals; highly migratory species, particularly tunas; anadromous species, especially salmon; straddling stocks (e.g., cod, pollock, orange roughy and hake), which move periodically both within and outside 200-mile fishery limits; Antarctic krill, a small, shrimp-like fish found in large quantities in the waters off Antarctica.

For several of these categories, specific global or regional conventions or treaties are in force. One such treaty is the 1946 International Convention for the Regulation of Whaling (IWRC); under its aegis, the International Whaling Commission in 1982 set a zero quota on the commercial harvest of whales throughout most of the world ocean. A second treaty in 1980 promulgated the Convention for the Conservation of Antarctic Marine Living Resources (CCAMLR) that adopted an ecosystem approach to the resources of the Southern Ocean, with a goal of conserving the as-yet under-utilized resources of krill.

There are regional tuna organizations,[34] whose operational areas extend both within and beyond countries' EEZs, a 1992 North Pacific Anadromous Stocks Convention directed toward salmon stocks in that area, and a 1994 Central Bering Sea Pollock Fishery Agreement to handle pollock and associated species in the high seas "Donut Hole" in the Bering Sea. One of the most important and controversial agreements is the UN's Straddling and Highly Migratory Fish Stocks Agreement, which deals with the issue of fish moving seasonally across the 200-mile fisheries boundaries.[35]

An effective management regime for all, or even a part, of the high seas living resources must, at a minimum, involve at least four processes. First is data collection and analysis concerning both individual species and the interactions of species with one another. Second is the establishment of conservation measures and their adoption by the principal high seas fishing states. Third are enforcement measures and fourth are feedback mechanisms to test and, if necessary, revise agreed-upon measures. Given the jurisdictional nature of the high seas, any real management of high seas resources is a highly complicated process; in addition to conservation, it may involve allocation—that is, within conservation limits, who gets what of a total global catch on certain stocks.

Issues of High Seas Management

Transforming the regime of the high seas from one of freedom of action towards a more managed system is an incremental process, where any restrictions placed on traditional freedoms must be justified by the benefits resulting from such actions. This process of weighing costs and benefits is difficult, since there are no global bodies with authority over the high seas, except for the United Nations and certain of its Specialized Agencies,[36] and for several international treaties, governing specific high seas areas,[37] or activities.[38]

The high seas freedoms should be interfered with as little as possible. This is particularly true of the freedoms of navigation and overflight (including military activities), and of marine scientific research. But the freedom to fish, and the implied freedom to pollute the high seas, must have some associated curbs.

This discussion of prospective high seas regimes does not extend to the seabed and subsoil beyond the limits of national jurisdiction, except regarding such issues as ocean dumping, scientific research, or arms control. Part XI of the 1982 Convention—as modified in the 1994 Agreement[39]—provides for the regime of the "Area", under the aegis of the International Sea-Bed Authority, although no mineral resources from the Area have yet to be commercially exploited.

What is not needed for the future is a complex, international management system, such as the Sea-Bed Authority, where approval of the organizational framework was considerably delayed by international politics, and where there is still jockeying among member states for position and power. Rather, specific high seas issues should be approached incrementally as need arises, and consensus can be sought on management measures.

However, there are several drawbacks to the incremental approach. For one, agreement on the scope and powers of international high seas organizations may take years to formulate. IMO, for example, after years of debate, adopted MARPOL[40] in 1973 and amended it in 1978, but the convention did not become operational until 1983, when, after ten years, it received sufficient ratifications by IMO members to enter into force.

A second problem is that agreements in force may weaken over time. The International Whaling Commission, which in 1982 established a moratorium on the harvest of whales world-wide to take effect in 1986, lost Iceland as a member in 1992, the same year that Norway resumed commercial whaling, particularly for minke whales. Japan has also objected to the moratorium, and harvests minke whales for "scientific purposes".

An additional problem with the incremental approach is the lack of coordination among international management bodies, particularly with respect to high seas living marine resources, but also with environmental protection and, in some cases, marine scientific research. Also important is the issue of enforcement of agreed-upon rules and regulations for the high seas.

A managed regime of the high seas is not a distant prospect; it is with us now and will only intensify with time. Current and anticipated progress in marine science and research will forge new dilemmas for the international community to face.

On the one hand, it is important to retain certain traditional high seas freedoms; on the other, piecemeal efforts at management have, for reasons noted above, often been unable to live up to their full potentials. Herein lies one of the great maritime challenges of the 21st Century.

Notes

1. As used here, the term "mile" refers to a nautical mile, equal to 1.15 statute miles.
2. "Shore" refers here to the baseline along the coast from which the breadth of the territorial sea is measured. See Law of the Sea Convention Art. 5 through 14.
3. The exclusive economic zone is a resource zone, extending beyond the territorial sea to a maximum distance of 200 miles from shore, in which the high seas freedoms of navigation, overflight and the laying of submarine cables and pipelines is retained. See LOSC Art. 55 through 75.
4. Thomas W. Fulton, *The Sovereignty of the Sea* (Edinburgh: William Blackwood & Sons, 1911), 523.

5.   The contiguous zone extends beyond the territorial sea, overlapping the EEZ, to a maximum of 24 miles from shore. In the contiguous zone the coastal state exercises control over customs, fiscal, immigration and similar functions. See LOSC Art. 23.

6.   In October, 1945, a month after the Truman Proclamation, Mexico declared "supervision, use and control" of the waters overlying its continental shelf. Panama followed suit in March, 1946, and five months later so did Argentina. Chile, in June, 1947 was the first state to claim fisheries jurisdiction out to 200 miles; two months later, Peru did likewise.

7.   Convention on the Territorial Sea and the Contiguous Zone, Convention on the High Seas, Convention on Fishing and the Conservation of the Living Resources of the High Seas, Convention on the Continental Shelf.

8.   By March, 1966, all four Conventions had entered into force.

9.   Article 16(4) of the Territorial Sea Convention reads, "There shall be no suspension of the innocent passage of foreign ships through straits which are used for international navigation between one part of the high seas and another part of the high seas ...". But what if the passage itself is not considered "innocent" by the strait states(s)?

10.   The Convention was adopted by 130 votes in favour, four (including the United States) against and 17 abstentions.

11.   The Convention enters into force 12 months after the date of deposit of the sixtieth instrument of ratification or accession. See LOSC Art. 308.

12.   An archipelagic state is one constituted wholly by one or more islands and archipelagos, which has, within its limits, a ratio of the areas of water to land between 1 to 1 and 9 to 1. The state is bounded by baselines generally not exceeding 100 miles each. Indonesia, The Philippines and The Bahamas are examples of archipelagic states.

13.   Part VI of LOSC (Art. 76 through 85) deals with the rights and duties of coastal states regarding their continental shelf.

14.   Section 2 of Part VII (Art. 116 through 120) refers to the conservation and management of the living resources of the high seas.

15.   Part XII (Art. 238-266) deals with rights and responsibilities of states conducting marine scientific research on the high seas and in various other jurisdictional zones.

16.   The bulk of the non-seabed provisions of the Convention had been agreed on by the Conference delegations by May, 1975, at which time the Informal Single Negotiating Text (ISNT) was issued. But seven more years would elapse before the final session of the Convention—years devoted primarily to deep seabed regime issues.

17.   There are approximately 21 "broad margin" states, whose legally defined continental shelf extends at one or more points beyond the 200-mile limits of

the EEZ. Among these states are Argentina, Canada, Ireland, United Kingdom, and the United States.

18. "Unauthorized broadcasting" (Art. 109) means the transmission of sound radio or television, contrary to international regulations.
19. e.g., Canada, Ireland, Japan, South Africa.
20. e.g., Ecuador, Liberia, Panama, Peru.
21. e.g., Albania, Greece, Sweden, Syria.
22. e.g., Finland, Italy, Saudi Arabia, Thailand, Cuba.
23. The 1982 Convention (Art. 121) makes no legal distinction between islands and rocks.
24. See, for example, William T. Burke, "Implications for Fisheries Management of U.S. Acceptance of the 1982 Convention on the Law of the Sea", *American Journal of International Law* 89, 1995, 804.
25. Among these are mercury, cadmium, silver, nickel, and lead.
26. Jon M. Van Dyke, "Sea Shipment of Japanese Plutonium Under International Law", *Ocean Development and International Law* 24, 1993, 399.
27. William T. Burke, "State Practice, New Ocean Uses, and Ocean Governance under UNCLOS", in Thomas W. Mensah (ed.), *Ocean Governance, Strategies and Approaches for the 21st Century* (Honolulu, HI: University of Hawaii, The Law of the Sea Institute, 1996), 230.
28. *Ibid.*
29. As, for example, university research vessels.
30. See James Kraska, "Oceanographic and Naval Deployments of Expendable Marine Instruments Under U.S. and International Law", *Ocean Development and International Law* 26, 1995, 311-357.
31. Treaty on the Prohibition of the Emplacement of Nuclear Weapons and Other Weapons of Mass Destruction on the Sea-Bed and Ocean Floor and in the Subsoil Thereof.
32. L.F.E. Goldie, "Maritime War Zones and Exclusion Zones", in Horace B. Robertson (ed.), *International Law Studies 1991: The Law of Naval Operations* (Newport, RI: Naval War College Press, 1991), 173.
33. *Ibid.*, 174.
34. e.g., Inter-American Tropical Tuna Commission, International Commission for the Conservation of Atlantic Tunas.
35. For a comprehensive survey of the straddling stocks issue, see Evelyne Meltzer, "Global Overview of Straddling and Highly Migratory Fish Stocks", *Ocean Development and International Law* 25, 1994, 255-345. See also Andre Tahindro, "Conservation and Management of Transboundary Fish Stocks", *Ocean Development and International Law* 28, 1997, 1-59.
36. e.g., Food and Agriculture Organization, International Maritime Organization, Intergovernmental Oceanographic Commission.
37. e.g, Convention on the Conservation of Antarctic Marine Living Resources.

38. e.g., International Convention for the Regulation of Whaling.
39. Agreement relating to the Implementation of Part XI of the United Nations Convention on the Law of the Sea of 10 December, 1982 (adopted 28 July, 1994).
40. Convention for the Prevention of Pollution from Ships.

3 Global Shipping Trends and Implications for Navies

DANIEL Y. COULTER AND ALAN GOLDMAN

The changes to global shipping in the past 30 years have been remarkable. During the same span, there has been a substantial shift in the balance of trade in both volume and value from the Atlantic Basin to the Pacific Rim. Perhaps the most significant change in the modern shipping industry has been the divorcing trend of the national maritime flag from the national economy. With rare exceptions, the flag no longer represents a manifestation of a nation-state's economic power. Shipping had already evolved from a pure national entity to a multinational enterprise, long before "multinational" became a buzzword.

Such changes have created tensions between the growing internationalization of shipping and the means of its protection and regulation, which remain largely national in scope. Nowhere are the tensions more acute than in the post-Cold War debate over the utility of a national naval force in managing a problem with "multinational" ramifications. What follows is an examination of emerging and future trends in shipping that have major implications for navies operating in the 21st century.

Significance of Shipping

Between 90-95 per cent of international merchandise trade by volume is carried on the oceans, which gives it a strong maritime character. Shipping is, in a sense, at the apex of world economic activity. Ocean-going ships provide the means for developing economic resources on an international scale, by allowing raw materials or finished products to be conveyed from areas of low utility to areas of production, assembling and high consumption (i.e., minerals from Africa to the Western industrialized nations). In his seminal book, *The Economic History of World Population*, Carlo Cipolla underscores the strategic importance of shipping by noting it as one of the prime forces responsible for shifting the world from an essentially national system to the global economy that exists today:

Fast and cheap transportation has been one of the main products of the Industrial Revolution. Distances have been shortened at an astonishing pace. Day by day the world seems smaller and smaller and societies that for millennia practically ignored each other are suddenly put in contact or conflict. In our dealings, in politics as in economics, in health organization as in military strategy, a new point of view is forced upon us. At some time in the past people had to move from an urban or regional point of view to a national one. Today we have to adjust ourselves in our way of thinking to a global point of view. As Bertrand Russell wrote, "the world has become one not only for the astronomer but for the ordinary citizen".[1]

History has also confirmed the continuing role of shipping as a stimulus of economic development. Adam Smith, better known as the father of modern economics, recognized shipping as one of the main drivers propelling economic development, whether in a local, national, regional, or global marketplace. In Volume I, Chapter III of *The Wealth of Nations*, he viewed water-based transport as an impetus to further economic development, since it can open up wider markets to specialization, offering regular deliveries of consumer products at affordable prices:

> As by means of water carriage a more extensive market is opened to every sort of industry than what land-carriage alone can afford it, so it is upon the sea-coast, and along the banks of navigable rivers, that industry of every kind naturally begins to subdivide and improve itself, and it is frequently not until a long time after that those improvements extend themselves to the inland parts of the country. A broad wheeled waggon, attended by two men, and drawn by eight horses, in about six weeks time carries and brings back between London and Edinburgh near four ton weight of goods. In about the same time a ship navigated by six or eight men, and sailing between the ports of London and Leith, frequently carries and brings back two hundred ton weight of goods....since such, therefore, are the advantages of water carriage, it is natural that the first improvements of art and industry should be made where this conveniency opens the whole world for a market to the produce of every sort of labour...[2]

Economic and technological advances have accelerated since Adam Smith wrote those words in 1776, and the ocean shipping industry has certainly not been impervious to such profound changes. What follows is a catalogue of trends in the shipping industry that have and will continue to play a major part as well as incorporate the current globalization phenomena.

Global Shipping Trends

Most noteworthy about the following trends is not so much the rapidity of the pace of change but the seeming irreversibility of the trends; that is the trends will not revert back to the past as we knew it. This has tremendous implications not only for commercial strategic planning, but also for naval planning, as will be explained in the next section.

The Decline of the National-flag Fleet

Throughout history, merchant ships served as economic plenipotentiaries in international commerce. With rare and often transitory exceptions, nationality of the ownership in the vessel, cargo and crew were inseparable from the ship's flag. In the post-Second World War era, the growing internationalization of trade combined with widespread de-colonization forced shipping to become increasingly divorced from direct national control, and this has had an adverse effect on the relative importance of the fleets of the traditional maritime nations. Today, the ship's flag more often than not gives no indication of the nationality of the controlling interests behind the vessel. In fact, more than half of the world's merchant vessels fly a flag that is different than the nationality of the owner.

This remarkable shift can be captured below in Figure 3.1. What is interesting is the domination by the national flags of the great powers in 1975. Today, only one remains in the top 10—Japan. Instead the list is dominated by open registers, better known as "flags of convenience" (FOC).

The flags of Liberia, Panama, Cyprus and Malta are considered "open" in that the flag is non-discriminatory on the basis of ownership nationality. National flags like Greece, China and Japan are more restrictive; those who opt to fly the flag must often provide proof of citizenship or residence that corresponds to that flag.

Figure 3.1 Top 10 Country Flags by Deadweight Tons (DWT)

1975		1997
Liberia	1	*Panama*
Japan	2	*Liberia*
United Kingdom	3	Greece
Norway	4	*Cyprus*
Greece	5	*Bahamas*
Panama	6	Norway
France	7	*Malta*
United States	8	China
Italy	9	Singapore
Former Soviet Union	10	Japan

Note: Countries in Italics represent flags of convenience
Source: US Navy

Why has the shift occurred on such a dramatic scale? Since ship-owners operate in a free-market environment, competitiveness becomes the rule of the game. In order to compete effectively, shipowners seek to cut costs or streamline operations wherever possible, and many have found the answers in flags of convenience. The advantages such FOCs offer in comparison to national flags include the following:

- Anonymity of ownership;
- Lower crew costs;
- Simple registration procedures;
- Less stringent regulations;
- No obvious weighting of insurance premiums or finances;
- Little to no corporation tax on profits from shipping; and
- Diffusion of liability.

A telling indication of the competitiveness or attractiveness of FOCs versus national flags can be derived from the influences of the foreign exchange markets. The dollar is universally accepted as the currency for which all international transactions in shipping are cleared; that is, the revenues of shipping companies doing global business are normally US dollar-denominated. At the same time the costs of shipping, (i.e., crew's wages and social insurance contributions) are mostly denominated in local currencies. Thus the movements of exchange rates, particularly the cross-exchange rates involving the dollar can have profound consequences on the national-flag fleets.

Figure 3.2 Net Outflow of JPN-Flag Tonnage (1980-1992)

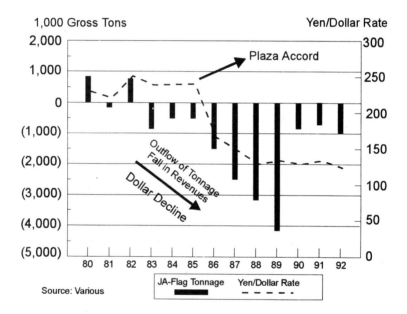

The volatility of the yen/dollar exchange rate in the 1985-1990 period in Figure 3.2 provides a good example. With the US dollar at record highs against the yen in 1985 contributing to massive and persistent US trade deficits, the G7 nations crafted the Plaza Accord to drive down the value of the dollar. The effects of the Japanese (JPN)-flag fleet and shipping companies were dramatic. The net outflow of JPN-flag tonnage increased as almost dramatically as the fall of the US dollar and only slowed as the dollar stabilized in the early 1990s. The revenues of the "Big 6" of Japanese shipping companies suffered a similar fate, as they plunged almost in tandem with the dollar movement.[3]

Today, there is more Japanese-owned tonnage flying flags of convenience than the Japanese flag; Japanese owners control roughly 40 per cent of all ships registered under the Panamanian flag. By registering their ships in Panama, Japanese owners do not have to man their ships with Japanese crews, avoid paying a host of what they consider excessive taxes imposed by the Japanese Ministry of Finance, and circumvent what they consider unfair and stringent regulations imposed by the Japanese Ministry of Transport.

Locus of Trade Shifting from West to East

Figure 3.3 World Merchandise Exports

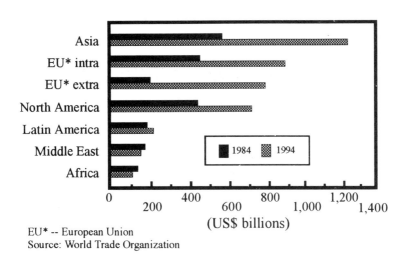

EU* -- European Union
Source: World Trade Organization

Equally dramatic has been the continuing shift in the volume of world trade from the Atlantic and Western Hemisphere to the Pacific and Far East. In the 1984-94 period, the value of trade between Asian countries increased in real terms by 125 per cent, compared to a 100 per cent and 60 per cent increase in intra-EU and North America trade, respectively, although only little trade of the former is maritime. This shift in trade towards Asia also holds true for most commodity trades, including crude oil and refined products, chemicals, iron ore, coal, grain and manufactured goods.

While the initial shift was powered by the Japanese economy from the 1960s to its first post-war recession in the 1990s, the rapid economic expansion of the Asian tigers (South Korea, Thailand, Indonesia, Malaysia, Taiwan, Singapore and Hong Kong), and more recently, India and China, has given rise to a sustained medium and long-term growth in seaborne trade to, from, and within this region.

Even more significant is that for the first time in modern history, world seaborne trade grew in spite of a slowdown in Gross Domestic Product (GDP) among the major western industrial powers (United States, Japan and the European Union) in the early nineties. The increasing presence of the Pacific Rim countries in the world economy is expected to accelerate the growth in world trade, as demonstrated below.

Figure 3.4 GDP Growth and Seaborne Trade

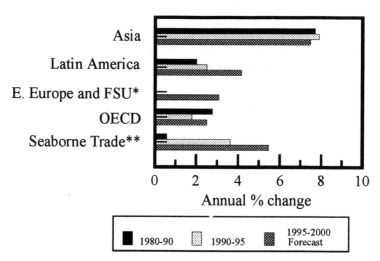

* Data unreliable for 1980-1995
** Growth measured in ton-miles
FSU -- Former Soviet Union

Several input-output models by private economic forecasting firms corroborate the ascendancy of Asia as the center-stage for world economic growth. According to one model of world activity, in 1990 the western industrialized nations produced some 40 per cent of the world's manufacturing employment. China and South East Asia had roughly 36 per cent. By the year 2020, the West will retain just 10 per cent while China and the rest of Asia will capture 65 per cent.[4] The numbers are certainly open to debate, but the trend is irrefutable; the economies of Asia may dictate the extent of future economic and job growth for the western industrialized powers.

Growing Containerization

Figure 3.5 Major Containerized Trade Flows

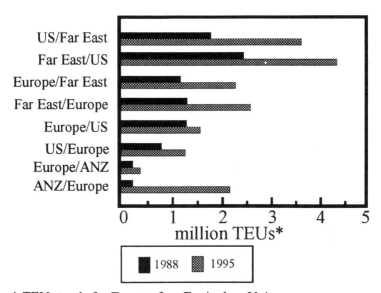

* TEU stands for Twenty-foot Equivalent Units
Source: DRI/Mercer World Sea Trade Service

Over the past 20 years, container shipping has been the fastest growing segment of the shipping market. According to the Institute for Shipping Economics and Logistics (ISL), between 1990-94, world seaborne trade rose by 3 per cent annually, but container traffic increased by roughly 9 per cent per year.[5] In contrast, seaborne trade in crude oil and iron ore grew only 3.5 per cent and 3.1 per cent, respectively.[6] As Figure 3.5 demonstrates, containerized trade has grown a whopping 70 per cent between 1988 and 1995, a yearly average of 8.75 per cent. The Pacific Rim figures prominently among the major containerized flows, again confirming the overall trade shift from west to east.

The containerization phenomena will continue to outpace world economic growth based on the following factors:

Increasing industrialization of Third World economies. As the economies of Latin America, Eastern Europe and, to a lesser extent, Africa continue to shift from producer of raw materials to technology and consumer goods, the ratio of containerized goods to break-bulk goods should increase significantly, since manufactured goods are synonymous with containerized goods.

Transplantation of manufacturing production processes. The worldwide dispersal of component manufacturing facilities, more commonly known as out-sourcing, has created additional demand for container shipping. In 1995, there were an estimated nine million TEUs (Twenty Foot Equivalent: standard unit of measurement of container throughput volume) trading worldwide that traversed multiple ports per year. This reflects the demand placed on container shipping to serve as the link between production facilities on different continents that require specific components for continued operation.

Containerization of break-bulk commodities. Traditional commodities like raw cotton, sugar, woodpulp, waste paper and even timber are increasingly becoming containerized. The prominent reason for such a conversion is the tremendous and chronic over-capacity in the container trades, forcing operators to search for ways to containerize goods previously thought uneconomical. Another and related factor is container operators seeking solutions to the "empty box" problem by containerizing cargoes for the backhaul to increase revenues per container unit. Figure 3.6 confirms the tremendous conversion taking place on a global scale in such a relatively short fashion.

Figure 3.6 Containerization of Global General Cargo Trade (million tons)

	1980	1985	1990	1995 (est.)
General Cargo	527	552	673	740
Containerized Cargo	120	172	269	408
% Containerized	23%	31%	40%	55%

Source: Drewry Shipping Consultants

Ocean shipping evolving into hub-and-spoke network. World trade flows are becoming much more concentrated with the mainline vessels calling at fewer ports worldwide, creating numerous "strings" of feeder vessels to disperse the trade throughout their specified locales. Such operations are not only cheaper, but more efficient. The net result is additional demand for containers and, by corollary, more container vessels, particularly feeders. The Zim Israel tri-continent service provides a good example. Utilizing Kingston, Jamaica as a hub, Zim's Caribbean feeders are effectively serving two trades, one to the US East Coast/Mediterranean and another to California and the Far East. A ship turning back from the Caribbean could only offer one of these, so Zim's feeders could either go twice the distance or be twice the size, thereby enjoying lower unit costs per container and better utilization of the mainline vessels serving the Kingston hub.[7]

Shift from Ocean Carrier to Total Logistics System

With the introduction of containerization, ocean shipping companies began to look beyond ports as an interface between land and sea, but rather as a total logistics chain involving the marine (including ports), road and rail infrastructure. The container makes this shift possible by virtue of its interchangeability among the various modes of transport. Containers packed with goods at the point-of-production can be transported over water and land without ever being opened until they reach their point-of-sale or final destination, creating a secure, seamless flow of goods.

Perhaps the most significant "enabler" of this shift has been the revolution in information technology. Advanced information technology allows businesses, government agencies and the military to improve the overall efficiency of transportation and reduce the number of transport requirements. As one industry consultant notes:

> Advanced information technology can integrate trade and trip transactions with financial management systems, as well as transportation systems planning, operations management of carriers, etc. By addressing the end-to-end flow time for information as well as for goods and people, dramatic improvements in the processes associated with all of the modes of transportation can be enhanced—at the nodes as well as in the links. In fact, applying such advanced information technology to intermodal transportation systems represents the critical competitive advantage that a [business] or nation can have, since it allows the optimization of the intermodal system from end-to-end in a seamless fashion. In many cases, it actually eliminates significant steps in the process; and, in other cases, it simply optimizes the transfer at the nodes and/or the selection of the best mode between the nodes.[8]

Since the primary customers for ocean carriers are businesses that compete on a global basis, the main drivers in this global approach have forced ocean carriers to shift from the traditional port-to-port focus to a door-to-door strategy. Some of those drivers are:

- *Speed and frequency of service.* Competitiveness is no longer just based on quality or pricing, but increasingly on the speed in which a product can be delivered to the market. Volvo provides a typical example of cost-savings from speed of delivery. The Swedish-based company estimates in a recent article that they spend $22/day per car en route from factory to showroom; adding 30 days to Volvo's transit time would cost them $660 extra per delivered car in interest costs.[9]
- *Global marketing.* The battle for market share has gone global, forcing companies to seek a competitive edge by employing the most efficient and cost-effective means of distribution.
- *Niche marketing and customization.* The consumers are becoming better educated with more discriminating tastes, creating a greater product mix. This forces companies to keep better track of inventory and seek out the best possible combination of transport modes to facilitate a quick and efficient response to the ever-changing and demanding tastes of a global customer base.

The door-to-door strategy facilitated the mergers of the various modes of transport into a seamless distribution chain from the manufacturer to the retailer. As a consequence, the carriers' customers no longer focused on which mode was the most cost-effective and efficient, but rather on the reliability of the deliveries. In effect, the burden of not only managing the costs of distribution , but also the selection of the mode, shifted from the customers to the carriers. This forced carriers from the various modes to not only compete with each other, but also within their own modes.

Consolidation within Shipping Industry

With the barriers of competition coming down between the modes of transport, the natural and inevitable response was to consolidate not only within the modes but also across the spectrum of modes. The motivation is simple: the larger the carrier is, the greater economies of scale afforded, leading to lower unit costs per ton or container offered.

Within the ocean shipping industry itself, consolidation has proceeded in recent years through alliances and consortia arrangements. These are extensions of ship-sharing agreements that started in the 1980s. Those agreements allowed for shipowners to charter spaces on each others ships plying certain trade routes. The current alliances took the system a step further with entire operations encompassing every asset from the vessels to the port terminals being pooled on a global basis.[10]

There are currently four alliances that dominate the container shipping industry:

- the Global Alliance of American President Lines, Orient Overseas Container Line, Mitsui O.S.K. Lines and Nedlloyd Lines;
- the Grand Alliance of Hapag-Lloyd AG, P&O Containers, Neptune Orient Lines and Nippon Yushen Kaisha;
- the partnership of Sea-Land Service, Inc. and Maersk Line, and;
- the consortia of Hanjin Shipping Co, Cho Yang Shipping Co. and DSR Senator Line.

There are other looser arrangements, such as slot-chartering among the remaining carriers. Conspicuously absent are two of the largest and independent carriers, Evergreen and the China Ocean Shipping Company. General industry wisdom has been that the independents' days are numbered; that either they will form an alliance or merge with existing ones.

In fact, the drive to secure greater economies of scale and cost rationalization has led to a new level of concentration—the merger, a fate that may well befall any and all in the container shipping industry. The merger of P&O Containers and Nedlloyd Lines in late 1996 and the announcement in April 1997 of the merger between American President Lines and Neptune Orient represent a harbinger of things to come in the industry in the next few years. The significance of the mergers lies in the view that such a complete integration of operations creates industry behemoths that can leverage economies of scale into per-unit cost of savings that force smaller competitors to either join forces with others or find marginal or niche trades.

Concentration in the form of mergers has not just been limited to the maritime industry, as attested by the digestion of Conrail by CSX and Norfolk Southern in early 1997. There is speculation that the merger is a preview to the formation of truly trans-continental railroads that will ultimately reduce the number of rail companies in the United States to just two, one on each coast.

The Richmond, Virginia-based CSX portends a further concentration in the making: a truly global transportation company that operates across national lines and modes of transport. CSX, already a major player in the US railroad market, owns Sea-Land, a major US player in the global container sweepstakes that joined forces with an even bigger container line, the Danish powerhouse, Maersk. In addition, CSX signed a letter of intent with Deutsche Bahn, the German state railway and NS Cargo, the Dutch rail freight operator, to run a door-to-door service across Europe.[11] Furthermore, CSX through Sea-Land provide freight forwarding services for the Trans-Siberian railway on behalf of the Russian authorities and has plans to offer warehousing, transport, cargo consolidation and freight forwarding services to its customers in China.

With up to 70 per cent of the total transport costs on land, the significance of CSX's strategy is obvious: A CSX combine would be in a position to offer a Shanghai-Frankfurt-Los Angeles through service that no shipping rival could match. CSX offers a glimpse into the future where global transport is dominated by a-national intermodal conglomerates, whose only motivation is carrying everyone's cargo, anywhere and at anytime.

Chronic Over-Capacity in Shipping Markets

Since the mid-1970s, over-capacity has been an enduring feature of the shipping markets. As Figure 3.7 shows, the gap between amount of demand for trade and capacity or supply of shipping has been in huge disequilibrium and will remain so in the next century. This raises the obvious question: when will the shipping markets reach a state of equilibrium? The answer in short, is possibly never; that is, the markets will always be in a state of over-capacity.

Two factors are evident. First, the corporatization of shipping beginning in the 1970s introduced asset play in the shipping markets where individual ships were being built for pure speculation and not traditionally for a specific trade that required it be based on cargo demand. Since then, advances in information technologies and a proliferation of financial instruments have facilitated the ease in which ships can be traded on the markets without regard for their specific trading requirements.

Figure 3.7 World Trade vs. Fleet Capacity

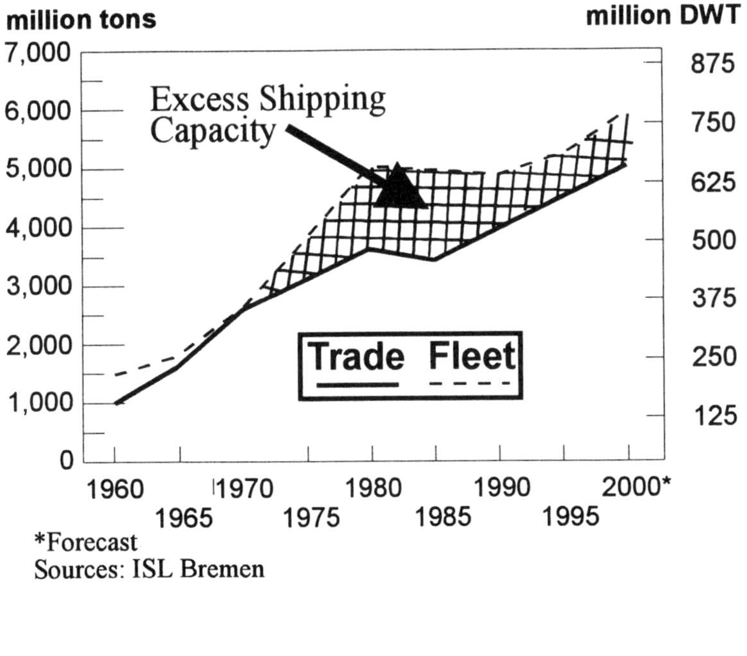

*Forecast
Sources: ISL Bremen

Second, some governments continue to subsidize the shipbuilding industries as they fear a political backlash from the unions (i.e., Lech Walesa's Solidarity movement in Poland). That is what created the massive over-capacity situation in Figure 3.7 after 1975, when the West European nations, who dominated world shipbuilding at that time, kept ordering ships to keep employment humming during a severe global recession, precipitated by the sharp oil price increases initiated by Arab-OPEC members. More recently, Bonn in 1996 created a limited partnership system, the KG company, that offered attractive financial terms for German shipowners if they ordered ships built in German shipyards. Bonn's motivation was partly to keep the Eastern German shipyards gainfully employed. A similar example can be found in Seoul's decision in the early 1990s to unilaterally expand the nation's shipyards' capacity to build more very large crude carriers (VLCCs), when the Europeans and Japanese shipyards agreed to keep their excess capacity mothballed.

In a global free-market environment like shipping, equilibrium in supply and demand remains an elusive, if not impossible, goal. There are not only too many dynamic market factors that operate independently of each other, but there are also many non-market decisions that influence the shipping markets. For planning purposes, it is prudent and, indeed, realistic to expect the shipping markets to always be in a state of over-capacity.

Implications for Navies

The protection and policing of maritime commerce has historically been one of the prime *raison d'être* for navies. The influences propelling the internationalization of the shipping industry pose a quandary for navies, since they represent a national policy instrument in a world where states are becoming globalized. That is, the policy orientation of the state has gradually shifted outward and beyond its territorial waters, and in the process, the nation-state's actions are increasingly being defined by non-territorial actors and global market forces.[12]

The difficulty, of course, for states and, by corollary, navies lies in recognizing that they can no longer operate in a vacuum where the only consideration is their national interests. This represents a sea change in culture, and there is enormous institutional resistance to such a revolutionary change. For navies to successfully manage radical change, the first step is to recognize the "problem" and then take steps to either reflect or incorporate those changes. That means—for policymakers and naval planners—broadening the focus from traditional threats, which are political or military in nature, to a more dynamic and unpredictable mix of scenarios, which include non-naval threats that often require the navies to participate in operations involving multiple organizations and multiple countries.

Globalization of the Navies

Given the internationalization of maritime commerce, every nation would require a navy capable of projecting power anywhere on the globe in order to ensure adequate defense of its national economic interests. For example, when roughly half of the world's oil exports come from the Middle East and combined with the transparencies in the global oil market, virtually all nations remain at risk to a disruption of the tanker trade out of the Arabian Gulf.

A quick survey around the globe reveals that few navies possess such a capability. In fact, today only one, the US Navy, conforms to traditional sea power theory. Yet, even the US Navy is facing budgetary disarmament. The choice for navies is stark: either seek multi-national cooperation or invest in power projection platforms. It is clear that only the former is a practical choice, since few nations have the economic resources to build and maintain a navy with truly global reach.

Hence, navies with their inherent national orientation must work together in scenarios that have adverse impact far beyond their territorial waters. Examples include trade interdiction, mining of harbors and straits, piracy, illegal migration, drug smuggling, arms proliferation, illegal fishing and nuclear dumping. The continuing integration of the global economy means that the source of the negative impact on the seas can occur from any point of the compass by virtue of the cascading effect generated by mutual interdependence of not just trade, but also banking, manufacturing, capital markets, etc. Thus, the states must "globalize" their navies in order for them to remain effective extensions of foreign policy in the 21st century.

Transnational Influences

A merchant ship today represent the ultimate trans-national corporation. Take for example a ship transporting a cargo of passenger cars from North America to Europe. Cars made in the United States from Japanese-owned plants, German-owned plants and US-owned plants with parts shipped in from Mexico and Brazil are loaded aboard a ship, owned by Sweden;

financed by offshore banks in the Cayman Islands; managed by a Singapore firm; registered in Panama; chartered to a US freight forwarder; crewed by a complement of Danish officers and Filipino and Indian seafarers; insured in London, re-insured in Germany and subsequently unloaded in several European ports.

With over 90,000 merchant ships plying the world's oceans and flying at last count 197 separate flags, the challenges are enormous for policy makers and naval planners in determining the multiple interests in a single ship; in short, separating friend from foe. Finding out "who's in charge" of both the ship and cargo can often take months of legal inquiry. Figure 3.8 below represents a model of an ownership structure based on a recent initial public offering (IPO) for shares in a oil tanker company.

Figure 3.8 Vessel Ownership Structure

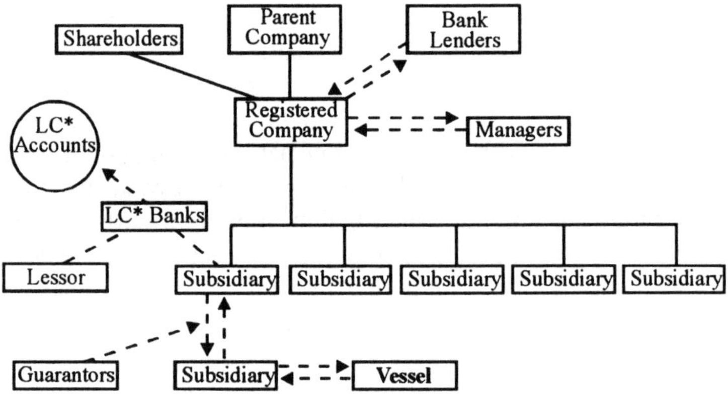

*LC - Letter of Credit
Source: Lloyd's Shipping Economist

In this example, the parent company based in the Netherlands decided to create a separate company in Bermuda under a different name and delegate management responsibilities to another company in Sweden. This bewildering complex web of interests is rapidly becoming the norm in the shipping industry for the following reasons:

- Borderless finance;
- Increased capital requirements for shipbuilding;
- Pressures to reduce costs and evade stringent regulations; and
- Expanding global trade and trade relationships.

This blurring of interests behind the ship and its cargo translates into a sobering reality for navies: interdiction of a ship in international waters creates an impact far beyond the flag its flies. The challenge then becomes how to determine precisely who is being affected and on whom may they call for assistance.

The Vessel Sharing Agreements (VSAs) among the major carriers in the liner service provide an excellent example of this challenge. These agreements allow for the participating carriers to pool and share their entire fleets and port terminals in some of the more competitive liner trades (i.e. Trans-Atlantic, Trans-Pacific and N.Europe to Asia trades). In the case of the current Global Alliance with the US-based American President Lines (APL), the Japanese-based Mitsui-O.S.K. (MOL), the Netherlands-based Nedlloyd and the Hong Kong-based Orient Overseas Container Line (OOCL) as participants in a VSA, the targeting of a ship assigned to this VSA affects all of the participants. So, if the US Navy is engaged in interdiction operations and stops a MOL ship, such an action could adversely affect APL, creating both a potential domestic political dilemma and an international incident for US policy makers.

The issue of protecting national trade in this context becomes confused. In a trans-national environment, trade can only be effectively protected by either a multi-national force or by one global navy. A multi-national force is often impractical and subject to changes in political emphasis within countries, especially in trade conflicts that produce winners and losers. For a global navy, such as the US Navy, the challenge then becomes practical in the sense of covering all potential scenarios or only those that affect its national interests and doing what it can with the assets at its disposal. It is clear that any one country cannot prepare for all possible contingencies, unless it is prepared to fund the highest common denominator.

There are those who argue that navies should not expand their missions to accommodate the "trans-national" environment, since the multi-national links are transitory and are a function of a peacetime environment. They believe that in times of large-scale, trans-oceanic conflicts like that of the Second World War, the ships will re-unite with their national navies.

Such arguments ignore not only the fact that these trans-national links cannot be liquidated in the short-term in the same manner as selling shares in a company on the stock exchange, but also the historical anomaly of the Second World War. One would be hard pressed to find in history books a conflict that approached the scale of the Second World War. The chances of a re-occurrence are extremely remote.

Strategic Sealift Planning

The traditional pillars of strategic sealift are coming under increasing assault from the present trends in shipping. Considering that merchant shipping has long been considered the fourth arm of national defense, it is not surprising that the trends have stirred much emotional debate over what has been perceived as the declining national control of shipping for future military logistics operations. The danger here lies in clinging to traditional and dogmatic notions of shipping that will ultimately preclude more advantageous and less expensive ways of planning a logistics campaign. Below are some of the issues that need to be addressed before an effective strategic sealift policy can be articulated for future overseas contingencies.

Decline of the national-flag fleet. Unquestionably, this trend has generated the most concern among governments, particularly among the great powers. Such concerns have been predicated on the assumption that only national-flag fleets can guarantee ships to move a nation's troops and war material in times of conflict, and that reliance on foreign-flag shipping is a risky proposition. Consequently, many governments have crafted shipping policies designed to ensure sufficient ships are flying the national flag. Yet, almost all have been expensive failures by granting subsidies without yielding a fleet that meets certified military requirements.

Too much attention has focused on the flag and not enough on the ability to access ships that are controlled or owned by domestic commercial interests. Just because the US carrier, American President Lines, decides that some of its ships will fly a non-US flag does not mean that those ships can not be made available in times of national emergencies. The key to an effective policy is to set up a mechanism that makes it economically attractive in the short-term for commercial carriers to switch ships to the national flag and give up control of those ships in specified crises. The Voluntary Intermodal Sealift Agreement (VISA) fashioned by the US Department of Defense with input by the US carriers may be a good example of this, since it stresses the availability of shore-side infrastructure as well as ships.

Nevertheless, the patriotic value of the national flag is, in many cases, overstated. In such a fiercely competitive sector as shipping, once a ship is removed from a trade for national security reasons, that ship will find it exceedingly difficult, if not impossible, to re-enter the trade, particularly in the liner trades that require a fixed schedule. As a result, the company will lose the corresponding market share, for which it had tremendous investments in securing and maintaining. It is essential for naval planners and policy makers to understand the limits of playing the "patriotic" card when requesting ships for service. Instead, they should closely monitor the open charter market and prepare to tender for those ships that meet the requirements.

Such an approach raises two counter-arguments. The first relates to the fears of relying on foreign shipping and foreign crews. They are unjustified, as demonstrated in past conflicts like the Tanker War from 1984 to 1988 and most recently, *Desert Shield/Desert Storm*. In both conflicts, the over-riding motivation for carrying cargoes into harm's way is money: the carriers and the crews make money only when they sail. So powerful is this urge that when the Japanese Seamen's Union held out for more hazardous pay during the Gulf War, the Japanese shipping companies promptly left them at home and hired Filipinos and other Third World nationals to man their ships. Those hired saw a terrific opportunity to make more money than they ever could have realized and conversely, the Japanese shipping companies made more money on those voyages, since with even the bonuses paid to the foreign crews, they were still a lot cheaper than Japanese crews.

Second, there are fears that the ships available for chartering do not meet "unique" military requirements. While such fears are occasionally justified, for example when outsized armored vehicles must be moved, the greatest physical bulk of material moved for a military operation is usually cargo readily containerized. Moreover, many—perhaps most—overseas operational deployments are of infantry or only lightly mechanized units (i.e., the Belgian and French airborne units which have deployed several times to Africa or the US 10th Mountain Division which deployed to Haiti in 1994), which do not require heavy or specialized equipment that cannot be containerized. The fact that most of the military requirements are converging with the commercial requirements should also be a consideration, which is noted below.

Role of containerization. Some military planners remain sceptical of the utility of containers in sealift operations. *Desert Shield/Desert Storm* proved that the overwhelming majority of the equipment and material was indeed containerizable—or in the case of some of the lighter-wheeled vehicles such as trucks and Humvees—could have been containerized had there been the proper support equipment, such as flatracks for example. Instead, the chosen alternatives were breakbulk and Ro/Ro (Roll-on/Roll-off ships) vessels that were much more expensive to operate.[13]

The continued reliance on non-container vessels is partly based on fears that containers require sophisticated port infrastructure not likely to be found in Third World countries. That is becoming less of an issue, due to the hub-and-spoke network in the global container trades that allows the commercial shipping world to make inroads into the Third World markets, but nonetheless remains a real constraint, as demonstrated in Operation *Restore Hope* in Somalia. However, it is not inconceivable that a reliable intermodal infrastructure will eventually be established in Somalia and other areas that are currently considered under-developed.

Decline of Ro/Ros. These ships have long been prized for their ability to carry tanks and other heavy equipment that require ramps of sufficient strength. With the commercial Ro/Ro market in decline, numerous national shipbuilding programs have been proposed to replace the declining availability of Ro/Ro in the open charter market for military sealift purposes. Such a strategy ignores the fact that much of the traditional cargoes for Ro/Ro have become containerized and that vehicle carriers have dramatically improved their ability to carry vehicles of mixed dimensions by incorporating strengthened ramps and hoistable decks. Most of the commercial vehicle carriers in operation today have ramps of 100-plus tons strength, which exceeds the military's requirements.

Reliance on intermodal systems. Military planners are loathe to concede control over cargoes to the commercial operators. They would rather contract for separate, independent modal moves than rely on existing integrated, container-based systems. Such an approach can result in significant economic and service penalties such as additional re-handling costs, inflexible routing, longer transit times and the loss or damage of cargoes. For example, during *Desert Shield/Desert Storm*, the US Department of Defense (DoD) took 40-60 days to resupply the same parts that Caterpillar guaranteed delivery anywhere in the world, including Central Africa, in just four days.[14]

Admittedly, there are unique military requirements that cannot be discounted. But that should not preclude military planners from taking advantage of commercial intermodal systems for the vast majority of the war material and equipment shipped by sea. Reducing the chances of "no-show" and damaged cargoes and delays in transit are already issues that the commercial world face everyday. To put it in perspective, Federal Express handles over 1.5 million orders world-wide every day, while the US DoD handled at maximum 35,000 orders per day during the Persian Gulf crisis.[15] By utilizing the existing commercial transport systems, military planners can free themselves to a large degree from the burdens of managing a complex logistics operation and instead concentrate on the business of fighting wars.

Conclusion

The growing internationalization of maritime commerce and shipping is forcing many nation-states to debate the utility of national naval forces in conflict scenarios that are not responsive to "national" approaches. Future disruptions to shipping and trade are certain to have international consequences and, therefore, are much more likely to demand multi-national naval cooperation. By gaining a fuller appreciation and closer monitoring of the drivers in the global shipping markets, national policy-makers and naval planners can make more informed choices that will impact on the effectiveness of their navies in the 21st century.

Notes

1. Carlo M. Cipolla, *The Economic History of World Population*, 7th ed. (Sussex, England: Harvester Press Ltd., 1978), 13.
2. Adam Smith, *The Wealth of Nations* (New York: Random House, 1937), Volume I, 18-19. The text printed here is that of the 3rd edition of 1784.
3. For more details on this theme and other influences on the decline of the national-flag fleet, see Charles N. Dragonette and Daniel Y. Coulter's *World Merchant Shipping: Multinationalism Triumphant* paper presented to the US Transportation Research Board Annual Meeting, 7-11 January 1996, Session 189.
4. John MacDonald, *Lloyd's List Maritime Asia* March 1996, 54.
5. *Lloyd's List*, 27 February 1997, 6-8.

6. Clarkson Research Studies, *Shipping Review & Outlook*, Autumn 1996, Section 3, 1-3.
7. *Lloyd's List*, 14 April 1997, 5.
8. J.S. Gansler, "Realizing An Intermodal Future: Research and Development Issues in the Commercial, Military, and Public Arenas", Paper presented to the US Transportation Research Board Committee, 15 November 1995, 3.
9. Lee Cisneros, "The Value of Time", *Intermodal Shipping*, April 1996, 40.
10. *Journal of Commerce*, 6 January 1997, 10-11C.
11. *Seatrade Review*, August 1996, 21.
12. Richard Falk, "State of siege: will globalization win out?", *International Affairs* January 1997, 129.
13. American President Lines, "Desert Shield, Desert Storm: Some Extraordinary Successes and Critical Lessons Learned in the Transportation of Military Freight," White Paper presented to US Department of Defense, 1.
14. Michael Rich, "Toward a New Government-Industry Partnership in Aerospace," Rand Corporation, Santa Monica, CA, Speech delivered in Orlando, FL, 24 February 1993, 6.
15. Gansler, 7.

4 Colbert's Heirs: The United States, NATO and Multilateral Naval Cooperation in the Post Cold War Era

JOEL J. SOKOLSKY

In late 1994, ships from ten NATO (North Atlantic Treaty Organization) nations joined vessels from Russia, Lithuania, Poland and Sweden in *Cooperative Venture 94*, the first Partnership for Peace (PfP) naval exercise which was held near the Norwegian port of Stavanger. Activities included "joint manoeuvring, refuelling from a NATO tanker ship sea, forming communications networks with other ships and groups of flights of naval helicopters".[1] The late Admiral Richard G. Colbert, USN (United States Navy) would have been pleased.

As John Hattendorf has noted, Richard Colbert was a rarity amongst officers of the United States Navy. In a profession and a service, which seemed synonymous with the projection of national power abroad, he was the champion of multilateralism. Elmo Zumwalt has called him "Mr. International Navy", the unofficial president of the global "fraternity of the blue uniform". A great believer in multilateral naval education, he created the Naval Command Course for senior foreign officers at the US Naval War College in 1955. As president of the college from 1969-1971, he began a course for mid-ranked foreign officers and inaugurated the Seapower Symposiums for foreign flag officers. Most importantly Colbert strove to put his multilateral vision into action. During his two tours on the staff of the Supreme Allied Commander, Atlantic (SACLANT) in the mid-sixties and early 1970s, Colbert was one of the moving forces behind greater allied maritime cooperation. He was especially active in the establishment of the Standing Naval Force Atlantic (STANAVFORLANT) in 1968. In his last post, as Commander-in-Chief Allied Forces, South

69

(CINCSOUTH) he was credited with lending "credibility to the NATO strategy of flexible response". He fostered "an enthusiastic spirit of solidarity" amongst the five allied nations of the region.[2] Central to his approach was that multilateral naval cooperation had to be approached from the stand point of partnership, rather than imposed by Washington.

Ironically, although Colbert saw his multilateralism as directed primarily against Soviet seapower, it was the end of the Cold War that ushered in an unprecedented era of naval cooperation as a growing number of nations (including former adversaries and non-aligned) became interested in collaboration with the USN and amongst themselves. A multilateral force supported land operations in the Gulf War. The old NATO maritime alliance has been given new life with its actions in support of United Nations (UN) peacekeeping operations in Yugoslavia, making use of the STANAVFORLANT and the Standing Naval Force Mediterranean (STAN-AVFORMED). New allied strategic concepts, such as the Combined and Joint Task Forces (CJTF), enhance the scope of naval operations. Most remarkable, the Alliance's Partnership for Peace program has expanded cooperation at sea to include the Russians and their former Warsaw Pact allies. Elsewhere, the USN has maintained a bilateral and multilateral exercise program that reached 200 per year by 1993.[3]

However, it is also important to remember that Colbert was not always successful in promoting his ideas for greater multilateralism. His plans for the Multilateral Nuclear Force, an Inter-American Military Force, the Free World Frigate Program, mix-manning of allied ships, and a combined marine amphibious force for the STANAVFORLANT, never came to fruition. By the early 1970s, many governments were suspicious of US schemes for greater cooperation at sea, especially those in the Third World. Older allies were not always anxious to assume the burdens of partnership, and Washington itself was wary of new joint undertakings. There were limits to what the fraternity could do.

The reason was that in Colbert's day, as now, navies remained first and foremost instruments of national policy, especially for the USN—now the "unipolar navy." For Colbert, it was always clear that multilateralism at sea was only attractive because it served US interests. Multilateral naval cooperation is an instrument used by a coalition of nations who deem it in their national self-interests to make use of seapower. Therefore, the tactical, strategic and above all political effectiveness of multilateral naval cooperation will always be dependent upon the cohesiveness of the coalition that stands behind, and especially upon, the will of the major contributing naval power. As Charles Krauthammer argues, when "America moves, the world moves...peace depends...on a balance of power. And with the structure of the world being what it is today, with the United States overwhelmingly dominant, that means American power and the will to use it".[4]

This chapter argues that much of the post-Cold War multilateral naval cooperation we have witnessed is very much the result of an American approach to its national security that has been, despite unilateralist temptations, directed towards maintaining older alliances and *ad hoc* coalition-building. The chapter begins with an analysis of trends in US national security policy, especially under the Clinton administration. It then turns to a discussion of the nature of naval collaboration consistent with these trends. While there is much potential, it can also be argued that without American leadership in this area, the future for multilateral naval cooperation might become less promising.

US National Security Policy and Multilateralism in the Post-Cold War Era[5]

The USN has been the focal point for multinational naval cooperation simply because the United States has not come home in the post-Cold War era. From the Persian Gulf to Somalia to Haiti to Bosnia, the United States has repeatedly led multilateral coalitions in armed interventions.[6] How can this be explained given that, as the world's sole superpower, the US faces no immediate threat to its national security interests?

Three interrelated factors can account for this. First, these interventions are the result of simple superpower inertia. The habits of fifty years are hard to break. No new overarching consensus or organizing principle similar to containment deterrence has emerged to guide Washington in the disorder of the new world order. Meanwhile, the predilection in favour of, and the capability for, intervention remains strong. This is especially the case when other powers and international organizations are unwilling or unable to resolve regional conflicts and turn to Washington for solutions.

Second, the United States does have interests in many parts of the world. Lacking a global challenge, these interests are less vital and more narrowly defined, but they span the globe nonetheless. Moreover, even if certain conflicts do not individually threaten US economic or military security, a mounting tide of regional instability combined with the proliferation of weapons of mass destruction could lead to a general break down in world order that would put vital American interests at risk.

Finally, there is the role of American idealism. Inertia and geostrategic interests cannot alone explain American intervention in places like Somalia, Haiti and Bosnia. In attempting to build a domestic consensus in favour of multilateral intervention, both Presidents Bush and Clinton appealed to the deeply-rooted American belief in the uniqueness of the United States and its special responsibility for promoting its ideals around the world. Indeed, Stephen Stedman has complained about the emergence of a new interventionist doctrine driven by moral and humanitarian impulses.[7] Michael Mandelbaum argues that the "seminal events of the foreign policy of the Clinton administration were three failed military interventions in its first nine months", in Somalia, Bosnia and Haiti. He accuses the President and his advisors of adopting the Mother Teresa approach to world problems, treating "foreign policy as social work".[8]

The Clinton administration has pursued an eclectic approach to the regional and ethnic conflicts that have characterized the post-Cold War international security environment. Sometimes it has sent in substantial forces, in others it has supplied supporting logistic and communications functions, while in others it has relied on diplomacy alone. A range of unilateral and multilateral responses have been carried out with a mixture of leadership and followership. Threats were made one day, only to be "clarified" on the next. The Administration's July 1994 strategic statement, *A National Security Strategy of Engagement and Enlargement*, called for an active policy directed toward enlarging the number of democratic countries with free market economies, while sustaining security "with military forces ready to fight".[9] Former national security advisor Anthony Lake stressed the need to contain so-called "backlash" states that are resisting the inevitability of the end of history.[10] However, the Clinton administration's early embrace of Wilsonian liberal internationalism seemed to flounder in the hard realities of the global environment and domestic politics. By the end of the first term, it had been replaced by what Lake now calls "pragmatic internationalism".[11]

The Renewal of Multilateralism: American Strategic Incentive?

It was unreasonable to expect Americans and their government to simply ignore fifty years of global leadership as if it never happened and to retreat into some mythical era of splendid isolationism. The habits of global leadership are hard to break. This superpower inertia has been reinforced by the nature of both the international and domestic environments.

The result has sometimes been US interventions, particularly, as a leader of multinational coalitions.

The alleged inconsistency and confusion in Washington has not been matched by clarity and firm purpose in other world capitals, or in the plethora of international organizations that now seem to clutter the diplomatic landscape. There does not appear to be any substantive effort by traditional allies to fill vacuums left by the contraction of American vital interests. In the Gulf War, in Haiti and Somalia and in the former Yugoslavia, allies seem willing to await the exercise of American leadership before acting forcefully.

Although it can be argued that superpower inertia has carried America into interventions in the post-Cold War era, it is also the case that the United States has not acted as one might expect the world's sole remaining superpower to behave. Mandelbaum contends that it was harder for American Presidents during the Cold War to decide on when and where to intervene because of the "spectre of nuclear conflict with the Soviet Union hovering in the background".[12] The collapse of the Soviet Union meant that Washington could intervene anywhere it wished, "without worrying that global rivals would back the other side and risk escalation into a global conflagration".[13]

Yet the United States has not seized the "unipolar moment" and imposed a new world order on allies and enemies.[14] It has sought to foster its security through international organizations or *ad hoc* coalitions. This is also a legacy of American Cold War policy. To be sure, the end of the Cold War meant that "automatic deference" to the United States has declined. Nevertheless, with the increase in the number of democratic governments and market economies, many more nations now share US policy goals, particularly in fostering regional stability, and "overseas acceptance of US policy positions has increased".[15] This has contributed to the perpetuation of American dominance, creating favourable conditions for Washington leadership, particularly when the international community seeks to collectively intervene with military force.

With the decline and fall of the Warsaw Pact and the Soviet Union, and with the success of the Gulf War, multilateralism seemed to have been given renewed life under different circumstances. It held open the possibility that, with American vital interests contracting, other nations might be persuaded, with some US financial and logistical support, to attend to regional instability. Initially, Washington appeared to look to the UN. With the success of the Gulf War, the United States found that the UN could again serve American foreign policy interests. President Bush "argued for a more activist role for the United Nations and pushed to pay US dues. He viewed the institution as capable of supporting American interests".[16] Then Secretary of State, James Baker declared that "We ought to recognize that we have spent trillions of dollars to win the Cold War and we should be willing to spend millions of dollars to secure the peace".[17] Between 1988 and 1993, the United States voted in favour of some twenty new operations, providing logistical and financial support.

As John Ruggie has observed, Clinton and his advisors became identified with "liberal internationalism", which saw international organizations as beneficial to American interests. This perspective came under increasing criticism from those espousing "conservative unilateralism," a view associated with the Republicans who regard international organizations as "inevitably constraining rather than enabling the pursuit of US interests." Finally, those who see themselves as "practitioners of real-politik" rejected "out of hand the idea that international organizations can make any significant difference in a world driven by self-seeking power politics".[18]

Congressional criticism, particularly of its involvement in multilateral peacekeeping, compelled the Clinton administration to retreat from its, and the Bush administration's, earlier enthusiasm for the UN. With Somalia and the Yugoslavian nightmare, support for peacekeeping began to erode in Washington. The UN was criticized for its poor financial management and bloated bureaucracies. Blame for the loss of American lives in Somalia was attributed to ineffective UN command arrangements.

In line with "pragmatic internationalism", the White House set out to set more narrow conditions for US involvement in peacekeeping but also to sustain domestic support for peacekeeping by asserting a new leadership role for America at the UN in order to make peacekeeping more responsive to American concerns and interests. In May 1994, the White House issued Presidential Decision Directive 25, *US Policy on Reforming Multilateral Peace Operations.*[19]

From the American public's standpoint, there is still strong support for this type of US leadership. Indeed, the Chicago Council of Foreign Relations poll indicated that:

> Despite the heightened emphasis on domestic concerns, American opinion does not reflect a new isolationism. Almost half the public and leaders say the United States plays a more important role as a world leader today

compared to 10 years ago—the highest numbers in the history of our survey. Almost three-quarters of the public believe that the United States will play a greater role in the next 10 years than it does today.[20]

The polls also show that unilateral intervention is to be avoided. Americans are:

Reluctant to shoulder the burdens of international leadership alone, but are willing to share responsibility through participation in multilateral organizations. Despite considerable Congressional opposition, especially after the debacle in Somalia, support for American intervention as part of a UN peacekeeping operation, including the placing of American forces under UN command is surprisingly high. The public is also more willing to support defence spending than it was at the end of the Cold War.[21]

Nowhere has the continuation of American leadership been more evident than in NATO. Washington has promoted changes in the Alliance's strategic concept and organization. It was the moving force behind the PfP program and the main champion for enlargement. And it was the Clinton administration which organized NATO Implementation Force (IFOR) to secure the Dayton accords it had negotiated.

There is little doubt that Washington continues to lead. There is, though, less agreement on whether such leadership is in American national security interests. If the "national interest" were clear, then there would be little debate about national security policy. However, in the post-Cold War era the United States is having a difficult time identifying what those interests are. In part, this accounts for the widely accepted criticism that Clinton administration has not articulated an overall, convincing vision to guide national security policy especially when it comes to identifying clearly which vital interests require armed intervention.

Nevertheless, it can be argued that a minimal consensus has emerged amongst the public and elites. It is that the sphere of vital US national security interests has been narrowed. American national security policy, however fitfully, has been moving since 1989 in the direction of a more disciplined discretion in foreign and defence policy. Thus, the July 1994 strategic statement notes that "We can and must make the difference through our engagement; but our involvement must be carefully tailored to serve our interests and priorities".[22]

There is general support for the notion that the United States has the "responsibility...for preventing nuclear war and helping to preserve global stability". There is also an understanding that "a forceful response to regional aggressions, such as Iraq's invasion of Kuwait and its threat to critical oil resources, may still be necessary".[23] America has a long-standing commitment to the security of Israel. The United States still maintains the legitimacy of the Monroe doctrine and thus the Caribbean, Central and Latin America will always be of special interest. There are some so-called "rogue" states, such as North Korea, Iran and Libya, which pose the threat of proliferation of weapons of mass destruction and/or terrorism.

American Idealism and Multilateralism

Yet, in reality, there are now very few countries that present an immediate or even longer-term indirect threat to American interests and there are fewer areas of the globe where American vital strategic and economic interests are at risk. As a result, the United States now has the luxury of greater choice about when, where and how it exerts its over-whelming military, diplomatic and economic power. Contrary to what might have been hoped for at the end of the Cold War, this has made decisions about intervention more, not less difficult. Many of the inconsist-encies associated with the Clinton administration are merely a reflection of the fact that, lacking an overwhelming challenge, there is less compulsion to mobilize and marshall American diplomatic and military resources. At the same time, the post-Cold War era also indicates that when Washington does choose to act, it prefers to pursue those interests in a multilateral context.

Thus, inertia and interests cannot alone account for American interventionism and multilateralism in the post-Cold War era. Even after the landing of American troops in Haiti, the public and leaders ranked Haiti's problems low amongst US "vital interests".[24] As Jonathan Howe has pointed out, in dealing with the "tangled ethnic struggles, civil wars and failed states spawned in a disorderly era" US obligations as a world leader and its interests are "less clearly defined and more open to ques-tion...Americans are confronted with a kaleidoscope of confusing conflicts in which the US interest is primarily humanitarian".[25]

President Clinton came under heavy criticism for what some viewed as a too idealistic, Wilsonian, approach. Somalia and difficulties in other peacekeeping missions tempered the earlier Bush and Clinton enthusiasm for the UN and multilateral solutions. Recent polls suggest that support for a humanitarian based foreign policy is shallow and easily turned.[26] But adjusting American idealism to harsh realities abroad is nothing new. To this extent, the Clinton administration's "pragmatic internationalism" represents the kind of approach which has always characterized US foreign policy, one of great ideals and uneasy compromises.

This mixture is apparent in the dispatch of troops to Bosnia. In his 27 November 1995 speech to the nation on the need to send American forces to Bosnia, the President cited US self interest in ending a conflict that might spread,and the importance of maintaining the credibility of the NATO alliance. The focus of his address, however, was an appeal to American idealism, its cherished belief in "liberty, democracy and peace" and humanitarianism. The conflict in Bosnia has "troubled our souls" as well as "challenged our interests". He invoked the deeply-rooted sense of American exceptionalism. The United States is a country singularly suited to make peace in the Balkans where others, including the UN, have thus far failed. "It is the power of ideas, even more than our size, our wealth and our military might, that makes America a uniquely trusted nation."[27] As Blechman has argued, "The impulse for intervention is not some fad, nor a plot foisted upon an innocent population by a liberal clique...It reflects the deeply held humanitarian values of democratic populations in the contemporary age".[28]

Rounding up the Posse: Leadership and Followership

This combination of inertia, interests and ideals has resulted in a post-Cold War American national security policy which has fostered multilateralism. When Washington does feel itself "bound to lead" multilateral coalitions it will seek out followers, or as Sir Brian Urquhart has put it, "round up the posse". Multilateralism is a tool to be used when it can support the achievement of American interests. For Clinton, as for previous Presidents, multilateralism has not meant the subordination of US objectives or control to the *ad hoc* coalition or international organization but the assertion of both. Thus, the price of American leadership is frequently acceptance of US command in the field and policy objectives at the negotiating table.

At the same time, if allies abroad do not feel themselves "bound to follow"[29] then it may be that the United States will circumscribe even more narrowly those regions where it is prepared to lead multilateral interventions. It will not adopt an isolationist stance but will move further toward unilateralism when its national interests are directly challenged and non-entanglement when they are not. As Madeleine Albright stated:

> When threats arise, we may respond through the UN, through NATO, through a coalition, through a combination of these tools or we may act alone. We will do whatever is necessary to defend the vital interests of the United States.[30]

The USN, NATO and Multilateral Maritime Cooperation

The pattern of US involvement in post-Cold War multilateral maritime cooperation reflects overall trends in US national security policy with all its successes, failures and inconsistencies. Here is a USN committed to supporting the engagement of American interests abroad, enlarging the range of contacts, yet whose activities are in keeping with the more narrow sphere of American vital national interests, imposed by foreign and domestic considerations.

Increasing Roles, Declining Numbers

The military capability to act, especially in a multilateral capacity, remains and has been demonstrated repeatedly since the end of the Cold War. Victory in the Gulf War was achieved by the forces built up in the 1980s. The Clinton administration is still holding to the ideas in the 1993 *Bottom-Up Review*, which held that the US had to be prepared to fight and win two major regional wars simultaneously. The two contingencies cited most often are conflicts in the Persian Gulf against Iran or Iraq and one against North Korea.

Questions have been raised as to whether forces will be adequate to meet these contingencies. After a decade of reductions, US defence spending is 35 per cent in real terms what it was in 1985. At 4 per cent of Gross Domestic Product this amounts to a 70-year low and the smallest proportion of the federal budget going to defence since Pearl Harbour. The active force is "smaller than at any time since the eve of the Korean War". Nevertheless, with a defence budget of $262 billion, the United States will spend on national security "more than three times what any other country" and "more than all its prospective enemies and neutral nations combined", some 37 per cent of global military expenditures.[31]

With the withdrawal of large numbers of American forces from overseas bases, all branches of the US military, have been shifted from "forward defence" to "forward presence" and power projection, the ability to dispatch forces, and if necessary intervene militarily, with forces based in the United States. This includes the US Navy, the focus of whose maritime strategy has shifted from the high seas to bringing force to bear ashore "from the sea".[32] Even the US Air Force now claims that it is especially well suited to sustain a "global presence", not only with forces that can be quickly deployed, but with the "virtual advantage obtained with space forces and information-based capabilities".[33]

Streamlining the American Military for Global Contingency Operations

Since the bulk of the fighting falls upon the US Army, it has re-oriented itself away from the Central European battle field to intervention scenarios. It even succeeded in overcoming US Marine objections and obtained Congressional approval for the deployment of an army heavy brigade afloat with more than 4,200 tracked and wheeled vehicles, able to carry out "sustained land combat" beyond the landing area. All of this is in the spirit of jointness.[34]

"Jointness" has become the watch-word for the US military. The emphasis on the overseas deployment of "joint" land, sea and air forces was evident in October 1993 when Atlantic Command, headquartered in Norfolk Virginia, was renamed United States Atlantic Command (USACOM) and became the joint headquarters for most forces in the Continental United States (CONUS). In shifting "from a predominately naval headquarters to a more balanced combatant command headquarters", USACOM is designed to "facilitate the identification, training, preparation and rapid response of designated CONUS-based forces currently under the Army's Forces Command, the Navy's Atlantic Fleet, the Air Forces's Air Combat Command, and the Marine Corps Marine Forces Atlantic".[35] Supplementing the rapid capability of the regular forces will be the reserves, whose use becomes more feasible when initial deployments, as the case of the Gulf War and Bosnia, extend over a period of several months. Indicative of the refocusing of the command was the appointment in October 1994 of a US Marine, General John J. Sheehan, as Commander-in-Chief, USACOM. Thus, for the first time SACLANT will not be a naval officer.

The USN articulated its post-Cold War strategy in *From the Sea* in 1992. It is an aptly named document for it constituted a shift in focus from the sea, as expressed in the 1980s Maritime Strategy, to the land where the real objectives of seapower have always been. For command of the sea is meaningless unless it could allow for the projection of force from the sea to the land. "Derived from" the National Security Strategy which emphasizes peacetime presence and engagement, promotion of stability, thwarting aggression, mobility and flexibility in meeting regional, rather than global threats to American interests, the USN's strategic direction was described as:

> ...A fundamental shift away from open-ocean warfighting *on* the sea toward joint operations conducted *from* the sea. The Navy and Marine Corps will now respond to crises and can provide the initial "enabling" capability for joint operations in conflict—as well as continued participation in any sustained effort. We will be part of a "sea-air-land" team trained to respond immediately to the Unified Commanders as they execute national policy.[36]

Revised and retitled *Forward From the Sea* in 1994, the document notes that the "cornerstones" of American seapower will be forward presence, power projection, strategic deterrence, sea control and maritime supremacy and strategic lift. Naval forces are "going to come from the sea. They are going to work near land and over land. They are going to work in the skies over land and sea". "And", declared the late Chief of Naval Operations, Admiral J.M. Boorda, "we are going to be joint and combined because warfare is joint and combined".[37] This approach to seapower lends itself to maritime multilateralism as the USN will be primarily focused on bringing power to bear on the littoral where the United States will usually be intervening in regional disputes on behalf of states, governments or peoples ashore and in circumstances where cooperation with regional or other outside actors is or may be desirable. This is fully consistent with the national military strategy which notes that "Our armed forces will most often fight in concert with regional allies and friends as coalitions can decisively increase combat power and lead to a more rapid and favourable outcome to the conflict".[38]

But it should be stressed that for the United States maritime multilateralism is a *policy option*, not a practical necessity. As Hirschfeld notes: "For now, there is virtually no mission that the US Navy could not perform by itself."[39] One of the key advantages which seapower affords the United States is the capacity to act unilaterally; "...the sea is the best avenue for US strategic mobility; Naval Forces are not subject to the political whims of foreign governments."[40] Despite this ability to conduct naval operations unilaterally, the United States has chosen to employ its unchallenged seapower in coalition and cooperative efforts when it has been in the US interest to do so. This has made maritime multilateralism possible in the post-Cold war era.

Streamlining NATO for Enhanced Military Operations

It has been considered to be in the American interest to sustain and expand NATO's long-standing tradition of multilateral naval cooperation. This has been particularly the case given the discernable shift in the Alliance southward, away from the central front and northern waters. In terms of maritime focus, the preoccupation with the Norwegian sea, open ocean anti-submarine warfare (ASW), and Soviet nuclear-powered ballistic missile submarine bastions have given way to heightened concerns about the situation in the Mediterranean basin.[41] This shift has come about because it is here, in the Balkans, in the southern republics of the former USSR, in the Middle East and potentially along the North African coast that instability might threaten allied interests, particularly those of Turkey and Greece. "The Mediterranean today represents perhaps the most important conduit linking East with West—the Adriatic with the Black Sea and the Arabian Gulf; and North and South—joining Europe with Africa."[42]

In terms of organization and strategy, NATO has taken steps which highlight the increased relative importance of seapower. By 1994, NATO had reduced from three to two Major NATO Commands by eliminating Commander-in-Chief Channel Command, leaving only Allied Command Europe and Allied Command Atlantic. In addition, a new Major Subordinate Command, under the Supreme Allied Commander, Europe (SACEUR), Allied Forces Northwest Europe, covering the UK and Norway has been created with a naval component. Still to be sorted out are specific naval responsibilities between this new command, SACLANT, and the Commander Allied Forces, Baltic Approaches, which will now shift to Allied Forces Central Europe. Under SACEUR the position of CINCSOUTH, held by an American,[43] will be retained as will the subordinate position of Commander Naval Forces, South (COMNAVSOUTH) held by an Italian admiral. Southern Command has always been predominately naval, dominated by the USN with its powerful Sixth fleet which continues to be forwardly deployed in the region. Overall, NATO will retain a command structure amenable to the day-to-day coordination of naval activities, especially surveillance, joint exercises and, if necessary, combined action in the event of a crisis.

The Alliance's new military strategy places emphasis upon smaller, flexible multilateral forces as well as mobilization. Reaction forces, comprising less than 10 per cent of the total, are designed for immediate or rapid response "to emerging military risks". Included here is the new Allied Command Europe multilateral Rapid Reaction Corps. These will be supplemented by standing Main Defence Forces, and mobilised Augmentation Forces or reinforcing units from Europe and North America.[44]

The Partnership for Peace (PfP) and Combined Joint Task Forces (CJTF) concepts, both of which were urged upon the Alliance by Washington at the January 1994 Summit, also represent dramatic change. Under the former, Russia and Eastern European countries were offered a kind of associated status which will permit consultation and coordination on security issues. Included here are joint exercises including at sea. For example in the North, the NATO nations, particularly Denmark and Germany along with the former Soviet Baltic republics, Sweden, Finland and Poland have conducted a number of exercises including *Cooperative Banners*. There is increased cooperation amongst navies in the Baltic Sea, where the *Baltic Eye* exercise tested combined search and rescue procedures and collaboration in mine counter measure capabilities has increased.[45]

Naval forces have also played a major role in PfP exercises in the South. For example, in July 1996 exercise *Cooperative Partner 96* was held in the Black Sea involving naval units from several allied nations as well as forces from Romania, Bulgaria and Ukraine.[46] In March 1998, the Alliance will hold *Strong Resolve*, its largest post-Cold War exercise to date. It will include a number of PfP countries and will simulate simultaneous crises north and south, peace support out-of-area and a UN operation handed off to NATO. As many as four carrier battle groups and 58 destroyers are expected to be in involved.[47]

The CJTF concepts calls for the reorganization of NATO forces into "combined joint task forces" which will allow different national contingents to serve under mobile commands "for specific operations", such as peacekeeping or be used by the WEU. In the spirit of "jointness" which now pervades American defence thinking and organization, the CJTFs could be composed of multilateral land, sea and air forces. They could also involve forces from Eastern European countries under the PfP.[48] At the same time, the task forces would allow the Europeans to "organize independently and, in some situations, take action within NATO but without involvement" of American (or Canadian) forces.[49]

For the allied maritime forces, the new NATO strategies and organizational concepts do not represent as dramatic and profound a change as they do for the land and air forces. At sea, the Alliance has had few standing forces and has always relied upon mobilized capabilities in the event of crisis or war. The NATO maritime component also has a long tradition of multilateralism with individual ships and aircraft from the allied navies operating closely together. In addition, the "Fraternity of the Blue Uniform" has always transcended national and even allied divisions, such that navies from very diverse countries, often find it easier to come together on an *ad hoc* basis for specific purposes and tasks. This will make it easier to implement the PfP and CJTF concepts with regard to units from former Warsaw Pact navies.

At SACLANT headquarters, planning has been underway to make seapower, based upon Multinational Maritime Forces (MNMF), part of the new NATO. The "concept of an overarching non-threat specific maritime force structure has been adjusted to support the new NATO strategy". Multilateral Standing Naval Forces (SNF) "together with individual national deployments" will provide presence and surveillance and constitute the Alliance's maritime immediate reaction forces in the event of a crisis.[50] Should the situation be prolonged and conflict become a possibility, the SNF would be joined by On-Call forces organized into a NATO Task Group (NTG). With the addition of more units from the naval component of the allied Main Defence Forces, the NTG would be expanded into a NATO Task Force (NTF) or with more units a NATO Expanded Task Force (NETF). It is estimated that the SNF would be available in as little as two days while the NTG, NTF and NETF would take from five to thirty days to assemble. In the event of a prolonged conflict, the Alliance would draw upon maritime units from its combined augmentation forces.

Even before NATO formally adopted its new ideas, the post-Cold era had already witnessed the employment of the MNMF concept. In the Mediterranean, the on-call force was transformed into the Standing Naval Forces Mediterranean under the Command of COMNAVSOUTH. Significantly, some of the first ships to sail with the new standing force did not come from the Mediterranean area, as the Netherlands and Germany sent units. In the fall of 1992, the STANAVFORLANT entered the Mediterranean to temporarily relieve the STANAVFORMED in the Adriatic where it was monitoring sanctions imposed by the United Nations against Serbia and Montenegro. The STANAVFORLANT later took part in NATO operation *Display Determination* 1992 and made port visits to the Black Sea.[51]

Multilateral Operations and Theatre Missile Defence

Still another dimension to maritime multilateralism is in the area of Theatre Missile Defence (TMD). For the last several years the United States has been promoting a NATO-wide approach to TMD, sponsoring allied workshops. The USN has pointed to the capabilities of its AEGIS ships including the SM-2 Block IVA missile as well as the lightweight Exo-Atmospheric Projectile and Cooperative Engagement Capability as a means of providing TMD from its Sixth Fleet in the Mediterranean. A number of allied nations are cooperating on TMD projects.

In the Southern region there is a TMD Working Group which meets on a "regular basis" to discuss "TMD Policy and Concept of Operations Documents". TMD is "regularly" included in Southern Command exercises and the USS LASALLE, the Sixth Fleet's flagship has a "TMD Cell which can act as a fusion centre and command and control centre for TMD operations".[52]

The Role of the USN and Other Navies in Multilateral Maritime Operations

This is not to argue that all maritime multilateralism is dependent upon the participation of the USN or even NATO. Small, regional navies can develop patterns of collaboration. As noted above, in the Black and Baltic seas, NATO countries and PfP partners have been conducting joint exercises. At Canada's Peacekeeping Training Centre, officers from a variety of countries study the use of navies in support of peacekeeping operations. Efforts are being made to foster closer cooperation in Southeast Asia, where the *Kaduku II* exercise in March 1995 brought together units from Australia, New Zealand, Indonesia, Singapore and Thailand. To the extent that regional navies of countries friendly to the United States develop closer working relationships, it will, if the need arises, make them better suited to join in larger coalition efforts with the USN.[53] The degree to which the effectiveness of joint naval operations requires American support will vary with the nature of the undertaking. For example, traditional peacekeeping, where a framework of consensus and consent exists and where no hostile action is expected, may be carried out entirely by the less sophisticated and more lightly armed maritime forces of smaller powers.

As James Tritten argues, the USN should use its position as the "inspirational leader of the navies of the world with the development of multinational doctrine" to improve ties with smaller and medium-size navies. Smaller navies can be especially useful in the monitoring of embargoes. In this regard, the long-standing relationship between the USN and the United States Coast Guard, which has experience in the tasks performed by smaller navies, should be used "to form the basis of how the US Navy might approach medium size power-navies from other nations" and assist in the formulation of multilateral naval doctrine[54].

However, as the level of hostility increases, and the maritime missions likewise escalate from monitoring to threatening action towards peace enforcement and intervention, then, as Eric Grove notes, "the roles of maritime forces...are identical to the normal combatant roles of navies as outlined in...*From the Sea*".[55] For these coalition actions, and indeed even for more restrained applications of seapower, participation by the USN seems essential. Only the United States can bring to bear the extended surface and sub-surfaces forces, carrier based air power and amphibious capabilities that might be necessary to secure the seas and project power ashore. Further, only the USN can call upon the vast command, control, communications, computer, intelligence and information (C^4I^2) networks that have become the "foundation of stone" of modern naval warfare at the strategic, operational and tactical level. "Any major international enforcement effort will probably have to rely" on US C^4I^2 assets, "even if most of the participating forces fly other flags".[56]

At the same time, other allied navies, in particular those of the NATO countries, can make a contribution to a coalition enforcement effort. Indeed, as evident in the Gulf War and more recently in the Adriatic, the ability of the USN to take advantage of maritime multilateralism is enhanced by the fact that naval forces from many countries can "fit together" in combined task forces with "relatively little difficultly". Most modern navies include ASW, anti-surface warfare and anti-air capabilities. The US and its allies "now have the benefit of global intelligence and data distribution system that can transmit a detailed intelligence picture to a work station in the operations room of warships deployed anywhere in the world". As Grove also points out, the long-standing NATO cooperative procedures can now be extended to other navies. The unclassified publication, EXTAC 768, *Maritime Manoeuvring and Tactical Procedures*, "provides naval manoeuvring and signalling instructions for units of different navies that have not historically operated together and do not have any prior agreement on procedures".[57] Some technical documents on *Standard Agreements on Operating Procedures* are also being made available.[58] Under the leadership of General Sheehan, Atlantic Command has adopted a set of "goals," which stress "joint operations", improved communications, cooperation with Allied Command Europe (ACE), PfP countries, "other international and security organizations" and "collaboration and dialogue with countries outside the alliance".[59]

In the tradition of Admiral Colbert, the US has gone to great lengths to foster an unprecedented capability for other nations' navies to operate with the USN. In a certain sense it is not so much that the international community relies upon the USN to sustain maritime multilateralism, but rather that maritime multilateralism is often the result of the deliberate policy of the United States to use its seapower in coalition settings in order to further its own interests. The distinction is important because what is offered so enthusiastically in some circumstances, making collaboration at sea work so well, can be withheld in others, thereby making it impossible.

US Foreign Policy and Multilateral Operations

The United States obtains several advantages from maritime multilateralism, some of which are inherent in the very nature of seapower with its intrinsic flexibility. First, in day-to-day peacetime conditions, it allows the US to maintain and cultivate security relations with the growing number of nations who are now interested, for political and technical reasons, in exercising with the USN. Not only does such cooperation provide "opportunities to influence the future development of other navies",[60] but it affords a means to sustain contact without the political complications associated with land and air collaboration. Moreover, with the withdrawal of American forces from around the world, a wide-ranging program of bilateral and multilateral naval exercises allows for a certain "continuity of forward presence" that could be useful in the event of regional crisis. It also might "foster the relationships that make it easier both to request assistance ashore and to grant such assistance".[61]

A second advantage of maritime multilateralism is evident in instances where Washington wishes to be involved in a particular cooperative effort, yet at the same time wishes to maintain a certain distance and independence of action. This was the case regarding the NATO/WEU operation *Sharp Guard* that enforced various Security Council resolutions imposing an arms embargo on the former Yugoslavia. The USN participated in this activity although Washington's policies with regard to the conflict and the efforts of the United Nations Protection Force (UNPROFOR) diverged from those of the UN and its NATO allies contributing ground forces to the operation.

Third, when the United States decides to take a more active role by intervening with significant forces, then maritime multilateralism, in addition to providing useful assets, also enhances the legitimacy of the operation abroad and at home. Within the international community, naval contributions are often the easiest way to multilateralize what would otherwise be an American only, or American, British and French, or NATO only operation. It is noteworthy that of the thirty-six nations participating in the Gulf War coalition, nine states contributed only naval vessels and aircraft, while only seven deployed ground forces "actually engaged in combat".[62] Similarly, several states were persuaded to participate in the Haitian embargo.

This maritime multilateralism, which enhances the "appearance of broad support", also serves a domestic legitimating function making it easier for the President to secure Congressional and public support. As noted above, in the present international security environment where vital interests are often not at stake in regional crises, the American people and the Congress are wary of foreign intervention. Thus, "acting alone will be increasingly difficult".[63] Domestic support is easier to secure when the administration can show that other nations are also contributing.

Each of these advantages has allowed maritime multilateralism to serve US interests in the post-Cold War era. However, because the main motivating considerations are political, those same interests and considerations may limit its future desirability and applicability in several ways.

While frequent joint naval exercises allow Washington to maintain security links with a variety of old and new allies, they do not bind Washington to firm security commitments in a way that forward based land and air forces once did. To this extent, the expansion of naval contacts can be viewed as consistent with the contraction, rather than expansion, of American vital interests. More nations may wish to obtain the benefits of closer contact with the USN, but without a global threat the imperative on the American side to make those benefits available has diminished.

In addition, although American involvement in maritime multilateralism has been evident in many coalition efforts in the post-Cold War era, including in support of UN peacekeeping, its impact has been limited by the nature of conflicts in which it has been employed. Overwhelmingly, the kinds of ethnic and national instabilities against which NATO now claims it must stand on guard, and where force might be needed, "are simply not maritime venues".[64] Unless Washington is prepared to bring force to bear "from the sea", that is to project power, including land forces ashore, the impact of naval-only operations may be limited. This is especially true where, as in Yugoslavia, the conflicts are over specific territories and where combatants may not depend heavily on sea-borne supply.

Operation Sharp Guard

This was the case regarding Operation *Sharp Guard*. The NATO naval forces collaborated with those of the Western European Union in support of the United Nations. The STANAVFORLANT participated under SACEUR's command. The operation also included ships from France and Spain. A multilateral forward logistic site was employed. All in all *Sharp Guard* is regarded by the Alliance as model for future allied naval collaboration in peace support operations.[65] From 22 November 1992 to 18 June 1996, 74,192 ships were challenged, 5,951 were boarded and inspected, and 1,480 were diverted and inspected in port.[66]

At the same time, it is not evident that the embargo had any serious impact on the level of fighting, especially given the Croatian offensive during the summer of 1995 and the failure of NATO and the UN to provide protection to a number of "safe havens". Once the Clinton administration persuaded allies to use force, sea-based airpower and other assets were able to contribute to air attacks which, combined with the Croatian victories, brought the Serbs to the table. However, it was always clear that any major allied effort, whether for UN peacekeeping or peace enforcement, would have to be primarily a land operation backed up by sea and air forces. This is evident in the NATO Implementation Force (IFOR) operations, where the maritime component, though important, is small relative to the ground and air forces.[67]

Moreover, the case of *Sharp Guard* highlights how USN participation in even the most advanced maritime multilateralism is circumscribed by US interests that may diverge from those of other contributing counties. In late 1994 the Clinton administration, acting in response to Congressional pressure, ended the participation of the USN in the arms embargo against the Bosnian government. Thus, while American Admiral W. Leighton Smith Jr. acting in his NATO capacity as CINCSOUTH continued to "oversee the embargo" he was not able to direct American ships to enforce the ban. Further, if he received American intelligence about weapons shipments he was not able to act upon that information.[68] While these restrictions did not seriously hamper the allied effort, they did highlight the political divisions behind those efforts.

This was only half the story. While the combined NATO\WEU fleets were enforcing the arms embargo, the Clinton administration was giving the green light to Iran to ship weapons to the Bosnia government forces[69]—weapons which were eventually used to launch the offensives in the summer of 1995 which paved the way for the Dayton Accords but in the process ended UNPROFOR's activities. The point is not whether the Clinton administration acted in bad faith, it clearly had reasons *both* to sustain allied cooperation *and* covertly arm the Muslims. This approach turned out to be essential in achieving the battlefield conditions which allowed Washington to broker a settlement. This simply showed that multilateral naval cooperation, being essentially a political undertaking, can be manipulated to serve the interests of the larger coalition partner.

Finally, the Bosnia experience points to the double-edged nature of maritime multilateralism as a political legitimatizing tool for the United States. As noted, naval cooperation can enhance the acceptability of US intervention in the eyes of the international community. This "appearance" of broad support is important if the administration is to secure the backing of the American people, and especially of Congress. However, to be fully legitimate in the domestic context, multilateralism must also mean the acceptance by contributing nations of US command in the field (or at sea) and policy objectives at the negotiating table. This is why President Clinton was prepared to offer only limited support to UNPROFOR, and even adopt policies that undercut the UN, yet has all but staked the future of his administration on the success of IFOR.

It is not that American interests are necessarily at odds with those of contributing counties—all may wish victory over an aggressor, or a settlement to a regional dispute, or the provision of humanitarian relief. It is really a question of which nations' approach to achieving these ends will prevail. In other words, it is Washington's view of how the shared political objectives are to be achieved which often determines the effectiveness of any maritime multilateralism in which the USN takes part.

Conclusion

As we approach the 21st century, the heirs of Richard Colbert have achieved a level of sophistication and importance in multilateral naval cooperation that not even he could have dreamed of. The core of this naval multilateralism continues to be the North Atlantic Treaty Organization. All of this has added a measure of strategic stability in an otherwise uncertain and unstable post-Cold War era. Much of the credit for this goes to the United States Navy, operating in accordance with an overall American national security strategy based upon a "pragmatic internationalism" which continues to stress multilateral approaches to the protection of US interests abroad.

From a practical point of view, multinational maritime operations are "not generally problematic".[70] If there are restrictions on what the "fraternity of the blue uniform" can do, they have to do with the often limited impact of seapower on many regional conflicts. This has clearly been the case in the former Yugoslavia. In addition, and perhaps more importantly, there are ever-present political constraints. The ability of naval forces to operate together, from traditional peacekeeping through monitoring to coalition peace enforcement efforts, is circumscribed by the willingness of nations to employ their national navies in cooperative ventures. Above all, it is contingent upon the extent to which the nation whose Navy now rules the waves like no other before is prepared to employ that vast seapower in further collaborative efforts. To the extent that the leadership of post-Cold War USN fosters maritime multilateralism in order to promote American interests and values, they are very much the heirs of Richard Colbert.

Dependence upon American naval power, combined with anxiety that America might choose to use that power unilaterally, or not at all when US vital interests and values are not challenged, leads allies old and new to accept US conditions as the price for maritime multilateralism in the post-Cold War era. Yet, given the alternatives and wide-spread benefits that have and can accrue from a US Navy actively engaged abroad, this new transoceanic bargain seems just as necessary as the one which won the Cold War.

Notes

1. Sergi Anisimov, "Cooperative Venture '94", *The Current Digest of the Post-Soviet Press* 46:16 November 1994, 22.
2. J. Sokolsky, *The Fraternity of the Blue Uniform: Admiral Richard G. Colbert, US Navy and Allied Naval Cooperation* Historical Monograph Series, No. 8 (Newport, RI: Naval War College Press, 1991), 59. See also, John B. Hattendorf, "Admiral Richard G. Colbert and International Naval Cooperation: The Intertwining of a Career and an Idea", in W.A.B. Douglas (ed.), *The RCN in Transition* (Vancouver, BC: University of British Columbia Press, 1988).
3. Thomas J. Hirschfeld, *Multinational Naval Cooperation* (CRM 93-44), (Alexandria, VA.: Centre for Naval Analyses, September 1993), 1.
4. Charles Krauthammer, "Peacekeeping is for Chumps", *Saturday Night* November 1995, 76.
5. Parts of this section appeared in Joel J. Sokolsky, "Great ideals and uneasy compromises: the United States approach to peacekeeping", *International Journal* 50, Spring 1995, 266-293 and "The Americanization of Peacekeeping: Implications for Canada", *Martello Papers* 17 (Queen's University Centre for International Relations, 1997).
6. Included in American military intervention in the post-Cold War era are the Gulf War as well as those instances, such as Somalia, Haiti and Bosnia where the United States used its armed forces in support of the United Nations Security Council resolutions. The latter went beyond classical "peacekeeping", the use of lightly armed multilateral forces to monitor an agreed upon peace agreement or armistices. There is no expectation that the peacekeepers will enforce the peace. To this extent, rather than debate the differences between peacekeeping, peacemaking and peace enforcement, the only distinction that now seems to count is between classic UN peacekeeping and armed intervention by a US-led coalition to secure a settlement followed by what amounts to military occupation. This is the kind of intervention that runs a high risk of leading to war. For however justified on international legal or humanitarian grounds, the imposition of the will of one country or a group of countries on another state or factions within that state by force of arms is war. Thus, although Clinton stated that he was not sending US troops "to fight a war in Bosnia", the size and power of the force indicates that he realizes that this could happen if there was resistance from any quarter.
7. Stephen J. Stedman, "The New Interventionists", *Foreign Affairs* 72, January-February 1993, 1-16.
8. Michael Mandelbaum, "Foreign Policy As Social Work", *Foreign Affairs* 74, January-February 1996 (Information Access Reprint), 1.

9. United States, White House, *A National Security Strategy of Engagement and Enlargement* (Washington, DC, July 1994), 1.
10. Anthony Lake, "Confronting Backlash States", *Foreign Affairs* 73, March/April 1994, 45-55.
11. See Stanley Hoffmann, "The Crisis of Liberal Internationalism", *Foreign Policy* 98, Spring 1995, 159-177.
12. Michael Mandelbaum, "Foreign Policy as Social Work", *Foreign Affairs* 74, January-February 1996 (Information Access Reprint), 2.
13. Charles Maynes, "Relearning Intervention", *Foreign Policy* 98, Spring 1995.
14. Charles Krauthammer, "The Unipolar Moment", *Foreign Affairs* 70, Winter 1990/91, 25-33. (Information Access Reprint), 1.
15. Jonathan Clark, "Leaders and Followers", *Foreign Policy* 101, Winter 1995-96, 49.
16. Victoria Holt, *Briefing Booking on Peacekeeping: The US Role in United Nations Peace Operations* (Washington, DC: The Council for a Livable World Education Fund, 1994), 14.
17. *Ibid.*, 20.
18. John Gerard Ruggie, "Peacekeeping and US Interests", *Washington Quarterly* 17, Autumn 1994, 175.
19. United States, White House, Presidential Decision Directive 25, *The US Policy on Reforming Multilateral Peace Operations* (unclassified version) (Washington, DC: 6 May, 1994), (hereafter, PDD-25).
20. John E. Rielly, "The Public Mood at Mid-Decade", *Foreign Policy* 98, Spring, 1995, 77.
21. Rielly, "The Public Mood", 77. See also, Steven Kull, "What the Public Knows that Washington Doesn't", *Foreign Policy* 101, Winter 1995-96, 104-106.
22. United States White House, *A National Security Strategy of Engagement and Enlargement,* 1.
23. Jonathan T. Howe, "The United States in Somalia: the limits of involvement", *The Washington Quarterly* 18, Summer 1995 (Information Access Reprint), 1.
24. Rielly, "The Public Mood", 86.
25. Howe, "The United States in Somalia: the limits of involvement", 1.
26. Rielly, "The Public Mood", 81.
27. *The New York Times*, 28 November 1995, A6.
28. Barry Blechman, "The Intervention Dilemma", *The Washington Quarterly* 18, Summer, 1995, 72.
29. See Andrew Cooper, Richard Higgott, and Kim Nossal, "Bound to Follow? Leadership and Followership in the Gulf Conflict", *Political Science Quarterly* 106, Fall 1991, 391-410.

30. United States, Congress, Senate, Subcommittee on Coalition Defence and Reinforcing Forces, *United Nations Peace Operations,* (S. Hrg. 103-772) (Washington, DC: US Government Printing Office, 1994), 5-6.
31. Lawrence J. Korb, "Our Overstuffed Armed Forces", *Foreign Affairs* 74, November/December 1995, 23.
32. United States, United States Navy, *From The Sea: Preparing the Naval Service for the 21st Century* (Washington, DC: September 1992).
33. United States, United States Air Force, *Global Presence* (Washington, DC: 1994), 1.
34. Captain James F. Pasquarette, US Army (USA) and Colonel William G. Foster, (USA), "An Army Brigade Goes Afloat", United States Naval Institute *Proceedings* (USNIP) 120, May 1994, 89-92.
35. United States, Chairman of the Joint Chiefs of Staff, *Roles, Missions and Functions of the Armed Forces of the United States* (Washington, DC: February 1993), III-4-III-5. See also, William R. McClintock, *USACOM Special History Study: Establishment of United States Atlantic Command as the Joint Force Integrator, 1 October 1993,* (Norfolk, Virginia: USACOM, Command Historian, USACOM, 1995).
36. United States, Department of the Navy, *From The Sea,* 2.
37. Admiral J.M. Boorda, USN, "The Art of the Long View: Enduring Naval Principles", *Vital Speeches* 61, 15 December 1994 (Information Access Reprint), 1-2.
38. *National Military Strategy of the United States* (Washington, DC: Department of Defense, February 1995).
39. Hirschfeld, *Multilateral Naval Cooperation Options,* 15.
40. Boorda, "The Art of the Long View: Enduring Naval Principles", 4.
41. Commander Michael N. Pocalyko, USN, "Future of Force In Maritime Europe", United States Naval Institute Proceedings, *USNIP* 118, August 1992, 46.
42. Admiral J.M. Boorda, USN, "The Southern Region: NATO Forces in Action", *NATO'S Sixteen Nations* 38, 2/1993, 7.
43. The French government has suggested that CINCSOUTH be an European admiral. But there appears to be little support for this in other countries.
44. General Vigleik Eide, Chairman of the Military Committee, "NATO In The New Era: The Military Dimension", *Canadian Defence Quarterly* 22, (March 1993), 8.
45. Interviews at AFNORTHWEST, 3 March 1997.
46. Allied Forces Southern Europe, *News Release,* No. 96-20, 24 July 1996.
47. Interviews at AFNORTHWEST, 3 March 1997.
48. "NATO's battle-plans for Survival", *The Economist,* 15 January 1994, 50.
49. Jim O'Leary, "O, Brave New NATO", *The Ottawa Sunday Sun,* 23 January 1994, 6.

50. Admiral L.A. Edney, USN, "Future Alliance Maritime Posture", *NATO'S Sixteen Nations* 37, 1/92, 4-6.
51. Boorda, "The Southern Region", 8.
52. "Theatre Missile Defense From the Maritime Operations Perspective" NATO document. See: also Summary of Report, *Fourth Allied TMD Workshop,* Brussels, Belgium, 23-24 February 1995, 3; "The Empire Strikes Back", *The Economist*, 23 March 1995, 87-88; Mark Hewish, "Providing the Umbrella", *International Defense Review,* 28, August 1995, 33-34.
53. Captain Brian Robertson, Royal Australian Navy, "Security Cooperation in Asia Pacific", USNIP 122 March 122, 65-68.
54. James Tritten, "Learning Multinational Doctrine At Home", *USNIP* 122, March 1996, 89-90.
55. Eric Grove, "Naval Operations: The Multinational Dimension", *Navy International* 100, January-February 1995, 15.
56. *Ibid.*, 17.
57. *Ibid.*, 16-17.
58. Interview, AFNORTHWEST, 3 March 1997.
59. North Atlantic Treaty Organization, Allied Command Atlantic, *ACTANT Goals 1995*, 2-3.
60. Taken from General Sheehan's Presentation, MC/CS, 12 September 1995.
61. Hirschfeld, *Multilateral Naval Cooperation Options*, 1, 3.
62. Cooper, et. al. "Bound to Follow?" 403.
63. Hirschfeld, *Multinational Naval Cooperation*, 15.
64. Pocalyko, "Future of Force In Maritime Europe", 46.
65. Interview AFSOUTH, 6 March 1997.
66. "NATO/WEU Operation Sharp Guard", *NATO Fact Sheet*, 2 October 1996.
67. *NATO Fact Sheet* "IFOR Maritime Component", 10 May 1996.
68. Michael R. Gordon, "President Orders End to Enforcing Bosnian Embargo", *New York Times* November 11 1994, A1, A10. Interview, AFSOUTH 6 March 1997.
69. Tim Weiner, "Clinton to Invoke Executive Privilege over Muslim Areas", *The Globe and Mail*, 18 April 1996, A15.
70. Sir Roger Palin, *Multinational Military Forces: Problems and Prospects*, Adelphi Paper No. 294 (London: International Institute for Strategic Studies, 1995), 52.

5 The Return of the "Small Wars": Technical Requirements for Multinational Naval Cooperation

STUART L. SLADE

Peacekeeping in an Uncertain World

The texture of military operations in the 1990s has become clear as the decade has progressed. Military deployments occurring over the last five years show that the roles expected of the forces involved differ radically from anything that had been expected during the Cold War period and its immediate aftermath. The Persian Gulf War, where large-scale engagements took place between regular forces in the context of a conventional (if very one-sided) campaign has proved to be unique. In its place, military forces are facing a significantly less well-defined series of military commitments where the circumstances, objectives and motivations are far from clear.

When the restraining hands of the superpowers were lifted after the end of the Cold War, regional and local differences, suppressed for decades, boiled over. In one sense, international tension was replaced by intra-national conflict. The disintegration of Yugoslavia was the first such incident. It was followed by others in Somalia, in Rwanda and many other, less publicized instances. The response of the United Nations in such cases has been to send peacekeeping and aid forces to the area. They have been tasked with keeping a lid on the military or paramilitary aspects of the conflict while distributing aid and disaster relief to the innocent caught in the crossfire. These objectives, both laudable in their own right, are often mutually exclusive.

The operations in Somalia, Bosnia and Rwanda were well-publicized; there have been many others which have failed to receive the spotlight

95

of media attention, either because the troops involved were not American or European or because the area in which they took place was remote and unfamiliar. Yet known or unknown, successful or failed, there are a number of common factors to these operations which directly relate to the problems they impose on the command, control, communications, computers and intelligence (C⁴I) sector.

Such situations have cropped up with little or no warning and have often required a rapid, improvised response. While there was an international political dimension to the Rwanda affair and the civil war in that country had been a long time in the making, the sudden need for disaster relief was unanticipated. The Rwanda situation also illustrated another unfortunate aspect of these situations—their inherent capability of spreading to neighboring regions. The Rwandan tragedy was a proximate cause (albeit by an indirect route) of the subsequent civil war in Zaire. This, too, had long been in the making but the flash point seems to have been a need for neighboring countries to eliminate the causes of border instability residing in the refugee camps along the Zaire side of those borders.

This inherent tendency for conflicts to spill over borders, combined with the unexpected nature of the conflicts seems set to become a common factor to future conflicts and suggests that strategic mobility using pre-packaged forces will be essential future elements. These nihilistic, chaotic and indiscriminately violent environments are likely to be the norm for the overwhelming majority of military operations over the next decade.

If this is the case, it is reasonable to project that multinational naval operations will be undertaken mainly in support of the UN initiatives intended to limit such conflicts. The role of naval forces in these operations will, therefore, be largely determined by the character of the peacekeeping and/or relief missions they support. These, in turn, will be largely decided by the precise nature of the situation in question.

The Role of Force in International Relations

Current military doctrine recognizes three distinctly different ways in which armed forces can be used. The recent Royal Navy publication "*The Fundamentals of British Maritime Doctrine*"[1] labeled these as being "military", "constabulary" and "benign".

The military role is one in which combat is used or threatened, or for which a real and tangible combat capability is required. All warfighting tasks require the military use of force. The same force can also be used in support of diplomacy by coercing, persuading or "sending a message" to an adversary. Although, under the latter circumstances, actual destructive force may not be used, it is the combat capability of the forces that underpins their use.

The constabulary role is where forces are employed to impose the rule of law or to implement some regime established by an international (usually United Nations) mandate. Violence is only overtly employed for self-defence or as a last resort in the execution of the constabulary task. The ways in which force can be used will normally be described in the law or mandate that is being enforced and are summarized in strict rules of engagement. These will be dominated by the general reluctance to employ violence. Combat is not, therefore, the means by which the mission is achieved, even though the situation may warrant combat preparations (in self-defence, for example).

The benign role includes such tasks as disaster relief, search and rescue, or ordnance disposal. Military forces contribute organized and self-supporting formations with specific capabilities and specialist knowledge. These can include logistic units capable of transporting large quantities of supplies over rough terrain; engineering units that can quickly rebuild destroyed bridges, build new roads and re-establish power/sanitation facilities; and medical units specifically trained to cope with large numbers of serious injuries under severe time and capability limitations. Although military units have repeatedly shown themselves to be both skilled and resourceful at benign role operations, the use of force has no part in their execution.

Although these three roles have distinctly different characteristics and requirements, the divisions between them are indistinct and tend to shift with changing circumstances. For example, benign disaster relief may require constabulary or military protection depending on the circumstances. The US involvement in Somalia stands as a classic example of a benign operation that escalated rapidly and unexpectedly into the military role. The US forces were optimized for the original benign function, and their inability to adapt to the requirements of a military role within the available time frame made their defeat inevitable. Had their original deployment been optimized for constabulary operations, the situation could well have been prevented from getting so disastrously out of hand. At least one prominent international strategist has suggested that the force needed in Somalia was not the US Marines but the New York Police Department.[2]

Somalia also illustrated the basic problem that the perceptions of any potential or real opposition, and of non-combatant civilians in the theatre, will also decide whether a particular operation can be restricted to benign or constabulary roles. This leads to very real problems where forces from the same country, or ostensibly representing the same coalition or agency, are simultaneously attempting to carry out coercive (military) roles and the distribution of aid (a benign role). As a result, the opposition can easily undertake reprisals for actions committed by the former group directed against troops or other personnel performing the latter function.

Although the boundary between the three roles is shifting and indistinct, they are not, in any sense, arbitrary or a matter of degree. The legal basis for each is quite different. Specific doctrine has to be crafted for each role, and a distinct attitude of mind is required from the command and military personnel involved in each type of operation.

Benign Roles

Disaster Relief Operations. If the context of the operation is simple disaster relief, for example after a typhoon or earthquake, the role of naval forces operating in the littoral regions will be that of carrying the needed supplies to the area and distributing them to the victims of the catastrophe. While an airlift can bring in food and medical supplies to a country very quickly, aircraft cannot lift the bulk supplies necessary in situations where the numbers of victims can reach hundreds of thousands. Experience has also shown that airlifting supplies also results in serious cargo handling and distribution problems at the point of arrival. In many recent cases, emergency supplies have been expensively airlifted to a disaster zone, then been left to rot due to inadequate distribution facilities to the point of need.

In contrast, the air-cushion landing craft has proved of inestimable value in such operations. Loaded with tons of supplies, it has shown a unique ability to deliver those supplies directly to the victims, cutting out transport delays and problems caused by shattered road or rail infrastructure.[3] This also has the advantage of eliminating losses of emergency supplies by theft or fraud to local racketeers. A less popular advantage is that supply distribution cannot be controlled by a local government and, therefore, cannot be used by them for political advantage. The naval C^4I aspect of this type of situation is the relatively simple task of administering the loading and delivery of the supplies and the provision of armed guards on the landing craft to deter hijacking. The command and control problems here are limited to those required for a low-level coordination of relief efforts, learning where the greatest need lies and ensuring that those areas receive the supplies needed. Existing amphibious forces are ideally suited to ship-to-shore transits required for this type of operation. After all, this is precisely what they were designed to do with the minor exception that they are delivering lifesaving food and medication rather than the traditional death and destruction.

Non-Combatant Evacuation Operations. Another aspect of benign role operations is evacuating one's own or neutral civilians from a situation that is in process of boiling over. Again, such situations tend to develop at short notice, although the crisis itself may have been developing slowly for a long time. In many ways, the challenges faced by this sort of operation are the reverse of aid distribution. The civilians to be evacuated are probably scattered over a wide area of the country and their precise locations may not be known. They have to be contacted, assembled into staging areas then brought out, usually either by helicopter or by land convoy. The attitude of the local population can also vary drastically. They might wish to prevent potential hostages from being removed, be glad to be rid of a potential embarrassment, or wish to curry favour with the evacuating forces. Throughout the entire process, good intelligence is essential if the operation is to be carried out safely.

Constabulary Roles

The evacuation scenario crosses the border between the benign role and the next manifestation of military presence, the constabulary role. This is when UN operations take place in an environment of popular disturbance, breakdown of civil order or where criminal activity has reached such a pitch that it has effectively displaced legitimate authorities. Although frequently carried out under an international mandate, the forces involved are acting in support of the civil power. The level of force that they may use and the conditions under which such use may be initiated are, therefore, determined by the legal system of the host country in question.

In theory, this is an easily understood and specified condition. In reality, the situation actually occurring is far from clear. Most civilians have only a limited understanding of the fine distinctions contained within their own legal systems; it is quite unreasonable to expect troops from different countries to do any better. A multinational force will, almost by definition, contain troops representing countries whose legal traditions and systems are radically different from each other and from the host country. At its most extreme, this could easily result in a soldier being arrested and charged with serious offenses when that trooper has (by his own country's standards) been acting with exemplary restraint and forbearance. This situation makes for a complex situation. Close coordination between the constabulary role forces and those of the host country are required.

Maritime Interdiction Operations. These may occur when a naval component is added to the multinational constabulary force. This force may, for example, be required to impose a quarantine on a specific location, to prevent drugs being smuggled out or illegal weapons in. A quarantine is not a blockade (the latter being an act of war with all the implications that contains). A search has to be legalized by the appropriate warrants; quarantine force ships have to be legally empowered to stop a given suspect. This may require a close and detailed interface to exist between the C^4I systems of the multinational force and the host country police intelligence files. It is easy to imagine a sufficiently ruthless group of criminals hijacking a civilian craft and operating it in an extremely provocative manner (with the original owners still on board). If things go wrong and the craft is sunk by the quarantine forces, a major incident would be almost inevitable. Given a few such incidents, the continued presence of the multinational constabulary force, may become politically impossible.

The real problem with attempting quarantine operations in a multinational environment is gaining agreement between the partners on what is to be covered by the restrictions. Modern industry is so complex and so interlocked that it is quite impossible to decide what constitutes a military weapon, what is a civilian product and what is humanitarian aid. In reality, virtually every aspect of a modern industrial state can be considered dual military/civilian use. Any multinational naval operation will be dependent upon continuous consultation and agreement as to the correct categories of goods to be quarantined. In a constabulary role, this will have to include the host country, whose aims and objectives may be far from clear even to itself. The evidence is that this will be the simplest common factor to all the partners in the operation.

Few would deny, for example, that preventing a rogue country making nerve gas by denying them the appropriate raw materials is legitimate. Yet, the problem is that the same raw materials are also required for pesticide production. Those pesticides are essential, not just to protect growing crops but to prevent insect and rodent infestation destroying stored food. In fact, in many tropical countries large scale food storage is impossible without using pesticides that bear a distinct family relationship to chemical warfare agents. Cutting the supply therefore, greatly increases the risk of famine.

It is not even safe to provide the final products in place of raw materials—any modern chemical industry could convert a relatively non-lethal pesticide to a chemical warfare agent with little difficulty. In most of the countries likely to be hit by trade sanctions, the choice between using "humanitarian aid" for humanitarian aid or for military production can only go one way. This factor may even be used as an additional weapon. Following the Second Gulf War, Iraq has made great play of the suffering inflicted on its civilian population by the UN trade sanctions. What is carefully not mentioned by that country is that its government and security forces have not been touched at all by those sanctions and hardship has been deliberately emphasized and concentrated on the most obvious parts of the population as an act of policy.

Even the most innocuous of products can be of dual use. The Iraqis place great emphasis on the shortage of baby milk being responsible for a great increase in child mortality (not failing to point out that a baby milk plant was flattened by US bombing). In reality, "baby milk" (actually milk concentrate) is a key nutritional culture medium in the production of biological weapons such as anthrax, botulism and genetically engineered products such as air-vectored rabies or influenza viruses that release cobra venom in place of the normal flu toxins. It is far from clear just what the Iraqi plant destroyed by bombing was producing—the evidence that it was a civilian installation was such blatant forgery that it insulted the observer's intelligence.[4]

If trade sanctions and embargoes are to have a direct effect on the military capability of a country, firstly they have to be watertight. This is almost impossible to achieve. Only if the country is an island with no land frontiers, and the multinational embargo enforcers are agreed absolutely on policy and have overwhelming sea power, can trade be cut completely. The second requirement is that all participants have to agree on the cut-off being complete; nothing can be allowed in or out. The interlocked and mutually dependant nature of modern industry means that no single class of product can be deemed as not having a military application.[5] Finally, all the evidence shows that the sanctions must be maintained for many years, probably decades, before the burden they impose becomes intolerable.

This is the key problem with using sanctions as a means of international coercion. The political willpower required to keep them in place and effective is almost impossible to maintain. This was almost certainly the gamble made by Iraq in 1990. It is easy to envisage the Iraqi leadership protesting the imposition of sanctions, then international military countermeasures being delayed "while sanctions are given time to work" (an argument very widely presented). The hardships inflicted on the civilian population would have been heavily emphasized leading to the softening, then removal, of the trade embargoes on "humanitarian" grounds. And Iraq would have got away with its aggression.[6]

The conclusion must be that, while sanctions and trade embargoes appear to present a viable alternative to military operations, the reality is that they do not and cannot work without inflicting massive hardship on the population of the country in question—hardship not shared by the military/political leadership and their security forces. In medieval times, towns and fortresses were taken by a siege in which the defenders would be starved into submission, a process accompanied by horrifying carnage and suffering. Where the modern equivalent is to inflict this fate on an entire country, a swift, effective military operation is (arguably) a far less brutal solution.

Piracy. Piracy and its suppression are another area where the constabulary role of multinational forces is likely to have a growing presence. Within territorial waters, suppression of piracy is a national responsibility. However, the ready availability of relatively sophisticated weapons, up to and including shoulder-fired anti-aircraft missiles, puts piracy elimination on much the same footing as other aspects of the trade protection role. Many of the techniques used to trap pirates could easily rebound if proper coordination of the C[4]I networks of the constabulary force and the host country is not achieved.

Where the local environment has deteriorated to the point of civil war or national conflict the situation for peacekeepers gets exceptionally complicated. In these cases, the UN troops are essentially committed to keeping the situation under control while the political powers manage to come up with some sort of conflict-resolving (or at least, conflict-limiting) agreement. The UN forces are then assigned to policing and enforcing that agreement. This has many implications for the operational texture of the deployment, none of which are even remotely good news for the troops involved.

UN-Sanctioned Peace Support Operations

A primary factor is that the troops deployed by the UN are essentially objective, their role being to observe, report and investigate. They are not an ally of one side or the other and cannot afford to be seen as such. If the UN is perceived as being strongly supportive of one side at the expense of the other, any hope of brokering an agreement is irretrievably lost. This absolute requirement is made more difficult if the international media, for whatever reason, decides that one side or the other are "the bad guys" and demands that they be "punished". Such perceptions of the situation are usually extremely simplified and rarely reflect the reality of the crisis.[7] This inherent characteristic of today's media generates severe pressure on the UN to take actions which may be immensely damaging to the chances of resolving the conflict. This translates into severe political restrictions on the military forces deployed, intended to prevent them taking actions damaging to the long-term political goals of the UN authorities.

The inevitable results of these considerations is the imposition of very tight Rules of Engagement (ROEs) on the troops involved. Often such ROEs are quite unrealistic,for example, troops may be required not only to hold their fire until fired upon but then only to engage any hostile unit which is actually seen to be in the act of firing upon them. Under battlefield conditions, this is usually quite difficult. Even where the Rules of Engagement are realistic, they require high-level authorizations to be received. Finally, there is the ever-present tendency of high-level political authorities to try to seize control of the minutia of a military operation from the hands of the professionals trained to undertake that role.

The Military Command Structure

As observers, reporters and investigators, the military forces deployed are operating in an unusual and alien environment. Typically, they will be deployed as small patrols, perhaps an infantry squad in a town or a three or four vehicle platoon in the countryside. Often the area will be poorly mapped; in Yugoslavia the available terrain maps are all severely distorted as an act of security policy by the previous government. Other areas may simply be too remote to ever have been mapped. In other cases, (Rwanda for example) the last maps had been made many years before and the terrain had changed significantly since then. The commander of these small patrols is placed in a truly hellish position. Often a junior lieutenant, only weeks or months from officer training school, he is not quite sure where he is, who the enemy are, what their intentions are, where his supporting units are or what their orders are. In addition, his small patrol is appallingly vulnerable to a well-planned ambush—which may, or may not, have him as its intended target.

This officer faces agonizing decisions which must be taken in the context of the exceptionally restrictive Rules of Engagement imposed upon him. Is that group of armoured vehicles over there friendly, hostile, undecided or are they one of our patrols which is also lost? Is the artillery fire aimed at me, at that group of civilians, or is it just random fire into the blue? Or is it our fire called in by one of my colleagues who does not know I am here? There is no doubt I am under attack, but can I get help quickly to get me out of here? Are there aircraft around that can support me? How do I contact them? By the way, where am I?

In effect, a UN peacekeeping initiative destroys the existing military command structure in which a platoon reports to a company which reports to battalion, all the way up to the supreme commander who has his orders. The need to respond quickly to a developing military situation makes using this chain of command impossible. By the time the necessary and essential procedures have been completed, the situation in question and, quite possibly, the troops involved, are history. Yet, the demands of peacekeeping are such that any authorization to do something must be cleared by the political authorities in question, that is, it must go right to the top. The inevitable conclusion must be that peacekeeping requires a new military structure in which large numbers of small units report directly to the military force commander who can access directly the political authorities.[8]

This strongly suggests that a comprehensive net communication system is required so that those in charge of a deployment can pass orders directly where needed. Yet, the ability of senior officers or politicians to bypass entire command levels is rightly anathema to the military tradition and has a catastrophic effect on good order and discipline. Striking a balance between applying the Rules of Engagement necessary to protect the military forces deployed, while ensuring that their necessary acts of self-defense do not disrupt attempts to resolve the situation in its widest context is a major challenge that defies easy response.

Intercommunications

A related problem is intercommunication between the units making up the multinational force. Where these forces are NATO derived, the problems are, loosely speaking, controllable. Years of NATO standardization have provided at least a basic level of interoperability, although cynics may suggest that forces of a single country still have grave difficulties in establishing cooperation. The real problems arise where *ad hoc* coalitions have occurred. Where the forces in question have no common links, the level of tactical communication between them is likely to be precisely zero. This inevitably leads to serious tactical misunderstandings.

Again, this problem is very hard to solve. Ideally, all the forces deployed as part of a UN sponsored operation would be re-equipped with compatible systems. This is impractical because of training considerations and, in any case, funding constraints mean that the resources necessary are simply not available. The solution may lie in some form of "transparent interfacing" at a senior command level so that the area communication administration system can receive signals transmitted in any format and can resend in any desired configuration. Transparent interfacing is already beginning to appear in warship command systems (so that a customer-selected weapon or sensor can be "plugged and played" into the desired command system) and this may give the kernel of a possible solution to this problem. It is filling this gap, between the structures required for effective military operations and those essential for effective peacekeeping operations that naval forces may have a key role in multinational operations on the ground.

The Utility of Warships for Peacekeeping Operations

Land-based communications structures are restricted in their capabilities by their need to be transportable in small armoured vehicles. They are also limited by the electrical power required to run them. A field headquarters must be mobile; its capabilities are therefore limited. A large, permanent headquarters can be of any size and have almost any desired electrical generating capability. The problem is that it is an extremely high value target for those not well intentioned towards the UN initiative and is extremely expensive to set up. There is an ever-present danger that it could end up as a besieged hostage with the primary attention of the UN force being diverted to defending their headquarters from, for example, a suicide truck bomb attack.[9] Once the emergency is ended, all the investment made in setting it up is wasted—indeed, further funding is required to take it away.

The Warship as a Command Post

Ships have none of these restrictions. They are mobile assets that can be deployed where and when required. In comparison with a land base, they have enormous reserves of power to run complex and massively capable command, control and communications suites. Most modern warships have satellite communications facilities which can be used to access the highest political authorities directly. Fully integrated communications suites capable of receiving large numbers of messages, and recording them for future reference are also common to the point of becoming standard. The message capacity of these systems is, as far as open information sources can reveal, entirely adequate to handle the message volume expected from the type of operations envisaged.[10]

It is quite easy to envisage a situation where the complex and comprehensive information management capabilities built into all modern warships of frigate size upwards, will be the first fully capable command and communications systems to arrive in a specific area of operations. At sea, they will be relatively safe; it would take a major military effort to penetrate the defenses of such a task group. The deployment of a modern warship provides unequaled facilities of just the type needed by the peculiar characteristics of a UN peacekeeping operation. It is also economical; the cost of maintaining a warship on station is far less than building an elaborate headquarters, only to tear it down again when the need has passed. The costs of operating a ship in this role will be minuscule in comparison with those incurred by attempting to do the same from an aircraft.

These integrated communications suites mean that large numbers of small units can be contacted directly by the most senior administrative levels—and since this is achieved by a different service, the deleterious effects of bypassing existing command structures are minimized. The same system is also capable of ultra-long range communications, dramatically reducing the response time of the communications chain. This will not necessarily reduce the time taken for distant authorities to make the decision, but at least one stage of the response loop timing has been minimized.

It may well be that the cramped accommodation and limited dimensions of a frigate are not best suited for the physical demands of controlling a diffuse and disorganized land operation—probably a larger and more capacious ship is required. The command systems and communications facilities projected for the new US Navy *LPD-17*-class appear to be entirely suitable and the ships have the size and volume to allow enhancements to be installed as necessary.[11] Where further additional facilities are required, it is even possible that these could be installed in caravans and fitted to the ships on a temporary basis.

The Warship as a Negotiation Venue

Warships may also have an unexpected value in the peacekeeping process. They are neutral yet very secure ground for meetings. Since communications out of the ship are subject to strict controllability, premature release of negotiation positions and "grandstanding" for the press can be eliminated. A subtle point is that any warship exudes an atmosphere of power to those unfamiliar with her capabilities. After all, any self-styled militia general who regards using a hand-held radio as evidence of his technical prowess will find the Combat Direction Centre of an Aegis cruiser sobering, to put it mildly.

Air Operations in Peacekeeping Operations

A related problem in peacekeeping operations is controlling airspace in the region of a multinational operation. These areas may be highly travelled with a dense concentration of civilian and neutral air traffic. To some extent, this problem can be resolved by installing secondary surveillance radars onboard warships. The overwhelming majority of civilian aircraft are not tracked by direct primary radar contact but by a secondary radar activating a transponder fitted to the target aircraft. This transponder response provides the course, speed and identity of the target, making for a much safer and more accurate track record. There is a problem with this situation in that many air traffic controllers have grown up with the secondary radar systems and do not have institutionalized memories of what actual radar tracks ("skin paints") look like. This can cause great confusion when an aircraft with a defective transponder enters the control zone. This has been noted with the loss of Flight TW-800 in July, 1996. A "mysterious" contact track crossing the area is prominent in most of the more outlandish theories about this tragedy. The track was, however, immediately recognizable as a skin paint to a veteran air traffic control officer who was able to identify it as a P-3 Orion that had previously reported a defective transponder.[12]

Fighter Control

A further factor that has to be considered is the problem of controlling the operations of fighter aircraft assigned to provide air cover to the ships operating in a specific area. Fighter control requires detailed and specific data on the inbound targets so that the interceptors can be manoeuvered out into an optimum position to make contact with the intended target and nobody else. The greater the complexity of the air tactical picture and the more subject that picture is to rapid change, the greater the demands placed on the instructions issued to the interceptor.

These demands mean that ships responsible for controlling fighters on combat air patrol demand radars capable of determining accurate bearings and elevations (in other words full and precise 3-D capability) and the ability to automatically extract and maintain track files on those contacts. They also need to continue such operations in the face of a fast-changing and immensely complicated tactical situation while under hostile attempts to disrupt these activities. Finally they require comprehensive communications and datalinking facilities so that data can be absorbed from different sources, correctly deconflicted and then relayed to the fighters and other ships in the formation.

This is not a new set of requirements. Such specifications evolved at the end of the Second World war in an attempt to cope with mass attacks by Japanese kamikaze aircraft. Originally, the task was assigned to destroyers stationed out along the threat axes. Later, the task was transferred to submarines that could submerge when subjected to heavy attack. Eventually, the function was devolved to airborne early warning aircraft.

This role may now return to surface ships. Relying on airborne early warning aircraft predicates the availability of aircraft carriers capable of operating them. This makes them unique assets to the US Navy (the Royal Navy helicopter AEW systems lack the range and endurance for theatre-level coverage and protection.) Although the French Navy has a single carrier capable of operating the E-2C, this is not a large enough force to be of any significance. The Aegis systems on the CG-47 *Ticonderoga*-class cruisers and DDG-51 *Arleigh Burke*-class destroyers provide adequate capability in the control area. These ships have demonstrated efficiency levels that have caused some task force commanders to prefer their cramped combat direction centers to the more spacious accommodation offered by an aircraft carrier.

For most navies, the existing classes of frigate with their two-dimensional radars and limited air warfare combat direction systems do not have the necessary levels of capability nor the internal volume required for its provision. A viable approach may be the provision of such equipment to suitable platforms as containerized kits. These could be delivered to amphibious assault ships or even cargo ships to provide the necessary facilities.

Safety of Friendly and Non-Combatant Aircraft

The problem of controlling this air picture is made more difficult still by the activities of friendly aircraft. Any multinational operation is likely to involve a wide range of air operations, including a variety of combat operations, logistic shuttle flights from ship-to-ship and ship-to-shore, patrol and liaison flights and special forces operations. All of these (and the last group in particular) may involve aircraft from different nations and armed forces. There is an ever-present risk that the correct identifications are not being detected due to equipment failure or incompatibility. This can have a subtle manifestation in that ships operating in different areas may build up marginally different tactical pictures. Where these operational areas overlap, merging those tactical pictures may either cause large numbers of phantom contacts (swamping the contact-handling procedures) or false data might be generated by merging non-related target tracks.

This latter point may not seem too serious, yet its real implications are very serious indeed. The obvious effect may be to cause a hole in the surveillance picture through which a single attacker can slip. A warship carries the political and military significance of a major ground or air formation, and its loss is correspondingly far more significant than that of a single aircraft or tank. If the Rules of Engagement permit the warship only to fire in its own defence, and that ship is not given an adequate level of warning, the "opening salvo" advantage means it is probable that the warship will be hit.

Yet, the converse of the situation can be even worse. Track confusion appears to have been a major factor behind the shooting down of the Iranian Airbus by the *USS Vincennes*. Reports in *US Naval Institute Proceedings* suggest that errors in deconflicting a tactical picture shared by datalink between two ships resulted in a track file merger under which the track number designating a military flight was applied to the track record of the Airbus flight. The combined data appeared to show the aircraft descending towards the cruiser. Other accounts point out that the *Vincennes* was engaged in a surface action at the time, was having systems problems and was also under observation by an Iranian P-3. Given the lack of transponder data from the Airbus, the combat direction center crew were attempting to identify the target by behaviour patterns. Under these circumstances, errors are understandable. Interestingly, an FFG-7 *Oliver Hazard Perry*-class frigate in the vicinity was able to identify the Airbus correctly; the austerely-equipped frigate did not have the datalink necessary to share tactical pictures and, therefore, its own picture was uncontaminated by the deconfliction problems. Sometimes there can be too much communication.

Power Projection and Multinational Naval Operations

The ability to strike at a target with overwhelming force is the ultimate expression of a multinational naval operation. This is where naval forces in general, and the carriers in particular, excel. If any sort of operations are to take place against serious opposition, the provision of capable and effective air support is essential. If the planners are in luck, there may be large land airbases within striking reach of the combat zone that can support adequate land-based aviation groups. However, such bases may not be available and, if they are, will be on allied territory subject to the political restrictions and demands of the allied government in question. Such demands are likely to affect policy issues such as targeting, geographical limitations on combat area and weaponry carried. Theoretical provision of air support from home bases hundreds or thousands of miles away is worthless—the aircraft cannot respond to an emergency quickly enough to be of any value.

An excellent example is the attempt to strike at targets in Iraq using air-launched cruise missiles fired from B-52 strategic bombers. Those bombers had to fly in from Guam. Had the Iraqi forces been capable of mounting a real defence against such attack, those defences would have been stacked and waiting for the bombers. As it was, the lumbering B-52s had to be given US Navy F-14 escorts for the last part of their flight. At best, such aircraft can be used for strategic bombing of infrastructure and logistic targets that can be pre-planned. If "doors have to be kicked in", the fleets doing the kicking have to carry their own air support with them, and this means they must use aircraft carriers.

Or does it? Recently, the Tomahawk cruise missile has become a weapon of choice for such punitive strikes. A political motivation for this is that, being unmanned, its crew cannot be held hostage if the weapon is shot down. Cruise missile bombardment also has an eerie robotic quality that is peculiarly demoralizing to the victim. The legends that have spread about the Tomahawk bombardments in Iraq and Serbia (for example, that the missiles following roads were seen stopping at traffic control lights!) bear witness to the degree of awe in which these weapons are held. Cruise missiles, however, have the same limitation as long-range bombers. They are only really effective when fired at pre-planned and static targets. Mobile facilities and those that have been carefully concealed are difficult targets for unmanned systems.

Targeting: The Cooperative Engagement Capability Concept

Targeting missiles or air strikes in the context of a multinational naval operation is a complex issue. The use of very long range weapons has always been a challenging proposition that has defied simple answers. The current US Navy effort is the Cooperative Engagement Capability (CEC). This envisages obtaining sensor data from a wide variety of sources, fusing that data to evolve an accurate and timely tactical picture, then using that tactical picture to isolate, designate and engage targets. At its most extreme, this means that the platform for a given weapon can fire on targets spotted and designated by other units remote from the firing point.

An early application of this technique was envisaged as a "magazine ship". The target handling capability of an Aegis warship far exceeds the weapons stowage on that ship. The magazine ship concept proposed an Aegis ship companion that was little more than a mass of vertical launch silos. This ship would fire its missiles and the Aegis ship would take them over in mid-air and direct them to the appropriate targets.

It was revived, some years later, as the Arsenal Ship, now an ongoing program with the US Navy. The Arsenal Ship was conceived as a means of providing missile deep strike and fire support for shore operations, at least in part as a replacement for the decommissioned *Iowa*-class battleships. The Arsenal Ship was seen as being the centerpiece of a complex targeting web, utilising a variety of sensors, including manned and unmanned aircraft, ships, satelites and troops. The weapons flexibility of the Arsenal Ship is limited only by the capabilities of its vertical launch silos, multiple-launch rocket system (MLRS) launchers and guns. The ship would have been capable of firing (though not controlling) air defense and anti-tactical ballistic missile weapons in addition to its shore bombardment capabilities.

The original Arsenal Ship concept was for the construction of a single prototype, followed by construction of five more ships and the modification of the original prototype to full service standards. However, during early 1997, rumours began to spread of serious shortcomings in the basic Arsenal Ship concept. Doubts had always been expressed about the wisdom of concentrating so many assets into a single hull.

These conceptual doubts are reported to have been reinforced by discovery of a serious technical deficiency. According to authoritative sources, the network of targeting data upon which the Arsenal Ship depends consumes so much data transmission volume that existing datalinks cannot handle it without a dramatic increase in bandwidth. Unless an entirely new, ultra-high-speed datalink system is developed (at a probable cost measured in US$ billions), a task force containing an Arsenal Ship has the choice of relaying target data to the Arsenal Ship or using its own sensors—but not both. This is essentially the same electromagnetic interference problem that was responsible for the loss of *HMS Sheffield* during the Falklands Campaign.[13]

The CEC Concept in Multinational Naval Operations

If this communications problem turns out to be real, it has dire implications for the whole of the CEC concept as applied to multinational naval operations. CEC depends upon the absorption of large masses of tactical data and its synthesis into a coherent tactical picture. If this is to be practical, the data has to be presented in a compatible form. This may not be too onerous a demand within forces derived from the NATO environment since the existing Link-11 and Link-16 data transmission systems are relatively standard. Even the incorporation of non-NATO ships is not too difficult since they can be equipped with relatively inexpensive stand-alone Link-11 receivers. Link-16 equivalents should not be too far down the road.[14]

The real problem is conceptual. If CEC is to work in a multinational naval operation, there has to be absolute consistency about the rules of enagement, fire authorizations and other administrative details. The danger is that a bureaucratic gridlock will evolve in which the rules and procedures adopted by one member of the operating team will be unacceptable to one of the others. It is easy to see fire instructions and targeting data being shuttled backwards and forwards until a mutually acceptable compromise is determined. Meanwhile, the original reason for the request fades into history.

Multinational CEC has another achilles heel. At present weapons guidance and targeting systems are designed to prevent outside interference. They may not do it too well, but that is the desired object. If weapons belonging to one navy are to be opened up to guidance from another, the whole system suddenly becomes very vulnerable. Where one enters the loop, another can follow.

With these considerations in place, it is probable that CEC will remain a national asset and true multinational participation in the loop is unlikely. In its place, it is likely that multinational command and control over the various national CECs will be established where the situation demands. This points to the virtues of multinational naval operations in support of UN initiatives being controlled from at-sea flagships.

Conclusion

There can be little doubt that the elaborate command systems installed on warships will be of great value, provided those capabilities are recognized and used to the full. The term "multinational operations" now appears to mean a UN peacekeeping operation in the overwhelming majority of cases. The evidence of deployments to date strongly supports the position that conventional, major-force wars will be rare indeed. The primary operational requirement will be much lower intensity tasks of the type discussed in this chapter. In the Victorian Era, these "small wars" were frequently resolved by "sending a gunboat" and lobbing a few shells into the appropriate government property. Now that small wars (in the Victorian sense) appear to have returned, perhaps the modern equivalent will be to send a command ship and lob a few well-chosen electronic messages into the appropriate ears. After all, the shells can always follow later!

Notes

1. *The Fundamentals of British Maritime Doctrine*, BR 1806, Directorate of Naval Staff Duties. Published by Her Majesty's Stationary Office.
2. Private communication with the author in July, 1996. There is a very serious point here—the skills that were needed to control the Somalia situation (gathering human intelligence, using informers, controlling what amounted to street gangs and arranging *modus vivendi* with such groups while under severe force restrictions) are all roles with which any city police force are intimately familiar. They are quite different from the superficially similar requirements of military operations.
3. See press accounts of the Bangladesh typhoon emergency relief operation for elaboration of the merits of air-cushion landing craft.
4. Dr. Norman Friedman discusses this point in detail in his book *Desert Victory: The War for Kuwait* (Annapolis: Naval Institute Press, 1991). The Iraqi attempts to label the plant as a baby milk producer were pathetic—hastily-painted signs were in English only, worker's overalls were also hastily labelled in English, yet the plant was camouflaged and had dummy bomb craters painted on the roof and was surrounded by military-style security fences. This is all quite irrelevant though. Even if the plant was producing milk concentrate, the real issue is what that product was being used for. Producing milk concentrate and being a biological warfare plant are by no means exclusive.
5. *Chemical Age Project File*, 1986, published by Pergamon Infolinc. This was a daily-updated list of all chemical industry construction projects world-wide, distributed to engineering companies with interests in that sector. The producers were highly suspicious of the nature of many Iraqi projects from an early stage. A number of facilities were co-located in ways that strongly suggested that their planned roles were quite different from the announced intention. The producers made their reservations known at the time but their doubts were only confirmed after the end of the Second Gulf War.
6. Dr. Friedman also discusses this possibility in *Desert Victory*.
7. Cynics may see the whole press coverage of the civil wars in the former Yugoslavia as an early example of "information warfare" or "infowar". Civil wars have always been horrific and barbarous. Press coverage that attempts to assert that one side is uniquely responsible for the atrocities in an attempt to bring about a desired course of action is not helpful. Any study of press

reports on this war will show how media coverage has been used to try and bring about international intervention on one side or the other.

8. These issues are explored in depth in the *C³I Market Forecast* published by Forecast International, 22 Commerce Road, Newtown, Conneticut, USA.

9. This can be seen in the wake of the attack on the US Marine Barracks in Beirut.

10. A good example of such systems is the ICS-3 equipment installed on HMS *Broadsword*. Over 20 years ago a sudden storm hit a yacht race being held off the Atlantic coast of the UK. Most of the amateur sailors taking part in the race were immediately in the direst of trouble and required help urgently. Not familiar with emergency procedures, they grabbed the nearest microphone and started yelling for help, often without giving positions or realistic estimates of their situation. The ICS-3 system on *Broadsword* was capable of descrambling this chaotic babble and directing help where it was most urgently needed. For 36 hours the frigate was the primary forward head-quarters for the rescue effort and her achievements in that role won her unstinted praise.

11. The provision of such command systems was specifically included in the LPD-17 program documentation from its earliest stages.

12. Private communication to the author, later repeated in most of the reliable coverage of the event. The conspiracy theories surrounding the crash of TW-800 are a classical example of "info-garbage" that betrays a total lack of understanding of how weapons systems operate. The same info-garbage can cause extreme problems for multinational forces by, for example, indentifying them with one side when they are trying to maintain neutrality.

13. The Arsenal Ship program is discussed (as part of the SC-21 program) in the *Warships Forecast*, published by Forecast International.

14. *The Naval Institute Guide to World Naval Weapons Systems*, edited by Dr. Norman Friedman and published by the US Naval Institute, contains the only authoritative and reasonably complete account of the various Link systems currently in service. This book should be regarded as essential reading.

PART II
THE ASIA-PACIFIC

PART II

THE ASIA-PACIFIC

6 Changing Strategic Environment and Need for Maritime Cooperation in the North Pacific: New Roles for Navies

SEO-HANG LEE

The end of the Cold War and the dissolution of the Soviet Union has undoubtedly had a profound impact on the security environment of the North Pacific.[1] While it has definitely promoted the welcome trend of a shift from confrontation to reconciliation and dialogue, the region's security outlook is more mixed and complicated than it appears. Against a background of the changing strategic environment, this chapter will examine the need for maritime cooperation in the North Pacific and explore new roles for navies which can contribute to the reduction of the level of uncertainty and anxiety, thereby promoting greater stability and prosperity in the region.

The Changing Strategic Environment in the North Pacific

The immense ideological barrier that gave rise to distrust and hostility among states for decades has ended. While this does not necessarily mean that peace has finally arrived, the improvements in relations between states in the region clearly provide new opportunities for the future. In addition, the preoccupation of virtually all countries in the region with accelerating economic development and enhancing their economic competitiveness has encouraged them to promote cooperative commercial relations with their neighbours, and this has also contributed to a reduction of tension. As a result, trade among the North Pacific countries has significantly increased in recent years, intra-regional interdependence is deepening.[2]

There are, of course, negative factors which are likely to affect regional peace and security, some from the legacy of the Cold War. The first group of negative factors include the territorial dispute between Japan and Russia, the tensions in the Taiwan Strait and the division of the Korean peninsula. Although some progress has been made in defusing these potential crises, none of these problems have been completely resolved.

Figure 6.1 The Northwest Pacific Ocean

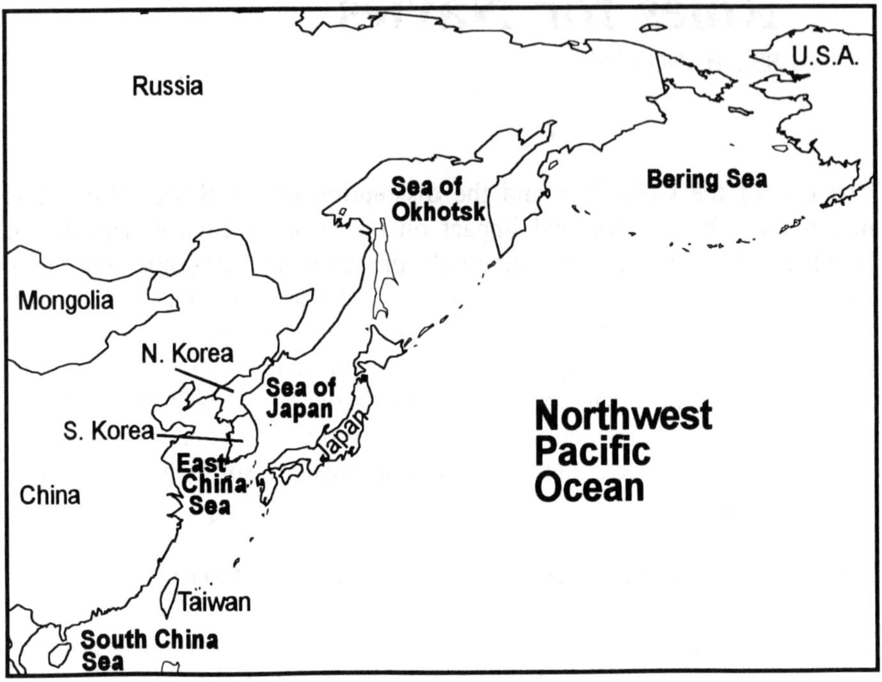

There is also a growing agenda of non-conventional security issues in the region, issues that do not involve direct military deployments, but could still give rise to the threat or use of force. These include the management of natural resources, the protection of the environment, in particular, transborder air pollution and nuclear waste dumping; the regulation of refugees; and the prevention of international criminal activities such as piracy, smuggling, drug trafficking and terrorism.

Probably the most serious challenge to the long-term security of the region may come from the internal factors. Major transformations—social, economic and political in nature—are taking place in key states in the region. The outcome of such transformations will determine to a large extent the nature of the future security environment in the North Pacific. The primary concerns are China and North Korea.

Finally, it should be noted that the countries in the region have been actively engaged in building up their military forces. Competitive acquisition of arms is being fuelled by the obsolescence of existing weapons stock and the general economic prosperity. The motivations behind the arms build-up are complex and vary according to country. The major causes for the military arms build-up in the North Pacific today no longer stem from ideological conflicts but rather from strategic uncertainty due to the collapse of the Soviet Union and the possible reduction in American deployment in the region, and conflicting national interests, that is, the urge to protect or expand a sphere of influence versus the fear of losing it.

A fragile peace was maintained in the North Pacific during the Cold War years with the United States playing a pivotal role in maintaining stability in the region. However, anxieties arise over the future security in the region with those negative security trends. At the moment, four points of strategic concern emerge when potential challenges to the North Pacific regional stability are discussed. They are:

* will the US reduce its military presence and what will be its future role in the region;
* will Japan expand its influence;
* will China extend its military capability;
* and how will the inter-Korean relations develop?[3]

The recent US-Japan Joint Declaration on Security Alliance provides, more or less, direct guidance on the first two concerns. The US will keep 100,000 American troops in the region and Japan will play a greater role in maintaining peace and stability in the North Pacific. Nonetheless, anxieties remain about the future security of the whole region and there are potential security challenges in all directions with the tradition of regional rivalries, unsettled territorial disputes and other sources of concern.

The Maritime Security Context

The North Pacific region, as the term itself implies, is dominated by the oceans. Maritime capabilities, therefore, provide the primary, but by no means exclusive, currency of power throughout the region. Three levels of naval forces presently exist in the North Pacific: the superpower level, the major regional level and the lesser regional powers level. The first level contains the US (combined with Japan and Canada in certain aspects) and Russia; the second includes Japan and China; the third is the two Koreas and Taiwan. The North Pacific security requirements thus need to be examined in light of the unique maritime considerations.

The Superpower Level

The maritime security context of the region dramatically changed after the end of the Cold War. The most important strategic change in the North Pacific involves the relative decline of the presence and influence of the two super-powers. For instance, the Russian navy has been hit hard by the economic restructuring imposed over the recent periods. It has been reported that many ships of the Pacific Fleet, with some four dozen nuclear submarines, some 50 major surface combatants and more than 400 naval fighter and bomber aircraft, are unfit to go to sea and their operational serviceability is in doubt.[4] There is likely to be substantial further deterioration in Russian capabilities in the Far East before any reconstitutive processes are able to take effect. The US Navy has also reduced its military presence in the North Pacific. The Bottom-up-Review requires further reductions in naval strength.[5] Most importantly, the bases, facilities and forces which were maintained in the Philippines have now all been removed. Some of these have been relocated elsewhere in the region, especially to Hawaii and the US west coast and to a lesser extent to Japan and Singapore, but some have been withdrawn from the region entirely.

These developments on the part of the major naval powers have certainly reduced tension and risks of confrontation at sea in the North Pacific. At the same time, however, they have led to the rather paradoxical situation where the navies of regional powers have begun to exert themselves, apparently to fill the power vacuum.

The Major Regional Level

China's naval capability is expanding from a coastal defence role to an ability to project power further offshore. With the relaxation of Sino-Soviet hostilities in particular, the focus in Chinese security planning today is on local rather than major conflicts, specifically along the maritime frontiers with the need to defend vital sea lanes and offshore assets. In order to implement this offshore defense strategy, the Chinese naval force structure is in the midst of substantial modification and modernization. The new naval program has established interim goals to transform its navy into an ocean-going one. The first stage, extending through the end of the century, places emphasis on the construction of major surface combatants (destroyers, frigates and submarines) equipped with guided missiles and advanced electronics. The second stage, through to about 2020, calls for the building of two aircraft carriers, and the requisite aircraft and warships to form carrier task forces. The third stage, from 2020 onwards, calls for the Chinese Navy to begin to approach global naval status and to be able to conduct large-scale naval operations anywhere in the world.[6]

Currently, the Chinese Navy has some 50 surface combatants and 52 submarines including one nuclear-powered ballistic missile-firing submarine and a variety of fast attack craft.[7] Such capability assumes great significance in the South China Sea where the territorial disputes over the Spratly Islands and the Paracel Islets remain unresolved. The Chinese Navy may try to establish large parts of the Yellow Sea and the East China Sea, as well as the South China Sea, as a zone of Chinese influence. Thus the rise of the Chinese Navy may prove to be a destabilizing factor on regional security.

On the Japanese front, the Maritime Self Defence Forces (MSDF) have also targeted air and sea-lane defense as the top defence priority into the 1990s. The MSDF has already in service an *Aegis*-class cruiser and more are likely to be procured by the late 1990s. The National Defense Program Outline, which was released in November 1995, particularly places an emphasis on the possession of one fleet escort force, maintenance of submarine units and creation of fixed-wing patrol aircraft units for the MSDF. The rationale for Japan to upgrade its naval capability is partly configured on geopolitical realities but also on the basis of Japan's realization that over the longer-term it should assume a more independent defence posture. Already virtually self-sufficient in key sectors of weapons development, the Japanese are likely to continue to emphasize the importance of a credible naval presence in the region.

Lesser Regional Powers Level

Other regional countries, including the two Koreas and Taiwan, are acquiring more powerful naval forces and developing their maritime capability. These countries are building a potentially formidable maritime strike capability provided primarily by aircraft and surface ships equipped with anti-ship missiles. For instance, the Taiwanese Navy is building twelve *Oliver Hazard*

Perry-class frigates through a technology transfer agreement with the US and buying sixteen *Lafayette*-class frigates from France.

The result of these trends is that, despite the decline in the US and Russian maritime presence, the maritime security outlook in the North Pacific region is now becoming more complicated. In essence, causes for such complication, as noted previously, stem no longer from ideological conflicts, but rather from growing concern with strategic uncertainty and differing national interests, that is, the urge to protect or expand a sphere of influence and the fear of losing it. At the regional level, there will be more navies of consequence. Warships will continue to navigate in distant waters in support of national political and economic interests, taking advantage of the exceptional mobility and flexibility of maritime power. In particular, the recent establishment of 200-mile exclusive economic zones (EEZ) under the UN Convention on the Law of the Sea and the growing exploitation of the seas, as well as the awareness of the vast unused resource potential of the seas, will increase the need for surveillance. Such activities may lead to dangerous situations and conflicts including an increased risk of incidents between maritime forces.

Need for Maritime Cooperation: New Roles for Navies

The changing security trends, particularly in the maritime context, certainly provide regional states with a challenging task of how to secure stability from the new form of instability arising in the post-Cold War era. Given the prevalent strategic uncertainty in which countries in the region could feel threatened by each other, although the definite causes or motives for conflict are difficult to pinpoint, what is needed are measures designed to reduce the risk of conflicts which could arise from misunderstanding or miscalculation in the unstable strategic environment.

In view of the importance of maritime issues in regional security and the emphasis recently given by regional states to maritime capabilities, naval activities deserve special attention. Maritime cooperation can help in dissipating tensions and making the region more stable. In fact, navies, by virtue of their inherent international nature, are more suitable for dialogue and cooperation than other arms of military forces.

The major reasons for encouraging maritime cooperation in which navies play an essential role are three-fold: first, cooperation helps build confidence and trust between maritime forces; second, cooperative structures can be used to maintain communications when tensions are heightened; and third, it can create an environment where maritime forces can combine to do real work on the high seas or within national jurisdiction, to achieve a so-called stable maritime regime. Cooperation also serves to prepare the ground for interoperability and harder-edged collaborative operations if the shooting starts.[8]

In the North Pacific during the Cold War, regional maritime cooperation involving navies was conducted largely on a bilateral basis between the US and Japan, the Republic of Korea and Taiwan to provide a deterrent and a war-fighting force to counter their common threat. Multinational exercises involving ships from Canada and US allies from further afield were also held regularly. The biennial RIMPAC (Rim of the Pacific) exercises, dating back to 1971, are one of the best examples.

Issues for Naval Cooperation

In the post-Cold War era, new forms of maritime cooperation have to be developed in order to materialize the above-mentioned interests and thus secure stability in the North Pacific. Given the existing suspicion among nations in the region and uncertainty about the future, the emphasis of maritime cooperation must be placed on nourishing the progress already made in economic cooperation and building the foundations—the cement and mortar—for holding potential security building blocs in place.

Since the early 1990s, a number of maritime cooperation proposals have been made for the North Pacific region. The proposals include measures to increase transparency, confidence-building measures (CBMs) and naval arms control. Many proposals have originated with non-governmental organizations (NGOs) and are now subject to official consideration. For instance, the recently established unofficial "track two" organization, called the Council for Security Cooperation in the Asia-Pacific (CSCAP), has identified a variety of naval issues for cooperation in the region (See Table 1), and the official ASEAN Regional Forum (ARF) is holding an inter-sessional meeting on search and rescue coordination and cooperation.[9] In addition, some proposals are much more practical than others, and several are simply unrealistic in that they lack official acceptance or cannot be meaningfully implemented across the region.

Table 6.1 Issues for North Pacific Naval Cooperation

- Exchange of Fleet Schedules
- Search and Rescue Cooperation
- A Regional Maritime Surveillance and Safety Regime (REMARSSAR)
- Regional Avoidance of Incidents at Sea Regime (INCSEA)
- Joint Patrol Arrangements
- Annual Conference on Naval Cooperation
- Development of Common Naval Doctrine
- Maritime Contingency Planning
- Shared Training Opportunities

In terms of feasibility, the following measures, which range from exchange of naval information and personnel through to more advanced operational measures such as surveillance cooperation or agreements on the prevention of incidents at sea between naval forces, are conceivable.

Exchange of Information and Personnel. Exchanging information on naval force structure and command organization would be extremely important for assessing the defensive nature of naval forces and the scope of naval exercises and would be a significant step forward in the field of confidence-building. Other areas where the exchange of information may be valid are shipbuilding programs and the operational status of existing ships. The effect that they could have is preventing a naval arms race based on incorrect intelligence. Exchanges of personnel, fleet schedules and ship visits would also contribute to removing the grounds for suspicion and mistrust, and to reaching a better understanding of other nations' intentions.

Prior Notification of Major Naval Activities. Prior notification of activities such as exercises, deployments and transits may be useful for promoting openness. However, advance information on various activities might also result in other states conducting similar activities in the same area, and thus trigger incidents which might not otherwise have taken place. Thus it is necessary to structure and provide notification of the exercises in advance in order to avoid unintended incidents.

Observation of Naval Activities. The purpose of observation is to confirm that the notified activity is non-threatening in nature, and that it is carried out in conformity with what has been laid out in the notification. However, inviting observers to naval exercises gives rise to many complicated administrative problems. In order for observation to be effective and meaningful, observers should be allowed to spread out among different naval units and meet after the exercise to discuss the scope and purpose of the exercise.

Constraint on Passage of Warships. Although the UN Convention on the Law of the Sea does not prohibit innocent passage of foreign warships or ships in government non-commercial service through the territorial sea, flag states could ensure that, barring exceptional situations, such ships should not normally pass within twelve nautical miles of the baseline of the coastal states. If the passage is necessary for the conduct of peacetime naval activities, the coastal state could be notified in advanced. A similar constraint could be suggested regarding all nuclear-powered ships as well as ships carrying nuclear or other dangerous or noxious substances.

Coordinated Participation in UN Register of Conventional Arms. The UN Register of Conventional Arms, which was opened on 1 January 1992, requests UN member-states to provide data annually on certain categories of arms (including warships)[10] imported into or exported from their territory. Since its inauguration, all the regional countries except North Korea have provided data and the experience of four years' reporting in the North Pacific has been encouraging. Hence, if it continues to develop, the UN Register will greatly contribute to enhancing confidence and transparency among governments in the region.

Multinational Naval Cooperation (MNCO). So far, most of the MNCO experience has been with blue water sea assertion operations, usually associated with the protection of shipping. However, most navies in the North Pacific are optimized for coastal water sovereignty protection or sea denial tasks which are focused on national security and not conducive to multinational cooperation. Therefore, it is a prerequisite for the regional countries to identify a common objective for joint operations. Only after that can the MNCO be expected to have mutual benefits. In the meantime, joint port visits and personnel exchanges between regional navies is something to be encouraged.

Incidents at Sea Agreement (INCSEA). In the context of the post-Cold War North Pacific where there is a heightened risk of incidents between regional naval forces due to the increasing naval presence in confined waters, agreements on the prevention of incidents at sea are urgently needed. The first agreement of this kind was concluded by the US and the Soviet Union in 1972. Known as the 1972 USA-USSR Incidents at Sea Agreement, it was negotiated to avoid the risk of collisions and other dangerous incidents, which had been occurring in increasing numbers when the naval forces of both powers encountered each other at sea. As the Soviet Navy grew during the 1960s, incidents between US and Soviet warships increased. The incidents included various dangerous manoeuvres in which ships violated the provisions of the International Regulations for Preventing Collisions at Sea. The agreement seeks to limit the number and dangers of naval incidents through regulation of hazardous manoeuvres, restriction of other forms of harassment, increased communications at sea, and convening regular naval consultations and exchanges of information. This agreement has been widely regarded as a success. One of the most critical factors contributing to the successful implementation of the agreement is considered to be the common interest of both states in avoiding incidents that could increase tensions and the risk of war.

The agreement has subsequently served as the model for several similar bilateral agreements: between the UK and the USSR in 1986; between West Germany and the USSR in 1988; between France and the USSR in 1989; and between Norway and Canada in 1989. It should be also noted that the Republic of Korea and Russia signed such an agreement to avoid the risk of collision and other dangerous incidents on 2 June 1994.[11] Given the apparent success of the US-Soviet agreement, it has been suggested that a similar type of multilateral agreement could be envisaged. The potential benefits of a sub-regional INCSEA-type arrangement in the North Pacific region are clear.

Developing a Harmonious and Solid Regional Maritime Regime. To build confidence in the North Pacific, it is important to enhance the openness and transparency and the practices of regional states on ocean affairs. In particular, some states need to make public accurate baseline and outer limits of their maritime jurisdictions by way of charts or lists of geographical coordinates.[12] The UN Convention on the Law of the Sea, which entered into force in November 1994, in fact requires a party to do this.

In addition, regional states could negotiate agreed understandings regarding those controversial rules of the law of the sea which are inconsistent with the policies of certain states. For instance, the US and Soviet Union in 1989 signed a joint statement on the innocent passage of warship in each other's territorial seas.[13] Attached to the joint statement, the two governments issued the uniform interpretation of the rules of international law governing innocent passage which sets forth in more detail the common interpretation of the UN Convention on the Law of the Sea governing innocent passage in the territorial sea. Similar measures could be taken among regional states with respect to various controversial issues. Considering that the several unfortunate incidents that occurred previously were mainly due to uncertainty on such issues, it is important to develop a more harmonious and solid maritime regime.

Conclusion

The end of the Cold War and the consequent improvement of relations in the North Pacific has provided a long-awaited opportunity for developing a uniform and stable regional maritime order. In this region, however, what appears to be most disturbing is a prevailing atmosphere of strategic uncertainty. Such uncertainty arises from a shifting balance of power such as the collapse of the Soviet Union, the reduction of the United States deployments and the rise of Japan and China as major powers, all in the context of historically-based suspicions and rivalries among the regional states. With such uncertainty looming large, regional states have been expanding and improving the qualities of their military capabilities for some years.

In this regard, a particularly worrying trend is that the important part of the improvements in military capabilities of regional states involve naval forces which are the most suitable for projecting force. Such a trend is all the more worrisome, given the fact that the maritime regime in the North Pacific is fragile and fragmented, lacking uniformity and transparency. Moreover, there are many conventional and non-conventional maritime security issues in the region, ranging from naval deployments and territorial disputes to the management of natural resources, navigational regimes and the protection of the marine environment. Such latent sources of conflicts, along with the strategic uncertainty prevailing in the region and the consequent increase of the naval presence of regional states, constitute a serious threat to maritime security in the North Pacific.

This current situation of the North Pacific definitely raises the need for maritime cooperation. In fact, more attention needs to be paid to measures aimed at strengthening the maritime regime and promoting cooperation among regional navies with a view to minimizing the risks of armed confrontation at sea. Building confidence among navies and strengthening maritime security may be one of the most urgent and needed tasks that countries in the North

Pacific should address in the post-Cold War era. In this regard, cooperative naval diplomacy, the expression of international solidarity and navy-to-navy cooperation for development, should become increasingly important options for navies in search of new roles.

The North Pacific is a region which lacks a habit of dialogue and mutual consultation on security issues among states. In this region, naval cooperation could have enormous rewards if it could be put into practice. Maritime cooperation, in which the navy plays an essential role, may encourage attitudes of collaboration having political, economic and security consequences that extend far beyond the maritime field. At present, although there is a proliferation of ideas for naval cooperation, it is a time for advancing opportunities unencumbered by an over-concentration on traditional difficulties and impediments.

Notes

1. Geographically, the North Pacific, which may be used interchangeably with the term Northeast Asia, is roughly that portion of the Pacific Ocean north of 30 degree north latitude. The region includes Canada, China, the two Koreas, Japan, Russia, Taiwan and the United States.
2. The speed and sheer mass of this region's economic growth, the rapid rise of the regional countries' economic interdependence and the concentration of those linkages in vast volumes of sea traffic, highlight the critical importance of shipping to this region.
3. Yukio Satoh, "Emerging Trends in Asia-Pacific Security: The Role of Japan", *Pacific Review* 8:2, 1995, 267-81; and Ralph A. Cossa, "Asia Pacific Confidence and Security Building Measures", in Ralph A. Cossa (ed.) *Asia Pacific Confidence and Security Building Measures* (Washington, D.C.; Center for Strategic and International Studies, 1995), 1-5.
4. *The Military Balance* 1994/95, 10.
5. *Ibid.*, 18.
6. Elizabeth Speed, *Chinese Naval Power and East Asian Security*, Institute of International Relations, University of British Columbia, Working Paper No. 11 (August 1995), 14-15.
7. See *The Military Balance* 1995/96, 177-178.
8. Capt. Russ Swinnerton, "Regional Naval Cooperation: An Australian Perspective", paper delivered at the CSCAP Working Group on Maritime Cooperation, 16-17 April 1996, Kuala Lumpur, 1.
9. The ARF's inter-sessional meeting on search and rescue (SAR) in the Asia-Pacific was held on 4-7 March 1996 in Honolulu, Hawaii. The ARF's search and rescue is aimed at promoting universality; enhancing multilateral SAR coordination

and cooperation in the Asia-Pacific within the ARF context; building mutual trust and confidence, and promoting transparency among the civilian and military agencies of the ARF participants engaged in SAR; and enhancing coordination and cooperation in the Asia-Pacific under existing operating procedures.

10. According to the UN Register of Conventional Arms, warships refer to a vessel or submarine with a standing displacement of 850 metric tonnes or above, armed or equipped for military use.

11. Agreement between the Government of the Republic of Korea and the Government of the Russian Federation Concerning the Prevention of Incidents at Sea beyond the Territorial Sea.

12. In proclaiming the Law on the Territorial Sea and the Contiguous Zone in February 1992, China employs the system of straight baseline. It was not until May 1996 when the location of baseline was made public. However, the Chinese baseline system in the South China Sea has not been made public yet, thus creating ambiguity about the exact extent of the Chinese territorial sea.

13. The text of the statement is found in *Ocean Policy News* (September/October 1989).

7 Strategic Issues Confronting Southeast Asia and the Future of Naval Power in the Region

BILVEER SINGH

While it is true that in post-colonial Southeast Asia, the army has tended to dominate the other services, a fundamental change seems to have taken place in the last few years, with more attention and resources being expended on the development of both the air force and navy.[1] In many ways, this is due to the shift in military mission from one based on counter-insurgency to one which is more focused on conventional warfare. The latter has required the development of a more "balanced force structure" and in the light of the emergence of concerns which are maritime in nature, in part, brought about by the coming into force of the United Nations Conference on the Law of the Sea, the naval component has been increasingly important. A better understanding of this can only be gleaned by examining the various elements of global and regional change that have come to affect the general military and strategic outlook in the region as a whole.[2]

Elements of Global Change

The world which the Southeast Asian countries are confronting today is a vastly different one than 20 to 50 years ago. In fact, the changes in the last one decade alone have been nothing short of revolutionary. The end of the Cold War has meant that the ideological conflict which dominated the world for the bulk of the post-Second World War era has ceased, freeing the countries of the region from various global pressures. While some have argued that the "clash of ideologies" has been replaced by the "clash of civilizations", what is even more poignant is the fact that economic issues have come to the forefront of the global agenda with ideology hardly a major factor any longer.

132

Related to the end of the Cold War has been the collapse and breakup of the former USSR. In its place has emerged 15 new republics with Russia accepted as the continuour state. Not only did Russia lose its "internal empire", the implosion of the USSR also saw the end of Soviet control over Eastern Europe. This provided the major impetus for the reunification of Germany. The dissolution of the USSR and end of Soviet control of eastern Europe also led to the dissolution of the Warsaw Pact. At the same time, Europe saw the "outbreak" of democratization taking place almost on a universal scale with capitalist and market-oriented economies replacing the former centrally-planned economic systems.

The most important consequence of the end of the Cold War has been the dramatic decline in international tension and the diminution of the threat of global nuclear war. Greater stability between the major powers has been achieved with the superpowers scaling down their overseas deployments and commitments. In general, what the end of the Cold War brought was "peace dividends" internationally as far as the superpowers were concerned. However, this did not mean that Europe, the principal theatre of Cold War conflict, entered into a "new peace era" as the region was increasingly torn apart by internal instability brought about by the rise of ethno-nationalism. The ethnic problems in the former Yugoslavia and parts of the former USSR testify to this new challenge.

This global transformation contains a number of elements for relations between states. The dramatically reduced possibility of great power conflict has already been noted. The prospects for arms reductions are also at their brightest ever for the last fifty years. Nevertheless, the uncertainty about the future of Russia and the former Soviet republics, has led to a latent fear that a "Versailles Syndrome" may develop, especially if Russia feels that it is being humiliated by the West. With both the United States and Russia, looking increasingly inwards, and suffering from emotional and psychological isolationism, security problems, resulting mainly from the regional power imbalances, are emerging on a worldwide basis. Ideological conflict has largely been supplanted by problems associated with nationalism and ethnicity. This has the potential to create insecurities worldwide as the existing security mechanisms, including the United Nations, are not adept in handling problems which are largely internal in nature. Finally, there has been a greater assertiveness on the part of the various regional powers and this has affected the security situation, especially in those regions where the regional powers have adopted a more military-first posture.

Figure 7.1 Southeast Asia

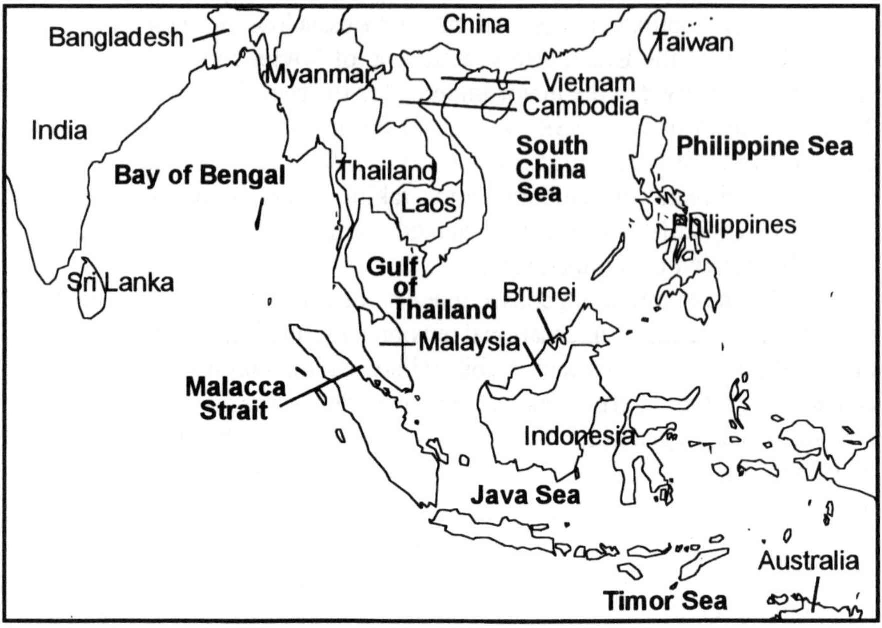

Fallouts for Southeast Asian Regional Security

Despite this extensive list of uncertainties and prospective problems in the new security environment, there have also been a number of positive developments in the region for relations between Southeast Asian states.

- The general warming of great power relations have greatly improved the security climate in Southeast Asia, blunting past rivalries which were largely associated with the Cold War.
- This has directly led to a warming of relations among past antagonists in the region, e.g. China and Vietnam, Thailand and Vietnam and Thailand and Laos.
- It created the environment for the settlement, though not the resolution, of the Cambodian problem, which had threatened regional security since 1979.
- The adoption of market-oriented reforms by all countries, especially those in Southeast Asia, has led to the diminished threat from

communism, providing better grounds for the improvement of relations between countries in insular and continental Southeast Asia.

- Vietnam and Laos accession to the ASEAN's Treaty of Amity and Cooperation in July 1992, followed by Cambodia and Myanmar's accession in July 1995, when Vietnam also joined ASEAN as its seventh member, provides the best opportunity ever for the rise of Southeast Asian regionalism, a dream which statesmen in the region have been aspiring since 1945.

Despite these developments, there remain a number of worrisome regional problems, some created by the global transformation in inter-state relations and others exacerbated by it.

- The rise of global economic rivalries have impacted negatively on ASEAN through reduced foreign investments and greater protectionism of Western markets.
- Tensions in American-Japanese relations, especially over commercial ties, have soured the overall climate.
- Global political warming has led the Superpowers to reduce their regional presence and this has created, in reality or in appearance, the notion that a power vacuum has been created in Southeast Asia, despite the presence of ASEAN, the Five Power Defence Arrangements (FPDA), and bilateral security pacts.
- The end of the Cold War/developing power vacuum has sharpened rivalries among the Asian great powers to be pre-eminent in the region, especially between China, Japan and India.
- It has also forced Southeast Asian countries to adopt greater "self-help" security policies with the negative consequence of the greater devotion of economic resources to arms purchases. Some analysts believe that an arms race has already broken out, or is about to break out in the region.
- The withering away of the "cork in the bottle" function of the dominant presence of the Superpowers in Southeast Asia has led to the rise of traditional conflicts, especially over territory, through the "decompression effect". The most serious conflict in the region is related to the many boundary disputes in the South China Sea.
- Finally, the global "democratic wave" is increasingly shaking the social and political fabric of many Southeast Asian societies which

generally have been accustomed to the "authoritarian developmental political system".

In the light of these developments, a number of features can be noted as far as the strategic environment and issues in the region are concerned. First, one can be cautiously optimistic about the future of Cambodia despite the "internal dimension" of the conflict remaining unresolved, especially as far as the future of the Khmer Rouge is concerned. There is also increasing hope that through ASEAN's policy of "constructive engagement" changes are taking place for the better in Myanmar. However, there will be a growing concern over bilateral territorial issues, both on land and at sea. The multilateral conflict involving the multiple and overlapping claims in the South China Sea will consume much of the region's attention. Those developments will have great implications for the world at large as any military conflict there would have serious implications for international maritime navigation. Both these developments emphasise the need to be careful about the arms purchases so that a "race" is pre-empted.

There is the potential for greater sectarian and ethnic politics in the region with conflicts among majority-minority groups becoming more intense in general, Islam becoming more assertive in "Small ASEAN" (Singapore, Malaysia, Indonesia and Brunei) and the overseas Chinese being increasingly targeted for discrimination. Layered on top of all these "hard" strategic issues, there is growing concern with internal political change, especially succession politics and development and distribution politics. Finally, there is concern with soft security matters, a post-Cold War by-product, with conflicts arising from environmental, labour, resource and values-related issues.

In view of these factors, governments in the region have responded to the need for security enhancement measures. In general, there is consensus that there is a need for the continued military presence of the United States and everything should be done to ensure that this is maintained. Countries in the region are also undertaking various measures to optimise and rejuvenate existing security arrangements, both within ASEAN, through bilateral exercises and other confidence-building measures, with third parties, including India, Great Britain, Australia and New Zealand. Finally, countries in the region are also supportive of various creative confidence-building measures at the bilateral and multilateral levels, particularly in the security arena, with ASEAN on the one hand and the ASEAN Regional Forum on the other having the brightest future and most important role.

Naval Power in Southeast Asia

The Southeast Asian region, essentially a maritime expanse, with only Laos as a landlocked state, has since time immemorial recognised the importance of the sea for both economic and security reasons. It is the medium through which the bulk of trade and communications are conducted and from where important food supplies and mineral resources are derived. At the same time, due to the region's unique location, on the crossroads of international maritime communications, it has also felt the impact of the major maritime civilizations, with the Indians, the Arabs, the Chinese and in the last 500 years, the Western powers, having dominated the region. Considering this past history, greater attention is being paid to maritime security and naval requirements by regional states, especially given the steep increase in the volume of trade passing through the area, the implications of the Law of the Sea Convention on boundaries and resources, and the growing overall economic interdependence between the region and the rest of the world.

While the role of navies in the region has always been important, since independence was obtained in most Southeast Asian states, naval requirements were subordinated to other military services, particularly the army. Even today, the army forms the primary component of the armed forces in the region. This was partly historical, as the dominant security concerns were land-based threats, either from across the border or within. For instance, almost all countries in the region were afflicted with subversive communist movements after the Second World War and counter-insurgency became the region's primary strategic priority. Even though naval power was acquired, it was mainly to assist in counter-insurgency operations. This inward orientation meant that the air and naval branches of the armed forces were largely subordinated to the army and the concept of a balanced force structure largely absent. This was true across the region, except possibly for Singapore, which did not face a similar insurgency problem and thus could devote its resources and energy to the development of a capability which was more conventional in nature. Generally, this meant that even if naval assets were being increased, it was accomplished in a very incremental fashion: navies played the role of "Cinderella" to the powerful regional armies. In compensation for their weak naval power, most Southeast Asian countries sought close bilateral links with external naval powers, especially the United States and Great Britain, a situation which lasted throughout the Cold War period.

Geopolitical Determinants

While recent interest within the region with naval power stems largely with concerns and developments linked to the post-Cold War era, certain enduring elements of the Cold War period continue to influence naval doctrine and procurements, however. The following points are worth noting:

Geographical Determinism. It is the geographical features and setting of the region which determines the importance of the naval dimension of warfare in Southeast Asia. Located at the crossroads of east-west communications, the region is the bridge between the Indian and Pacific Oceans as well as home to some of the most important sea routes in the world. Naturally there has been a realization that the protection of the maritime region with all the attendant assets is an important aspect of national security.

The Decline of Offshore Revolutionary Threats. The withering of land-based threats, especially following the transformation of Vietnam from a "Cold War adversary" to a post-Cold War partner has meant that the region could develop a force structure that catered to all aspects of national security rather than a unidimensional strategy focused on the land alone. This, too, increased the attention paid to the naval dimension.

Containment of Internal Insurgencies. Related to the removal of the "land-based threat" was the defeat and successful containment of most insurgencies in the region, especially those associated with communism—presently, only the Philippines remains troubled by this. As such, resources were freed for regional states to develop balanced force structures which were more oriented towards conventional warfare.

The Effect of UNCLOS III. The enaction of the Law of the Sea Convention was also an important factor for the growing concern with the naval dimension of warfare. This was primarily due to the fact that almost all countries benefitted through the expansion of their maritime frontiers with 12 miles of territorial waters and 200 miles of extended economic zones. As many countries acquired new boundaries, this meant that they had to protect newly acquired lucrative oil, gas and fishery resources as well as the new territories themselves. At the same time, a number of countries were brought into conflict by territorial disputes arising from the emergence of overlapping boundaries. All these factors led to greater attention being focused on the naval aspects of warfare.

The Role of the Great Powers. The post-Cold War also saw the rise of greater insecurity in the region, with the next major wars expected to be on the "seas" rather than on "land", and between states rather than within them. Here, in addition to the surfacing of bilateral territorial disputes among states in the region, such as between Singapore and Malaysia over Pedra Branca and between Malaysia and Indonesia over the islands of Sipidan and Ligitan, there has also been growing concern with the policies of the great powers.

During the Cold War period, the naval presence of the Superpowers, especially the US Seventh Fleet and Soviet Pacific Fleet, provided some semblance of predictability and stability in the region. With the Cold War over, both Washington and Moscow downsized their military presence in the region due to both the disappearance of their adversarial relationship as well as exigencies of domestic politics which paid increasing attention to the strengthening of national economies. Under these circumstances, the downsizing of the Superpowers provided the opportunities for the Asian powers, especially China, Japan and India to become more pro-active in the region, partly motivated by the object of filling a perceived power vacuum. Here, the policies and actions of China have been perturbing, forcing states to both engage China, as well as to build up their defences to "balance" China's military capability. China's aggressiveness with regard to the South China Sea issue, where she has indicated her willingness to use force, and where Vietnam, Malaysia, Brunei and the Philippines, all members of ASEAN, are also parties to the dispute, account, in part, for the greater attention being paid to the maritime dimension of security.

The Modernization of Fleets. (See Annex A) The drive for expansion and modernization of naval assets is also influenced by a set of inter-related factors. First, fleet modernization is long-overdue because of obsolescence or neglect, and the countires in the region can now afford to undertake such a modernization financially. Second, the region lacks structures for conflict resolution. Finally, although no identifiable threat presently exists, countries in the region are bracing themselves for conflict at sea and hence the greater focus on the maritime dimension.

The Future of Naval Cooperation and Maritime Conflicts in the Region

Future Assessment

The future of naval power in Southeast Asia will be largely determined by the nature of "demand" for such a capability. In the last 50 years or so, the role and importance of the navies in the region has been somewhat downplayed due to the nature of security concerns in the region which placed greater emphasis on the need for a lop-sided army with only a skeletal air force and navy. To what extent a balanced-force structure will emerge, with a proportionate role for the navy, expressed in terms of assets acquisitions and operational doctrine, remains to be seen. To a large extent, this will be determined by the nature of conflicts and challenges facing the countries in the region, in turn, influencing the resource allocation therein.

In many ways, the new power constellation will play a major role in this regard. At the global level, to what extent will the drawdown of the major maritime powers continue and what this would mean for the security of the region, will be the most important determinant. With Russia still embroiled in internal problems and the US pursuing comprehensive engagement through a concept of "places, not bases", how the reduced visibility of the American naval power in the region will affect the security environment, especially maritime security, will be an important factor to consider in this regard.

At the same time, how the major Asian naval powers, especially China, Japan and India behave in the region remains to be seen. The key question here is whether a power fault line will emerge with the assertive Asian powers attempting to become the new hegemons and how this will affect Southeast Asia's security. In particular, the role of China takes on a critical importance. The key question among security and policy makers will be: is China a status quo or revolutionary power; will it be a foe or friend?

In Southeast Asia, China is critical for the following reasons:

- historically, it has longstanding relations with the region with many Chinese leaders viewing Southeast Asia as a "Chinese backyard", in the same way, American leaders have viewed South America through the "Monroe Doctrine".
- geographically, Southeast Asia is directly contiguous to China with Vietnam and Myanmar sharing land borders with her while Vietnam,

Malaysia, Brunei, Indonesia and the Philippines have common maritime boundaries.

* demographically, more than 20 million "overseas Chinese" live there and critical for the economic success of countries in the region.
* economically, Southeast Asia is also closely intertwined with China, where in addition to the "overseas Chinese" link, there has been a major rise in state-to-state relations, especially following China's decision to undertake its "Four Modernizations".
* strategically, China considers Southeast Asia to be a region of vital importance and it will do all it can to ensure that threats from that part of the world are reduced, making it vastly important for Beijing to be engaged.

China is expected to become a major economic, political and military power in the coming years. The existence of many unsettled security issues with Southeast Asian countries makes China a critical player as far as the region is concerned. Here, maritime concerns will loom large, in turn, affecting the directions of naval acquisitions.

Naval Force Structures

In general, what the regional navies have been undertaking is a policy of catch-up. In many ways, a number of features are worth noting. First, with regard to surface ships, the ASEAN region as a whole has been keeping abreast with the latest technologies. Thus, the region has seen the purchase of corvettes and frigates with state of the art missile systems. These ships are, however, not equipped with the latest electronic warfare systems. However, even though the purchases are not uniform in character, with vast differentiation in quality and quantity, injection of new naval vessels and technologies have taken place with a new sense of mission present.

Notwithstanding this, the region continues to suffer various shortcomings in a number of areas. First, Southeast Asian navies lack afloat support systems, such as support vessels, logistic ships and landing ships. In modern conventional warfare, the existence of a good logistics support system is critical for naval operations. Second, the sub-sea dimension is extremely weak to almost non-existent. Within the ASEAN region there are only four fully functioning submarines with Singapore just about to acquire a second-hand training submarine. Compared to countries located directly adjacent to Southeast Asia, such as China, Japan, India and further south,

Australia, Southeast Asia is extremely weak in this dimension of naval assets. This is a necessary tool for the navies, especially for countries which are essentially maritime in nature. The submarine is an extremely versatile asset as it has a big multiplier effect, being able to tie down a large component of an opponent's fleet, thereby enhancing its offensive character. The near-absence of this dimension is all the more stark as it takes between six to eight years to train a good submariner for operations, making the deficiency in the region all the more critical.

In addition to logistics support and sub-sea deficiencies, countries in the region also need to think about two other aspects of naval power, namely, the need for naval aviation and rapid reaction troops, such as marines, to deter any aggressor from the sea. A number of countries have already begun developing this aspect of naval power. At the same time, as the maritime area of operations has expanded vastly, through the rapid expansion of the EEZ, there has been a serious need to undertake surveillance and enforcement, forcing countries to develop both the sea-borne and air-borne components to protect their new territories. Presently, the "best low end" solution has been use of corvettes and off-shore patrol vessels to handle sea-borne surveillance duties. At the same time, there has been an interest in acquiring air-capable ships for their potential capabilities in anti-submarine and amphibious operations as well as maritime policing and humanitarian assistance tasks.

Prospects for Naval Cooperation

Under these circumstances, the future of naval cooperation as well as acquisitions of naval assets will be largely determined by the various national assessments of the potential for regional stability or instability, on the one hand, and the possibility of peace or war, on the other. Whether various navies will have to confront crises in the region will also loom large. For instance, Vietnam must consider whether the Chinese will use force to dislodge its troops from islands in the Spratly group and the Philippines will have to consider whether another "Mischief Reef" incident will be provoked by China. China's recent sabre-rattling over Taiwan must have also been registered strongly in the region. For countries which are faced with maritime territorial disputes, be they bilateral, as those between Singapore and Malaysia, Malaysia and Indonesia, Malaysia and Brunei, Malaysia and the Philippines and Malaysia and Thailand, or multilateral in nature, as in the South China Sea, involving Vietnam, Malaysia, Brunei and the Philippines, the need to boost their national maritime capability will continue unabated. This will also affect the force structure and doctrine. Additionally, there will also be the need to enhance confidence-building measures among the disputants and this is likely to see greater naval cooperation taking place. Already, the ASEAN states have an excellent track record of naval cooperation even though most of this is undertaken on a bilateral basis. The expansion of this is viewed as a valuable in trust-building, thereby reducing the possibility of misunderstandings between the various navies, especially during manoeuvres.

Conclusion

What the above indicates is that Southeast Asian naval power is being given a boost, something it has not experienced for a long time. The object of the fleet modernization in the region is essentially to acquire a balanced capability by exploiting the air, surface and sub-surface dimensions. To a large extent, this modernization is technologically driven by balance of power considerations as well as security concerns with regard to the EEZ. In the present circumstances, the quantity aspect is not that critical. The idea being, it can be small as long as it is effective and potent. Despite this, there appears to be a lack of the air and sub-surface element and this will remain for sometime to come.

Annex A: Southeast Asia's New Maritime Assets

Southeast Asia's interest in the naval dimension of warfare can be best gleaned from the following purchases, already acquired or on order:

Malaysia[3]
- 2 F-200 2270-ton missile frigates armed with MM 40 Exocet anti-ship missiles.
- 2 guided missile corvettes armed with vertical Sea Wolf air defence missiles.
- keen interest in the purchase of 12 New Generation Patrol Vessels (NGPVs) and possibly some Off-Shore Combatants.
- 4 Assad Corvettes.
- 1 training submarine with another 3 in the next development plan.
- 1 oceanographic survey vessel.
- an unspecified number of maritime surveillance aircraft of the IPTN-235 model.
- 1 logistic vessel.

Indonesia[4]
- 5 frigates
- 16 Parchim 1 type (*Pattimura*-class) corvettes
- 12 Frosch 1 Project 103 landing ships
- 9 Kondor 11 Project 89 minesweepers
- 2 HDW/IKL Type 209/1300 Cakra submarines with another 5 Type 206 class being considered.
- 1 hydrographic survey ship (Baruna Jaya IV)
- major upgrading of the German-made frigates and corvettes with Western avionics and radar systems.
- a sizeable number of maritime surveillance aircraft of the IPTN-235 type.

Singapore[5]
- 1 training Sjoormen submarine with another 3 under consideration.
- 4 360-ton Mine Counter-Measure Vessels
- 6 56 metre gun-armed patrol craft
- 12 *Fearless*-class anti-submarine patrol vessels of which 6 are already operational.
- 5 Fokker-50 Maritime Enforcer MK25 Maritime Patrol Aircraft.
- 4 140m landing ship tanks.

Thailand[6]
- 18 A-7 naval fighters
- 10 Harrier jump jets
- 1 11,400 ton Bazan light aircraft carrier with another under consideration.
- 2 *Knox*-class frigates
- 1 *Naresuan*-class frigates
- 4 Chinese-made frigates.
- 4 submarines under consideration

Philippines[7]
- 3 Corvettes with another 6 under consideration.
- a number of 45m patrol crafts.

Brunei[8]
- 3 95m 1,500-ton OPVs
- 3 Yarrow Corvettes

Vietnam
*   2 *Tarantul*-class Corvettes.

Notes

1. For details, see Bilveer Singh, *The Challenge of Conventional Arms Proliferation in Southeast Asia* (Jakarta: Centre for Strategic and International Studies, 1995), 26-60 and Bilveer Singh, "ASEAN's Arms Procurements: Challenges of the Security Dilemma in the Post Cold War Era", *Comparative Strategy* 12: 2, 199-223.
2. For details on this area, see Bilveer Singh, "The Challenge of the Security Environment in Southeast Asia in the Post-Cold War Era", *Australian Journal of International Affairs* 47: 2, October 1993, 263-277; D. Banerjee, "A New World Order: Trends for the Future", *Strategic Analysis* 17: 2, May 1994, 150-152 and Swaran Singh, "Post-Cold War Order and India's National Security", *Strategic Analysis* 18: 4, July 1995, 524-525.
3. Details on Malaysian naval procurements can be found in Abdul Razak Baginda, "Malaysia's Armed Forces in the 1990s", *International Defence Review* 4, 1992, 305; Abdul Razak Baginda, "Arms and Defence Planning in Southeast Asia: A Malaysian Perspective", paper presented at the Arms and Defence Planning Workshop, Institute of Southeast Asian Studies, Singapore, 5-7 December 1991, 13-14; Major (R) R. Sachi, "Malaysia's Future Naval Requirements", *Asian Defence Journal* 12, 1990, 76; Anthony Preston, "Naval Review", *Asian Military Review* 3: 1, February-March 1995, 42; Anthony Preston, "The Royal Malaysian Navy", *Asian Military Review* 3: 5, October-November 1995, 13-22; and J.N. Mak, "The ASEAN Naval Build-Up: Implications for the Regional Order", *The Pacific Review* 8: 2, 1995, 303-325.
4. Anthony Preston, "The Submarine Threat to Asian Navies", *Asian Defence Journal* 10, 1995, 20; Anthony Preston, "EEZ Protection and Surveillance", *Asian Military Review* 2:3, June 1994, 15-16; Anthony Preston, "Naval Review", *Asian Military Review* 3:1, February-March 1995, 42.
5. See Anthony Preston, "The Submarine Threat to Asian Navies", *Asian Defence Journal* 10, 1995, 22; "The Republic of Singapore Navy: Naval Defence for the Island Nation", *Asian Military Review* 2:6, December-January 1994-1995, 4-9.
6. "The Royal Thai Navy", *Asian Military Review* 3:5, October-November 1995, 4-10; "Thailand's Navy Sails Into a New Era of Security", *The Nation* 15 February 1993; "Bazan Wins Thai Carrier Deal", *Military Technology* 4, 1992, 92.
7. J.N. Mak, "The ASEAN Naval Build-Up: Implications for the Regional Order", *The Pacific Review* 8:2, 1995, 303-325; and J.N. Mak and B.A. Hamzah, "The

External Maritime Dimension of ASEAN Security", *The Journal of Strategic Studies* 18:3, September 1995, 123-145.

8. "Brunei Picks Yarrow for Offshore Patrol Vessels", *Jane's Defence Weekly* 9 December 1995, 5.

8 Multinational Naval Cooperation in the Indian Ocean

RAHUL ROY-CHAUDHURY

The Indian Ocean is the third largest of the four major oceans in the world, after the Pacific and Atlantic Oceans. It covers an area of 74 million square kilometres, comprising some 20 per cent of the total area of water in the world, and includes, amongst others, the Red Sea, the Persian Gulf, the Arabian Sea, the Bay of Bengal, and the Andaman Sea.[1] Although its waters border four major land bodies of the world—Africa, Asia, Australia and Antarctica—it is considered to constitute a distinct region.[2] It is also the only ocean to be named after a major state whose shores it reaches.

A special feature of the ocean is that it is virtually surrounded by land on three sides; in the west by the eastern and southern parts of Africa and the south-western part of Asia; in the north by Southern Asia; and in the east by South-eastern Asia and Western Australia. It is only the southern part of the ocean which easily links up with both the Atlantic and the Pacific Oceans. In view of the vast distances of these sea routes for the countries of Asia and Africa, the importance of alternative sea lines of communication increase considerably.

Such sea routes not only enable the supply of crucial energy resources and the transportation of trade within the Indian Ocean, but provide for shorter, and more economical, routes for shipping between the Atlantic and Pacific Oceans. The more important of these in the western part of the Indian Ocean include the Straits of Hormuz, which link the Persian Gulf to the Gulf of Oman, the Suez Canal, which connects the Red Sea to the Mediterranean Sea and onwards to the Atlantic Ocean. In the east, the Indian Ocean is linked to the Gulf of Thailand and the South China Sea via the Straits of Malacca and Singapore, the Java Sea via the Sunda Straits, the Flores Sea via the Straits of Lombok, the Savu and Banda Seas via the Straits of Ombai-Wetar and onwards to the Pacific Ocean.

Multinational naval cooperation is strongly influenced by geopolitical, economic and cultural factors. In this chapter the prospects and challenges of naval cooperation in the Indian Ocean are examined in the context of political and geographic features, security challenges, naval trends and the evolving structure of international cooperation in the region.

Figure 8.1 The Indian Ocean

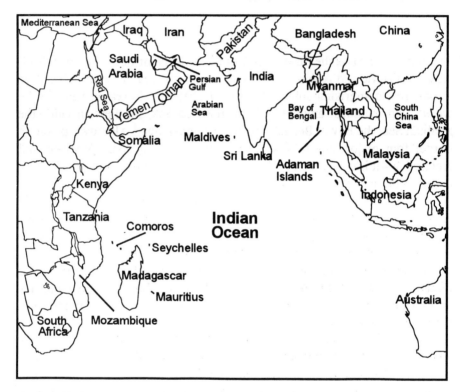

Major Features of the Indian Ocean Rim

The first challenge in thinking about the Indian Ocean region is its geographic diversity, while its geopolitical significance lies in energy and the strategic importance of its shipping lanes.

Political and Geographic Features

There continues to be considerable confusion as to the number of states which could actually be considered part of the Indian Ocean. This is due primarily to the geographical complexities of the eastern boundaries of the ocean, which preclude any formal legal delimitation of the area, as well as political differences amongst states. It is not clear, for example, where the Indian Ocean stops and the Pacific Ocean begins. Does the Indian Ocean include the Gulf of Thailand, the South China Sea and the Java Sea, amongst others, which would make even countries like Cambodia, Vietnam, the Philippines, Brunei and China rim states of the ocean? Or does it simply cease at the Strait of Malacca itself, in which case even Singapore would not qualify as an Indian Ocean rim state? While the former definition appears unrealistic, the latter is too restrictive. In this respect, whereas Singapore can be considered a rim state of the Indian Ocean, other countries like China and Cambodia can not.

Even within such a geographical framework, there are major political differences in defining the "rim", "region", or "community" of states of the Indian Ocean. The number of "rim" (including island) states considered to be part of the Indian Ocean vary from a low of 28 to a high of 39. The former appears to restrict itself to most of the littoral states alone, excluding the island states. The latter, meanwhile, includes major French possessions in the area, as well as the island of Diego Garcia, which is claimed by Mauritius, possessed by Britain, and leased to the United States as a military and communications facility. Moreover, none of these French possessions, nor Diego Garcia, are states. In effect, therefore, it would not be amiss to define the Indian Ocean "rim" as constituting 35 states, comprising all the 29 littoral states and six island states of the Indian Ocean.[3]

In a similar manner, the states comprising the Indian Ocean "region" vary from a minimum of 35 (all the rim states) to an intermediate figure of 47 (including 12 landlocked countries dependent on the ocean), and a maximum of 52 states (by further including the five Central Asian Republics). Meanwhile, the Indian Ocean "community" could be stated to comprise as many as 60 states, including those not dependent on the ocean, and even located some distance from it. At the first international conference on "The Making of an Indian Ocean Community", held in New Delhi in November 1995, for example, representatives from countries such as China, Japan, Russia and Britain, took part. At another conference on "The Indian Ocean Community" held in Tehran a year later, representatives from the Caspian and Caucasian regions participated, along with those from Brunei-Darussalam and Japan.[4]

A common feature of virtually all these countries is that, at one time or another, they were colonised by major European powers, especially the British, French, Dutch and the Portuguese. While a few of these countries became independent in the late 1940s and early 1950s, the majority received independence only in the 1960s and the 1970s. This indicates a relatively limited period of time as sovereign entities in the world. All of them are categorised as developing states, with the exception of Australia and Israel (industrial countries).[5] The population of the Indian Ocean rim is approximately 1.87 billion, comprising a third of global population.

Another major feature is the sheer diversity amongst the countries of the rim. This relates to their size (Australia vis-à-vis Singapore), their population (India's 950 million people vis-à-vis the 72,000 people of the Seychelles), and the nature of their political systems (the world's largest democracy vis-à-vis authoritarian and military regimes). In terms of economic development as well, considerable differences are present. This area consists of countries whose Gross Domestic Product (GDP) varies from US $294 billion in the case of India, to US $1.5 billion for Mozambique, and GNP per capita of US $19,760 for Singapore to US $74 for Mozambique.[6] This area includes a number of weak economies, as well as the fastest growing ones of Southeast Asia. The continuing pace of liberalisation and globalisation in India is also expected to make the country a powerful economic force in the world in the near future.

Security of Energy Resources and Supplies

The Persian Gulf remains the single largest source of oil, and an important source of natural gas, worldwide. In terms of oil, the eight Gulf states accounted for 18.56 million barrels per day or 28.5 per cent of total production, and 657.30 billion barrels or 65.1 per cent of total proven reserves in the world in 1993. In terms of natural gas, they collectively accounted for 4,120.40 bcf (billion cubic feet) or 5.3 per cent of total production, and 1,557.76 tcf (trillion cubic feet) or 31.1 per cent of total reserves worldwide. In terms of the rates of production, their oil reserves are expected to last for about 21 years for Qatar, 84 years for Saudi Arabia, and over a 100 years for Kuwait, Iraq and the UAE. Meanwhile, their gas reserves are expected to last for over 100 years.[7] Huge deposits of a number of other mineral resources, such as 40 per cent of gold, 90 per cent of diamond and 60 per cent of uranium deposits worldwide, are also found in the Indian Ocean rim.

The oil and gas from this area is sent to countries of the Indian, Atlantic and Pacific Oceans, dependent on them for their economic growth and prosperity. The vast majority of these supplies are shipped through the Straits of Hormuz to the Indian Ocean and beyond; accounting for over 39 per cent of global imports of crude oil.

Although the extent of dependence of countries on Gulf oil vary in North America, Europe, Asia and Africa (for example, a figure of 76 per cent for Japan, and 36 per cent for India), the nature of this dependence for a majority of countries is expected to increase in the future. This is due to their growing demand for oil and the shortfall in the rate of domestic production, along with their relatively limited reserves.[8] The ability to ensure the security of these energy supplies from port of origin to destination, therefore, will remain a critical feature of the geo-strategic environment of countries in the Indian Ocean.

The importance of ensuring a secure supply of energy resources can be seen from the huge amount of oil carried by ships in the Indian Ocean. In 1994, 14 million barrels per day of Gulf oil was sent across the Straits of Hormuz; of this, just over half passed through the Straits of Malacca and Singapore.[9] Meanwhile, the sea routes off the Cape of Good Hope account for 30 per cent of Persian Gulf oil bound for Europe and the Americas.[10]

Security of the Sea Lines of Communication (SLOC)

The geographical position of the Indian Ocean, and its strategic waterways, provide the shortest and most economical lines of communication between the Atlantic and Pacific Oceans. It is not surprising to note, according to one estimate, that the ocean accounts for the transportation of the highest tonnage of goods in the world.[11] The vast majority of this trade is extra-regional by nature, with intra-regional trade accounting for only 20 per cent of total Indian Ocean trade. This is in marked contrast to the Asia-Pacific economies around the Pacific Ocean, where intra-regional trade accounts for 66 per cent of total trade.[12] The Straits of Hormuz are, by far, the single most important waterway in the Indian Ocean, accounting for a vast proportion of energy supplies, as well as other commodities of trade. This is followed by the Strait of Malacca and the Strait of Singapore. It has been calculated, for instance, that in a one year period, May 1993-April 1994, there were over 30,000 oil tanker movements in Southeast Asian waters.[13] Meanwhile, some 840 tankers travel around the Cape of Good Hope annually.[14]

This trade, both extra-regional and intra-regional, reflects the dependence of countries of the Indian Ocean on the sea. This is true even for a country with long land borders like India, which actually resembles an island when it comes to trade; for, over 97 per cent of its trade in volume is seaborne.[15] Similarly, over 90 per cent of Kenya's and South Africa's, and around 97 per cent of Malaysia's, trade is seaborne. In effect, it is in the interests of the countries of the rim to maintain the safe and secure transportation of goods across the waters of the Indian Ocean.

Regional Security Challenges

The maritime dimension of regional security concerns in the Indian Ocean region span classic inter-state tensions, the stability of energy supplies and new, post-Cold War security challenges of the "non-traditional" variety.

Stability in the Indian Sub-continent

Considerable concern continues to be expressed over the perceived threat of a major war between India and Pakistan especially one which could well take the form of a nuclear exchange in the region. The development and acquisition of sophisticated conventional weapons, and the nuclear weapon capabilities of both countries, add to these concerns.[16]

Although India has been forced to fight three major conventional wars against Pakistan in 1947-48, 1965 and 1971, the last 25 years have witnessed the longest period of relative peace in the region. The perceived crises of the late 1980s and mid-1990 were considerably exaggerated in the international media. Admittedly, this period of armed peace has been strained by Pakistani support to militant activities, and the launch of a full-fledged low-intensity conflict (proxy war) against India since mid-1988 (including the series of bomb blasts in Bombay in March 1993). Nonetheless, this is being successfully countered internally through tightened border controls, an attempt to bring about political reforms in the province of Jammu and Kashmir, and the resumption of formal talks with Pakistan in March 1997, after a gap of three years. Although India has the capability to build nuclear weapons, it has shown considerable restraint in not doing so, despite substantial evidence that Pakistan may already have built up to 15 nuclear bombs with Chinese assistance.[17]

A situation of deterrence, therefore, can be said to exist between the two countries at present. It is in neither country's interest to resort to a full-fledged war against each other. It is also important to note that India's defence policies are directed not only to Pakistan, but to its larger and more powerful nuclear-weapon armed neighbour to the north, China, against which it fought a war in 1962. This war has had a considerable psychological impact on India's security policies over the years.

SLOCs and Oil: Stability of Energy Supplies

Although both Iraq and Iran may like to ensure the supply of their own energy resources to the world, they possess the capability to restrict the supplies to others; they are also actually in a position to do so, as they are located strategically astride the Persian Gulf. Although the 1991 Gulf War considerably dampened Iraq's interest in intervention, and destroyed a vast proportion of its military and economic infrastructure, its political leadership still retains the ability to threaten the stability of the rim.

Iran's revolutionary fervor is also perceived to be inimical to western interests in the region. The recent increase in defence spending and the expansion of its armed forces have raised alarm bells. This is especially true of its navy, which is perceived to be capable of blocking the Straits of Hormuz, thereby threatening the supply of oil worldwide. Much of these concerns are focused on Iran's acquisition of three modern *Kilo*-class conventional submarines from Russia.

These perceptions, however, appear exaggerated. While it is clear that the submarines could be of nuisance value to shipping in the area, they would not be any match for the firepower of American naval forces in the region, which have only recently been reinforced. The Iranian Navy remains limited to five principal surface combatants, in addition to the submarines. The level of maintenance and operational capability of these warships are low. Moreover, the political leadership of Iran appears to be increasingly prudent and practical in its relations with a number of countries in the Indian Ocean rim.

Proliferation of Small Arms and the Spread of Narcotics

The proliferation of small arms and the growth of drug trafficking is of increasing concern to countries of the Indian Ocean rim. Not only do these factors encourage and exacerbate the dominant form of warfare globally at present, but increase tension in the area. Indeed, the term "small arms/light weapons" is highly misleading, and often tends to give a misplaced sense of complacency to strategic analysts. Small arms are quite clearly no longer "small" in lethality, range, accuracy, or effect. In NATO terminology, for instance, these weapons embrace all crew-portable direct fire weapons of a calibre less than 50 mm, and include a secondary capability to defeat light armour and helicopters.

Such weapons comprise land mines, automatic assault rifles, rocket-propelled grenade launchers, shoulder-fired surface-to-air missiles and high explosives. In terms of the spread of land mines, for example, nearly 110 million of these weapons are deployed in more than 60 countries. Of the nine most seriously affected countries, five (Iraq, Kuwait, Mozambique, Somalia and Sudan) are located in the rim, and another one (Afghanistan) in the region of the Indian Ocean. Moreover, 500 million guns are believed to be in circulation in the world, including 55 million Kalishnakov automatic assault rifles. Some 1.5 million AK-47 rifles are stated to be unaccounted for in the Indian Ocean rim state of Mozambique alone. With such developments, it is not surprising that non-state actors in many of these countries are increasingly challenging the structure and the institutions of the state.

In view of the nature of the war fought against the Soviet Union in Afghanistan during much of the 1980s, the vast quantities of weapons supplied to the Mujahideen forces were of the small arms variety. A large proportion of these weapons, over the years, were diverted to Pakistan itself, and have been used in the Indian provinces of Punjab, Jammu and Kashmir. During the seven year period from mid-1988 to mid-1995, for example, the weapons and ammunition seized by the Indian security forces in Jammu and Kashmir included 13,894 AK series of assault rifles, 844 machine guns, 601 rocket launchers and 1,667 rockets, 4,999 pistols/revolvers, over 2 million rounds of assorted ammunition and 8,622 kgs. of explosives.[18] Some of these arms were also transported across the sea and off-loaded on the Indian coast, as was seen from the Bombay blasts of 1993.

Such a state of affairs is further exacerbated by the connection between the supply of arms and the production and trade in narcotics in the region, resulting in the lethal mix of narco-terrorism. All the three countries comprising the world's largest drug growing area, the Golden Crescent, are in the Indian Ocean region—Pakistan, Afghanistan and Iran. To make matters worse, two of the three countries of another vast drug producing area, the Golden Triangle, are also of the Indian Ocean region—Myanmar and Thailand. The cultivation and trafficking of drugs encourage the establishment of alternative powerful non-state actors, as well as covert channels of distribution, within the region. This essentially provides funds for the purchase of sophisticated small arms and light weapons, and their distribution amongst militant groups in the region, for disruptive purposes.

Security of Small Island States

The Indian Ocean is dotted with six island states of varying size, spread over hundreds of kilometres. They have limited, if any, defence against internal or external military threats, or even organised attempts to overthrow their political regimes. The Maldives, for example, consists of some 2,000 low-lying coral islands, of which only about 220 are inhabited with a total population of 214,000. Its paramilitary force consists of 1,400 personnel, equipped with light arms. It has no navy; the coast guard consists only of six patrol boats armed with guns, the largest of which is less than 40 tonnes. Four of these six island states—Sri Lanka, Maldives, Comoros and the Seychelles—have, at one time or another, faced considerable domestic disruption and the threat of coups d'etat.

The island of Sri Lanka continues to suffer from an insurgency which has affected it for the past 14 years. Moreover, the most powerful Tamil militant organisation, the Liberation Tigers of Tamil Eelam (LTTE), controls large areas of territory, has a parallel administration and wages a determined battle against the Sri Lankan armed forces. Even the deployment of an Indian Peace-Keeping Force (IPKF) in northern and eastern Sri Lanka in 1987-90 was not able to control this insurgency. At one time the Indian force consisted of over 300,000 military personnel (in view of normal rotation procedures), and over 100 armoured and 7,000 other vehicles.[19] Negotiations between the Sri Lankan government and the LTTE have not made any progress in bringing the fighting to an end.

A few years earlier, in November 1988, timely Indian military action had, however, played a crucial role in maintaining the sovereignty of the Maldive Islands. At the request of the legitimate Maldivian government, the Indian Navy had sent armed forces to the area to bring to an end the coup attempt in progress. The Indian Navy's warships were successful in locating, and then apprehending, the mercenaries who had set sail aboard a captured merchant ship.

The most vivid example of a coup attempt took place in the Comoros in September 1995, planned and led, by a well known French mercenary, Bob Denard, and his gang of thirty men. Each of them had been paid 80,000 French francs for their role in the plot. This attempt to oust President Djahor and Prime Minister El Yachroutu, was finally brought to an end with the intervention of French armed personnel, and led to the capture of the mercenaries. Just over two months later, in December 1995, another attempted coup in Comoros was suspected. The personnel involved were believed to have been paid over a million Comoros Francs each, as well as provided 150 litres of motor fuel.[20]

Maritime Security and the Law of the Sea

The new legal regime of the sea, formalised in November 1994, legitimised the claim of a number of countries of the Indian Ocean to an extended maritime zone. This includes an Exclusive Economic Zone of 200 nautical miles (nm.) for the mainland and island territories, as well as a legal continental shelf of 200-350 nm. As a result, about 30 per cent of the Indian Ocean is presently under the EEZ of coastal states.[21] The EEZ of these countries could increase further to 300 nm. by the year 2004, if the preliminary exploration of the extended zone is completed by then.[22] The prospect of these changes in the international law of the sea set in motion attempts in the 1970s and 1980s to delimit maritime boundaries amongst littoral and island states. In view of the relatively limited distances amongst states, and conflicting claims on territory, it is not surprising that a number of maritime disputes are prevalent in the Indian Ocean.

None of the eight Persian Gulf states, for example, have completely delimited their maritime boundaries. More than 15 bilateral maritime boundaries, and at least five tri-junction points, are yet to be negotiated. An authoritative assessment took note of thirteen maritime disputes/problems amongst these states.[23] Meanwhile, India has not delimited its maritime boundaries with either Pakistan or Bangladesh. Two segments of Australia's boundaries with Indonesia, as well as with New Zealand, have yet to be determined. With the growing importance of marine resources to a country's economy, claims for potentially rich areas of the seabed could well lead to heightened tension amongst countries.

In addition, traditional claims of conflicting sovereignty prevail, especially over French island possessions in the south-western part of the Indian Ocean. Whereas the French territory of Mayotte is claimed by Comoros, Tromelin is claimed by three island states—Madagascar, Mauritius and Seychelles. Also, sovereignty over the British Indian Ocean Territory (BIOT), including Diego Garcia, is claimed by Mauritius. Other disputes of a maritime nature concerning the south-western Indian Ocean include the demarcation of maritime boundaries, the exploitation of mineral resources and overfishing.

Naval Trends in the Indian Ocean

In this part the impact of naval seapower exercised by states from outside the area is assessed together with the modernization of the naval forces of states along the Indian Ocean littoral.

Extra-Regional Naval Forces

The demise of the Cold War and the disintegration of the Soviet Union ended an important aspect of American naval presence in the Indian Ocean, that of rivalry with the erstwhile Soviet Navy (since the late 1960s). Nonetheless, the United States as a global power continues to maintain other equally important interests there, especially the reliability of oil supplies and trade through the Persian Gulf and the Indian Ocean, as well as the security of friendly states. The importance of these interests were clearly brought out during the Gulf Crisis in 1990, and the subsequent "Operation Desert Storm" in early 1991. In view of the absence of superpower naval rivalry, the United Nations resolution of the Indian Ocean as a Zone of Peace (IOZOP) has been rendered obsolete.[24]

The establishment in 1995, for the first time, of a permanently deployed independent fleet in the western Indian Ocean, indicates increased American commitment, and represents a crucial aspect of American interest. American military presence in the Indian Ocean has also increased considerably; with the new Fifth Fleet in the Persian Gulf, warships of the Seventh Fleet deployed in the central and eastern Indian Ocean, additional rotationally deployed forces and logistics support facilities in the Persian Gulf and at Diego Garcia.

American naval doctrine in the post-Cold War world has also undergone a dramatic transformation. From its focus on open-ocean war fighting, it has increasingly shifted to one of power projection and the employment of naval forces to influence events in the littoral regions of the world. This strategic concept has been further expanded to encompass the employment of naval expeditionary forces and joint operation missions. In essence, therefore, the creation of the Fifth Fleet represents this fundamental aspect of American naval policy. This is especially true in relation to the two countries in the region with which the United States has difficult relations at the best of times, Iraq and Iran.

The only other major power which maintains a standing naval force in the Indian Ocean is France. The French Indian Ocean squadron, deployed in the south-western zone of the ocean, comprises about eleven surface warships, including four principal combatants, and aircraft.[25] French interests in the area include island territories; links with neighbouring island and littoral countries; and defence arrangements with some of the states in the area.[26]

The Chinese Navy in the Indian Ocean

While China's assertive policies towards the South China Sea, and more recently, Taiwan, have gained international publicity, its increased interest in the seas around India have not been adequately noted. Since the middle of 1992, reports have persistently indicated Chinese assistance in the construction of naval and electronic facilities in Myanmar. These essentially relate to the modernisation of the naval base on Hianggyi island at the mouth of the Bassein river, the construction of a Signals Intelligence (SIGINT) facility on Great Coco island, and the development of existing naval infrastructure at Akyab and Mergui.

Although preliminary assessments indicate that the Hianggyi base, when fully built, will be too small to host Chinese surface warships of the size required for effective operations in the Indian Ocean, it may be too early to reach such a conclusion. Moreover, it could be used to support Chinese submarine operations in the area.

Chinese activities on the strategically located Coco island, at a distance of only 30 nm. from the Indian Andaman chain of islands, is of particular concern to India. In 1993, some 70 Chinese naval and technical personnel were believed to have arrived on the island to install new radar equipment. This could enable Chinese military personnel to monitor Indian naval communications in the area, and possibly even India's ballistic missile tests off its eastern coast. In the past five years, China has also provided Myanmar with over $1.6 billion worth of arms.[27] Chinese interests in the region include important defence ties with Pakistan, Bangladesh and Myanmar, as well as shipping in the Indian Ocean.

Littoral Naval Forces

Amongst the navies of the 35 littoral and island states of the Indian Ocean, only fourteen possess principal surface or sub-surface combatants. The majority of the navies consist of minor war vessels, especially patrol and amphibious craft, with a few corvettes; only some of these are armed with anti-ship missiles. Five of the major Indian Ocean navies are located in the Persian Gulf/Red Sea region; three in Southern Asia; and five in South-east Asia/Australia. None of the navies of eastern or southern Africa, with the exception of South Africa, possess principal combatants. Amongst the fourteen major littoral navies of the rim, the Indian Navy continues to remain the largest, followed by those of Pakistan, Australia, Indonesia, Thailand, Egypt, Iran, Saudi Arabia, Bangladesh, Malaysia, Israel, South Africa, Singapore and Iraq (Table 8.1).

Evolving Force Structures of Littoral Navies

During the five-year period 1991-96, the Indian Navy suffered considerable budgetary constraints and problems over the supply of spare parts; the former due to its new economic policies, and the latter due to the disintegration of its primary supplier of weapon systems, the erstwhile Soviet Union. Although the Navy's financial situation is expected to improve in the near future, it will, nevertheless, face an alarming reduction in force levels; accounting for almost a third of its principal combatants till the year 2000.[28] Such a sorry state of affairs is due largely to a lack of decision-making by the government, as well as bureaucratic delays. This will have a grave effect especially on the aircraft carrier component, and the submarine force of the Navy.

Meanwhile, the Pakistani Navy continues to improve its combat capability, with a US $1 billion order for three advanced technology submarines from France (September 1994), and the provision of a much delayed naval arms package from the United States, including the supply of three P-3C Orion maritime strike aircraft. The supply of three conventional Agosta 90-B French submarines equipped with the MESMA Air Independent Propulsion (AIP) system and Exocet SM-39 anti-ship missiles, will also decrease the Indian Navy's edge over the Pakistani Navy in warfare.[29] In terms of the United Nations Register of Conventional Arms, Pakistan was the second largest recipient of warships in the Indian Ocean, and the fifth largest in the world, during the 1992-95 period. Six of the seven warships procured were Type-21 frigates from Britain, subsequently armed with Harpoon anti- ship missiles. In contrast, the Indian Navy did not acquire a single warship from any foreign source in the 1992-95 period.[30]

Table 8.1 Major Littoral Navies of the Indian Ocean (in terms of principal combatants)

Country	Aircraft Carriers	Patrol Sub-marines	Destroyers	Frigates	Rotary Aircraft	Fixed-Wing Aircraft	Manpower
India	1	16 + (2)	5+(3)	14+(3)	Yes	Yes	54,000
Pakistan	0	6+(3)	3	8	Yes	Yes	22,800
Australia	0	4+(5)	3	9+(7)	Yes	Yes	13,700
Indonesia	0	2 + (2)	0	17	Yes	Yes	30,000
Thailand	0+(1)	0	0	14	Yes	Yes	43,000
Egypt	0	3+(2)	1	4	Yes	Yes	20,000
Iran	0	3	2	3	Yes	Yes	18,000
Saudi Arabia	0	0	0	4+(2)	Yes	No	12,000
Bangladesh	0	0	0	4+(1)	No	No	8,050
Malaysia	0	0	0	3+(1)	Yes	Yes	12,000
Israel	0	3	0	0	No	Yes	6,000
South Africa	0	3	0	0	Yes	Yes	5,000
Singapore	0	1 + (2)	0	0	No	Yes	4,000
Iraq	0	0	0	1	No	No	2,000

Notes: Figures in bracket indicate warships being acquired, but not yet commissioned.
Figures updated from *Jane's Fighting Ships 1996-97* (1996).

Considerable naval activity is also taking place in two other areas of the Indian Ocean, the Persian Gulf and Southeast Asia. In view of the perceived threat emanating from Iran's acquisition of conventional submarines, countries in the region are in the process of substantially upgrading their anti-submarine warfare (ASW) capabilities. The most prominent is the United Arab Emirates (UAE), which is believed to have provided $2 billion for this purpose. The UAE Navy has already signed an arms deal with France for seven Eurocopter Panther helicopters and five super Puma helicopters, and is seeking new Maritime Patrol Aircraft (MPA), minesweepers and additional patrol and coastal combatants. A formal requirement for up to four modern frigates has also been issued.[31]

A major naval arms build-up is also currently taking place amongst the Association of South-East Asian Nations (ASEAN) member states. This may be due to a number of factors, including the additional coastal state responsibilities in the new international law of the sea; uncertainties due to a perceived American military withdrawal from the region; rivalry amongst the states themselves; the rapidly growing economies; and perceptions of threat from an assertive Chinese Navy in the region.[32]

The most dramatic naval expansion has been that of Thailand, which has nearly doubled its strength in recent years.[33] During the 1992-95 period, Indonesia was, by far, the largest recipient of warships in the world, according to the United Nations Register of Conventional Arms. All the 27 warships received from Germany during this period, however, were patrol or coastal combatants. Malaysia and Singapore are also enhancing their naval capabilities.

A critical aspect of this naval arms build-up is expected to take the form of modern submarines. At present, only two ASEAN states possess submarines in their navies; this is expected to increase to four, with the addition of Thailand and Malaysia; and the number of boats are expected to increase from the three at present to as many as 14 by the year 2002-2003.[34]

In view of the nature of the major warships to be acquired in the near future, the order of naval forces in the region is expected to change. The most notable would be those of Australia, which could become the second largest littoral navy, and Thailand, whose acquisition of an aircraft carrier by the middle of 1997, will make it the first country in Southeast Asia, and only the second country in the Indian Ocean rim, to operate a warship of this class. The acquisition of submarines by a number of states in the near future would also affect the order of naval forces in the region.

Evolving Structures of Regional Cooperation

Since no state can exercise autonomous command of the sea in such a vast region, the case for naval cooperation in maritime surveillance and enforcement is compelling. However, combined maritime activity does not happen in isolation from over-arching international political arrangements, which are examined here.

Formation of an Association for Cooperation

During 5-7 March 1997, the Indian Ocean Rim Association for Regional Cooperation (IOR-ARC) was formally inaugurated in Mauritius. Ministers and representatives of fourteen member states participated in the event, which also adopted the 11-Article Charter of the Association. This is the first time that an association for cooperation for the entire Indian Ocean rim has been formed, notwithstanding the historical trade and cultural interactions amongst them for centuries. In contrast, the sub-regional organisations existing in the Indian Ocean, such as the Indian Ocean Commission (IOC), the Gulf Cooperation Council (GCC) and the South Asian Association for Regional Cooperation (SAARC), are all limited in terms of scope and/or membership.

The process for the establishment of the IOR-ARC had been initiated as early as March 1995, when Mauritius invited seven states—Australia, India, Kenya, Mauritius, Oman, Singapore and South Africa—perceived to represent their respective areas, to attend a meeting in Port Louis. However, within five months it was decided to double the membership of the Association to fourteen states.[35] The additional seven member countries were Indonesia, Madagascar, Malaysia, Mozambique, Sri Lanka, Tanzania and Yemen. Meanwhile, countries like Iran, Pakistan, Bangladesh, Thailand, and even France and Japan are keen to become members or associated with the IOR-ARC in one form or another.

However, the rationale for involving a limited number of countries during the early stages of the Association has been to initiate successfully concrete means of cooperation through a core group of countries. This approach was preferred to one which would simultaneously have involved a large number of countries, thereby possibly hampering the degree of cooperation. Nonetheless, the Charter of the IOR-ARC has kept open the possibility of expanding further the membership of the Association at a future date. Article 4 of the Charter states,

> All sovereign States of the Indian Ocean Rim are eligible for membership. To become members, States must adhere to the principles and objectives enshrined in the Charter of the Association. Expansion of membership of the Association will be decided by Member States.[36]

At the First Ministerial Meeting in Mauritius in March 1997, it was further agreed that a Working Group be set up to go into all the issues relating to membership and other forms of association such as observership, guest status and dialogue partnership. The Working Group is expected to submit its recommendations for the next meeting of the senior officials of IOR-ARC.[37] As this needs to be formally endorsed by the Council of Ministers, additional membership of the Association has effectively been frozen for the next two years.

Economic Cooperation

The IOR-ARC is aimed exclusively at bolstering economic cooperation amongst the countries of the Indian Ocean rim. This is a major task in itself, especially in view of the low level of intra-rim trade. Economic cooperation is to be carried out through the implementation of projects relating primarily to trade facilitation, promotion and liberalisation; promotion of foreign investment; scientific and technological exchanges and tourism; and the development of infrastructure and human resources. In addition, close interaction of trade and industry, academic institutions, is to be encouraged and cooperation and dialogue amongst member states in international fora on global economic issues to be strengthened.[38]

In this endeavour, in August 1995, the Indian Ocean Rim Business Forum (IORBF) and the Indian Ocean Rim Academic Group (IORAG) were both formally constituted.[39] By May 1996 it was agreed that the Action Plan to be followed would initially cover the major themes of trade development and investment facilitation, along with institutional capacity building and human resource development. As a result, the IORBF agreed to address a number of issues including the mutual recognition of accreditation systems; harmonisation and recognition in the fields of standardisation and quality certification, and laboratory testing; and the provision of a central database on trade policies, procedures, etc. Meanwhile, the IORAG agreed to focus on twelve economic related projects, including offshore processing zones, the management of megacities, and a directory of databases on Indian Ocean matters.[40]

As the focus of IOR-ARC is clearly on economic cooperation, it was felt best to concentrate wholly on these activities, and not burden it through the introduction of extraneous issues. As a result, all the fourteen members of the Association have agreed to exclude the discussion of bilateral and political issues from the agenda, as they could hamper economic cooperation. Article 2 (iv) of the IOR-ARC Charter makes this quite clear. Regional security issues are also excluded from discussion.

Multinational Naval Cooperation

Whereas multilateral maritime cooperation in the Indian Ocean in a limited form is carried out through sub-regional organizations like the IOC, naval cooperation in sensitive areas such as joint naval exercises, continues to largely remain bilateral in form. In terms of actual operations, the only exceptions were "Operation Desert Storm", when a multinational coalition of thirty states, led by the United States, went to war against Iraq; the United Nations operations off Somalia; the multinational maritime interception force presently in place in the Persian Gulf/Arabian Sea to enforce the blockade against Iraq;

and cooperation amongst Indonesia, Malaysia and Singapore, to combat piracy in the Straits of Malacca and Singapore.[41] In terms of joint naval exercises, the only exceptions are the "Starfish" series of exercises carried out in Asia-Pacific waters under the auspices of the Five Power Defence Arrangement (FPDA), and the Kakadu-series of joint training exercises, off Darwin.

In addition, since 1995 the Indian Navy has twice hosted a multinational gathering of warships from five to seven countries at the sensitive Port Blair naval base of the Andaman and Nicobar islands in the Bay of Bengal. This event had initially been proposed, by the then Indian Chief of Naval Staff in 1993, as joint naval exercises with some of the ASEAN states. However, the Indian government and ASEAN formally reduced it to a bi-annual gathering (appropriately called "Milan") of warships in what is coyly described as a "social and cultural event".[42] In February 1995, four warships from Indonesia, Thailand, Singapore and Sri Lanka, along with one from India, participated in "Milan 95". Two years later in February 1997, thirteen warships from seven countries (including Malaysia and Bangladesh) were involved in various activities (excluding joint naval exercises) for a five-day period.

Numerous bilateral naval exercises, meanwhile, continue to take place in the Indian Ocean. In 1991, the Indian Navy resumed the conduct of joint naval exercises, after a period of virtually twenty five years. Since then, it has conducted 25 bilateral naval/ coast guard exercises in the Indian Ocean, with 13 countries. In terms of the rim states, the Indian Navy's emphasis continues to be placed on the Bay of Bengal/eastern Indian Ocean. Joint bilateral naval exercises have been conducted with all the four ASEAN states of the Indian Ocean rim. Indeed, the Indian Navy has conducted the largest number of joint naval exercises with the Republic of Singapore Navy; the fifth such exercise took place in February 1997. However, only one joint bilateral naval exercise has taken place with the navies of Indonesia, Malaysia and Thailand. The scope of these exercises, however, continue to remain limited, involving, at present, only one or two warships on each side. The largest and more successful, of these exercises (three during 1992-97) have been with warships of the American Navy.

In terms of port visits, the Indian Navy, for example, has visited ports in Indonesia and Malaysia virtually every year since the mid-1980s. This included the visit of two warships to Penang in 1990-91, to take part in the international fleet review that marked the fiftieth anniversary of the Royal Malaysian Navy.

Indian ports also continue to host visits by foreign warships, including those from Australia, Indonesia, Malaysia, Russia and the United States. In November 1993, the first visit in recent times of a Chinese warship, a destroyer-size training ship, took place at Bombay. On the earlier Chinese naval visit to the Indian Ocean in the mid-1980s, no Indian port had been visited. In March 1995, the first visit of a South African naval ship, a combat support vessel, also took place at Bombay.

In an important development, sensitive Indian naval establishments have also been opened up to warships of foreign countries on a selective basis, including those from ASEAN states. Since 1991, naval ships from Indonesia, Malaysia and Singapore have visited the naval establishment at Port Blair in the Andaman islands; Republic of Singapore Navy warships also visited the submarine base at Vishakapatnam for the first time in 1995.

The problems with joint multilateral naval exercises amongst the countries of the Indian Ocean, whether by conception or extension of bilateral exercises, are not difficult to see. Not only is there an absence of an agreed upon single common perception of threat/uncertainty, but the defence of the shipping routes in the Indian Ocean does not necessarily require the conduct of formal joint multilateral naval exercises.[43] Moreover, the formation of a multilateral organisation in the Indian Ocean with a specific mandate of avoiding political issues, such as regional security, complicates matters further. There is clearly no political organization under which truly multilateral naval exercises could satisfactorily be conducted. In such a situation, any attempt at serious multilateral naval exercises would necessitate the inclusion of some countries and the exclusion of others. This could be misperceived as the beginning of a military alliance of sorts, targeted against a specific country/ countries, and would only serve to increase tension in the area. The development and growth of a web of bilateral naval relationships could, however, evolve into a loosely-defined multilateral set of activities.

Multilateral naval cooperation in non-sensitive areas could clearly enhance confidence and trust amongst states.[44] The broad areas of naval cooperation identified and suggested since the early 1990s by naval personnel, commentators and analysts, include the following—greater transparency in procurement plans, and the future shape and size of naval forces, as well as the rationale for naval deployment; and a multilateral agreement on the prevention of incidents at sea.

In this respect, the Maritime Cooperation Working Group of the Council for Security Cooperation in the Asia-Pacific, a "second track" organization whose ideas feed into the "first track" 21-member (including

India) ASEAN Regional Forum, has also suggested specific proposals for future naval cooperation. These include the exchange of fleet schedules and joint maritime contingency planning; surveillance operations, regional crisis response planning and shared training opportunities; joint patrol arrangements; a multilateral Incidents at Sea agreement, naval representation at the ARF, development of a common doctrine and defensive SLOC exercises; the improvement of the Western Pacific Naval Symposium (WPNS); and warship maintenance and construction, naval hydrographic training and operations, naval training, increased emphasis on ship visits and an annual conference on naval cooperation in the Indian Ocean.[45]

While some of these proposals are clearly too ambitious to implement in the Indian Ocean, the major success for the CSCAP Maritime Cooperation Working Group has been the formulation of a set of Guidelines for Regional Maritime Cooperation. This is a unique 28-point document which has been developed for the first time. Its non-binding principles encourage cooperation for the Asia-Pacific countries in areas such as SLOC; humanitarian assistance; search and rescue; marine safety; law and order at sea; maritime surveillance; the protection and preservation of the marine environment and marine resources; and marine scientific/technical research.[46]

Clearly, the most contentious issue in these guidelines concern maritime surveillance, in view of the security implications of such activities. Nonetheless, there has been agreement amongst the representatives of the Working Group in the adoption of the following two points:

> Parties recognise that maritime surveillance may be conducted for peaceful purposes as part of the exercise of freedom of navigation and overflight in areas claimed as exclusive economic zone or continental shelf, and on the high seas. This should be conducted without prejudice to the sovereign rights of the coastal state within its exclusive economic zone or continental shelf.

> Parties are encouraged to work towards arrangements for the sharing of surveillance information with other Parties to these Guidelines.[47]

Conclusion

Notwithstanding the common interests of most of the states in the security of energy supplies and trade, there remain a number of factors and issues which could threaten stability and increase tension in the region. The level of multilateral naval cooperation which exists at present is clearly insufficient to constitute a credible confidence and trust-building mechanism. This is exacerbated by the absence of a unified perception of threat/uncertainties, or even an ocean-wide forum for the discussion of these issues. These factors pose a considerable challenge to effective and sustained multinational naval cooperation in the Indian Ocean into the twenty-first century.

Notes

1. P.S. Jayaramu, "India and the Indian Ocean", in Rama S. Melkote (ed.), *Indian Ocean: Issues for Peace* (New Delhi: Manohar Publishing, 1995), 33.
2. William L. Dowdy, "The Indian Ocean Region as Concept and Reality", in William L. Dowdy and Russell B. Trood, *The Indian Ocean: Perspectives on a Strategic Arena* (Durham: Duke University, 1987), 3-23.
3. The 29 littoral countries are Australia, Bahrain, Bangladesh, Djibouti, Egypt, Eritrea, India, Indonesia, Iran, Iraq, Israel, Jordan, Kenya, Kuwait, Malaysia, Mozambique, Myanmar, Oman, Pakistan, Qatar, Saudi Arabia, Singapore, Somalia, South Africa, Sudan, Tanzania, Thailand, United Arab Emirates (UAE) and Yemen. The six island countries are Comoros, Madagascar, Maldives, Mauritius, Seychelles and Sri Lanka. The 12 landlocked countries are Afghanistan, Bhutan, Burundi, Ethiopia, Lesotho, Malawi, Nepal, Rwanda, Swaziland, Uganda, Zambia and Zimbabwe. The island possessions of France are Mayotte, Tromelin, Reunion, St. Paul, Amsterdam, Kerguelen and Crozet. At present, the island possession of the UK consists only of the British Indian Ocean Territory (BIOT), of which the largest island, Diego Garcia, has been leased to the United States.
4. See Rahul Roy-Chaudhury, Report on the International Conference on "The Indian Ocean Community", Tehran, Iran, November 10-12, 1996 (Unpublished).
5. *UNDP Human Development Report* (1995), 229.
6. The World Bank, *World Development Report 1996* (1996), 188-89, 210-11, 220-22.
7. *International Petroleum Encyclopedia* (1995), 9, 90, 274, and 317.
8. Air Commodore Jasjit Singh, "Critical Resources and the Ocean", in *The Indian Ocean—Challenges and Opportunities* (Bombay: Indian Navy Foundation, 1992), 184-87.
9. *International Petroleum Encyclopedia* (1995), 198.
10. Robert Simpson-Anderson, "The South African Navy", in Greg Mills (ed.), *Maritime Policy for Developing Nations* (Johannesburg: South African Institute for International Affairs, 1995), 274.
11. Vice-Admiral Marcel Le Cicle, "Opening Speech", in Pierre Maurice and Olivier Gohin (eds), *International Relations in the Indian Ocean* (1994), 28.
12. Keynote Address by Senator Gareth Evans at the International Forum on the Indian Ocean Region (IFIOR), June 11, 1995, reproduced in *The Indian Ocean Review* (June/September 1995), 7.

13. Sam Bateman, "Maritime Cooperation in East Asia", 161.
14. Simpson-Anderson, "The South African Navy", 274.
15. Rahul Roy-Chaudhury, *Sea Power and Indian Security* (London: Brassey's, 1995), 88.
16. Paul Dibb, "Key Strategic Issues for Asia and Australia", in Sam Bateman and Dick Sherwood (eds), *Australia's Maritime Bridge into Asia* (St. Leonards, Australia: Allen and Unwin, 1995), 21-23.
17. *The Times of India* (India), February 1, 1995.
18. Air Commodore Jasjit Singh, "Light Weapons and Conflict in Southern Asia", in Air Commodore Jasjit Singh (ed.), *Light Weapons and International Security* (New Delhi: Institute for Defence Studies, 1995), 55-56.
19. Roy-Chaudhury, *Sea Power and Indian Security*, 140.
20. *The Indian Ocean Newsletter*, No. 700 (January 6, 1996), 4.
21. Vivian L. Forbes, "Legal Extensions to Australia's Maritime Claim", *The Indian Ocean Review* (December 1994), 15.
22. See *The Times of India* (India), November 12, 1995.
23. Edgar Gold (General Editor), *Maritime Affairs: A World Handbook* (Harlow, UK: Longman Group, 1991), 373-79.
24. D. Banerjee, "Indian Ocean Zone of Peace: Need for a New Approach", *Strategic Analysis* November 1992, 722-23.
25. See, for example, *The Military Balance 1994-1995* (1994), 49.
26. Le Cicle, "Opening Speech," 30-31.
27. Rahul Roy-Chaudhury, "The Chinese Navy and the Indian Ocean", *Maritime International* January 1995, 21-22.
28. Rahul Roy-Chaudhury, "The Indian Navy: Past, Present, and Future", *Asian Strategic Review 1995-96* December 1996, 100.
29. Rahul Roy-Chaudhury, "Advanced Technology Submarines for Pakistan: Implications for the Indian Navy", *Strategic Analysis* December 1994, 1097.
30. Rahul Roy-Chaudhury, "The Naval Arms Trade in the Indian Ocean", *Maritime International* March 1996, 13.
31. Rahul Roy-Chaudhury, "Indo-UAE Joint Naval Exercises: Passage to the Persian Gulf", *The Pioneer* (India), December 13, 1995.
32. See J.N. Mak, "ASEAN Maritime Insecurity: Contingency Planning in an Uncertain World", *International Defence Review - Defence 95*, 58-65.
33. See Robert Karniol, "The RTN's Two-Ocean Ambition", *Jane's Defence Weekly* December 3, 1994, 17-22, and "Thailand", *Jane's Sentinel: South China Sea* (1995), 17-19.
34. Rahul Roy-Chaudhury, "Submarines in the Indian Ocean", *Maritime International* May 1995, 14-15.
35. See *Indian Ocean Rim Initiative, Second Meeting of the Working Group*, Port Louis, Mauritius, 14-16 May 1996, Document 1.

36. "Membership", Article 4, *Charter of the Indian Ocean Rim Association for Regional Cooperation (IOR-ARC)*, First Ministerial Meeting, Mauritius, 5-7 March 1997.
37. Chairman's Statement, First Ministerial Meeting of the IOR-ARC, Mauritius, March 6, 1997, 3-4.
38. Article 3, *Charter of the IOR-ARC*.
39. Indian Ocean Rim Initiative, First Meeting of the Working Group, Port Louis, Mauritius, 15-17 August 1995, 2-3.
40. Documents 1-3, *Indian Ocean Rim Initiative*.
41. See Sam Bateman and Anthony Bergin, "Building Blocks for Maritime Security in the Indian Ocean: An Australian Perspective", in Dipankar Banerjee, *Towards an Era of Cooperation: An Indo-Australian Dialogue* (1995), 327.
42. Sanjeev Miglani, "India Reassures Region as it plans to Bolster Forces", *Asia Times* February 20, 1997, 16.
43. Charles A. Meconis and Commander Stanley B. Weeks (Ret'd), *Cooperative Maritime Security in the Asia-Pacific Region: A Strategic and Arms Control Agreement* (Monograph), 1995, 63-65.
44. Michael C. Pugh, "Multinational Naval Cooperation", *Proceedings of the US Naval Institute* March 1994, 72.
45. Rahul Roy-Chaudhury, Report on the Second Meeting of the CSCAP Maritime Cooperation Working Group, Kuala Lumpur, Malaysia, April 16-17, 1996 (Unpublished).
46. CSCAP Maritime Cooperation Working Group, *Guidelines for Regional Maritime Cooperation*, Jakarta, Indonesia, 3-4 December 1996, 1-6.
47. *Ibid.*, 4.

9 Small Island and Archipelagic States

PHILLIP SAUNDERS AND HUGH WILLIAMSON

Small island and archipelagic states present special challenges in the development and maintenance of multinational naval cooperation, but they may also have unique opportunities. They are likely to have a very high degree of "oceans interest", in the sense that their land-based opportunities may be small and their reliance on marine resources quite high. In addition, they are often faced with controlling very large jurisdictional zones with restricted financial and human resources. The ability to devote extra effort to multinational efforts may consequently be severely limited. On the other hand, the potential benefits of cooperation for such states, through resource sharing and increased efficiency, may be significant.

There is some degree of overlap between these two groups, in that many small island states are also archipelagic states. The problems which arise for the two groups are, however, sufficiently distinct that they will be given separate treatment in this chapter. The situation of small island states is explored through a case study of the island states of the South Pacific, while the problems of archipelagic states are reviewed without detailed reference to specific countries or regions. Consistent with the discussions of the workshop group upon which this chapter is based,[1] the primary focus is on the small island state problem as reflected by the South Pacific, with a briefer overview of the archipelagic issue.

Small Island States: The Case of the South Pacific

Multinational naval cooperation in the South Pacific dates back at least to the Second World War, and the various operations involving forces from a number of allied navies, including the US, Australia, New Zealand and the Netherlands. In more recent years, however, the focus of cooperation has changed both with respect to the players involved and the objectives and modes of cooperation.

Figure 9.1 The South Pacific Ocean

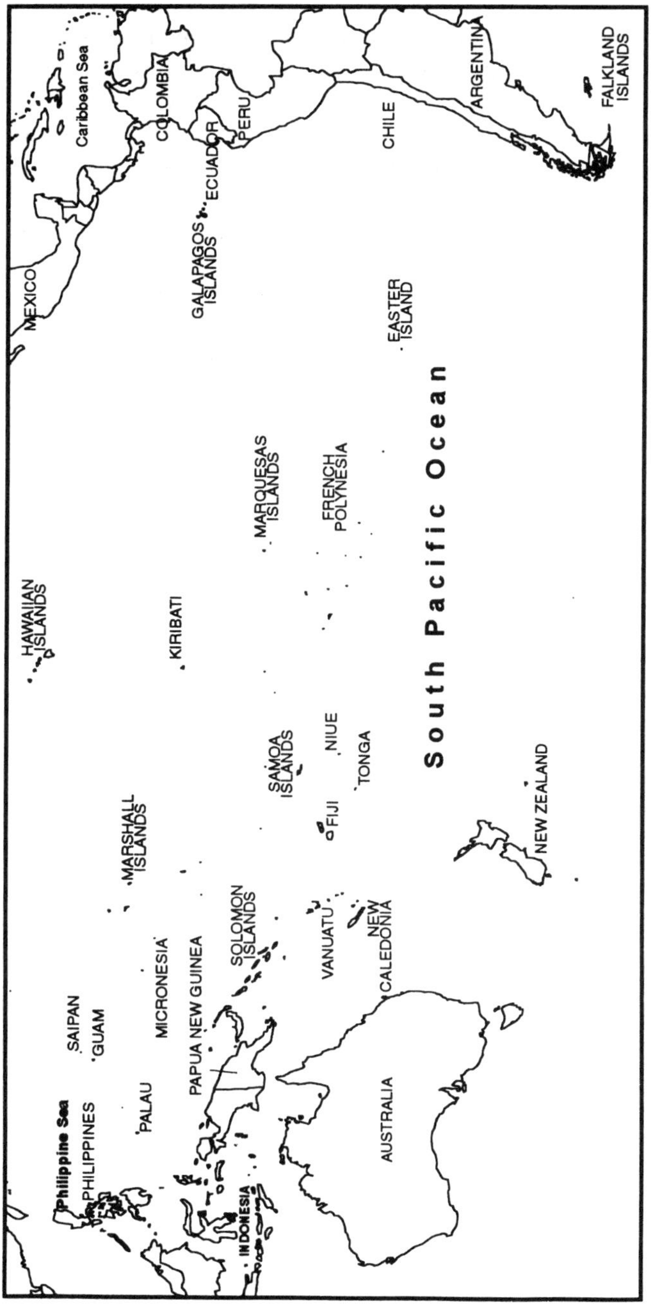

The Regional Setting

With a degree of ambiguity suited to its occasionally opaque politics, the very term "South Pacific" is subject to a number of possible definitions. For the purposes of this chapter, the term "South Pacific" is taken to encompass the states, self-governing territories and other entities set out in Table 1.[2] The main concentration of the study is on what will be referred to as the "island countries" or the "Forum Island Countries (FICs)". These terms both denote the 14 island country members of the South Pacific Forum (SPF).[3]

Table 9.1 States and Territories of the South Pacific

Independent and Self Governing	Population
Australia	18,260,000
Cook Islands (NZ)*	19,500
Federated States of Micronesia	125,300
Fiji	782,000
Kiribati	80,900
Marshall Islands	58,300
Nauru	10,200
New Zealand	3,500,000
Niue (NZ)*	2,170
Palau**	16,950
Papua New Guinea	4,400,000
Solomon Islands	412,000
Tokelau (NZ)***	1,480
Tonga	106,400
Tuvalu	10,146
Vanuatu	177,500
Western Samoa	214,300
Other Territories	
American Samoa (US)	59,500
French Polynesia (France)	224,900
New Caledonia (France)	187,700
Pitcairn Island (UK)	56
Wallis and Futuna (France)	14,650

*	Cook Islands and Niue are self-governing territories in free association with New Zealand, which controls external affairs.
**	Palau achieved independence in 1994, in a Compact of Free Association with the US.
***	Tokelau is a territory of New Zealand, with membership in SPC.

Source: *CIA World Factbook 1996*, accessed at http://www.odci.gov/cia/publications. Population figures are rounded.

This grouping (almost all of which would classify as small island countries) is both massive and minuscule, depending upon one's frame of reference. The FICs have 200 nm. Exclusive Economic Zone (EEZ) claims of between 20-25 million km^2, but in many cases their land masses and populations are exceedingly small. Apart from Australia (18 million), Papua New Guinea (4.4 million), New Zealand (3.5 million), Fiji (782,000) and the Solomon Islands (412,000), the remaining countries of the Forum have populations ranging from 214,000 down to 2,170. (see Table 1 below). By way of practical example, the Cook Islands, with a population of 19,500, has an EEZ of roughly 1,830,000 km^2.

Naval forces in the region are quite limited. Outside Australia and New Zealand (and any forces deployed by France or other metropolitan powers), only Papua New Guinea and Fiji have formal naval units, and these are very limited in capability beyond their own coastal requirements. Some other states have police or coast guard-type units, and a number of patrol boats have been supplied to the region under the Australian Pacific Patrol Boat Programme, which has included training, running costs and communications facilities (see discussion below). This paucity of formal naval forces means that we must look at cooperation which is broadly "maritime" in scope, and not just naval in a strict sense.

One important distinguishing characteristic of the South Pacific has been the extent of regional cooperation, both institutional and otherwise, that has occurred in the post-war period. This is evidenced by even a partial listing of regional intergovernmental organizations and other agencies which have been influential in the region's development:[4]

South Pacific Commission (SPC). Established in 1947, the SPC maintains a wide range of social, technical and scientific programs, including fisheries science and extension services. Membership of the SPC extends to metropolitan powers.

South Pacific Forum. The Forum, established in 1971, is the senior "political" regional organization, and is supported by a Secretariat. Membership includes the independent and self-governing island countries, as well as Australia and New Zealand. The forum has maintained subsidiary programmes in areas such as shipping, tourism, communications and energy, although a recent review has resulted in a shift of programme activities outside the main Secretariat.

Forum Fisheries Agency (FFA). The FFA was established under the Forum as a separate agency in 1979 with a mandate in harmonization of approaches and cooperation in control of foreign fishing in the region.

South Pacific Regional Environment Programme (SPREP). SPREP was originally established as a UNEP regional programme in 1975, but since 1993 has been a full intergovernmental regional organization. It has a broad mandate to foster cooperation in environmental protection and sustainable development.

South Pacific Applied Geoscience Commission (SOPAC). SOPAC was also an outgrowth of a UN-supported programme, which achieved full status as an intergovernmental agency in 1989. Its mandate is to assist member states in the management of non-living marine resources and in the management and protection of coastal areas.

University of the South Pacific (USP). Although not an intergovernmental organization, the USP serves an important role as the regional university for most of the island countries (Papua New Guinea maintains a separate institution).

South Pacific Organizations Coordinating Committee (SPOCC). Since 1988, this committee of heads of regional institutions has played an important part in the coordination of development assistance and other policy matters relevant to the regional institutional structure.

Main Players in Regional Cooperation

In considering naval and maritime cooperation involving the island countries, it is important to recognize the different categories of actors who are the potential participants in cooperative activities. The first group might be called the solely "regional" actors; that is, the island states themselves. Second, "quasi-regional" actors would include other powers present in the region but not part of the island country group. This would include primarily Australia and New Zealand, but could extend to metropolitan powers such as the US and France, if acting through their regional territorial presences. Finally, we have extra-regional powers operating in the region, which could include metropolitan states such as the US or France, when operating in their broader global roles. One important factor to note here is the absence of a single power extensively involved in the region as a dominant presence. Australia plays this part in a limited way at times, but is lacking in capacity, while the US has the capacity to do so when it chooses, but has not actively assumed the role in recent years. There is nothing in the South Pacific to match, for example, the US role in the Caribbean.

The presence of the three categories of actors set out above could conceivably generate a number of patterns of cooperation: island states among themselves; island states and the "quasi-regional" states; island states with extra-regional powers; and fully extra-regional, in that no island states are involved at all. The extra-regional options have been pursued (as, for example, through the ANZUS alliance, which does not involve the island countries, or through bilateral Australian-New Zealand arrangements). Clearly, however, it has been the first two options, island states among themselves and island states with the quasi-regional powers, which have the most direct relevance for the states which are the focus of this chapter. Before turning to a consideration of maritime cooperation in the region, however, it is necessary to complete the regional setting with a review of some of the issues which have helped to structure that cooperation.

Regional Issues and Challenges

The relevant challenges facing the island countries of the South Pacific in recent years can be grouped as internal, regional and external in nature. The following is a brief overview of some of the more salient socio-economic, security and resource management issues which have confronted these states.

Internal. Internal or domestic concerns for most states in the region have focused on pervasive problems of inadequate resource bases and under-development, which are linked to inherent problems of size, vulnerability to natural disaster and economic disruption, as well as a serious imbalance in power when dealing with most of the rest of the world. This has been described by Richard Herr as follows:

> Three particular limitations were, and remain, considerations with regard to the national capacity of South Pacific microstates. These are:
> * the diseconomies resulting from diminutive scale;
> * the extreme levels of vulnerability; and
> * the comprehensive asymmetry of their external relations.[5]

In addition to the daunting prospects on the economic front, some states have experienced bouts of internal instability. The two coups in Fiji, the attempted secession of the northern island group in Vanuatu in the 1980s, and the continuing civil conflict in Bougainville in Papua New Guinea are the main examples.

Regional. Regional conflict of a military nature has, fortunately, been absent from the South Pacific in recent years (although there have on occasion been tensions between Papua New Guinea and the Solomon Islands, associated with the Bougainville situation). There are, however, other regional-level phenomena which have been of concern. Economic migration, primarily but not exclusively to Australia and New Zealand, has continued to be an important factor both for originating and recipient states. In recent years, transboundary crime (ranging from drug smuggling to piracy in some of the more northern parts of the region) has emerged as a matter of sufficient concern as to attract the attention of the political leaders of the Forum countries.[6]

External. Two marine-related challenges have dominated the external horizon insofar as the island countries are concerned, one more critically than the other. Environmental threats from sources such as shipping routes and, more recently, global warming[7] have caught the attention of Pacific policy makers. Clearly, however, it was the need to assert control over marine resources within the region's EEZs which most directly engaged the region through the 1980s and into the 1990s. In particular, the activities of Distant Water Fishing Nations (DWFNs) in exploiting the valuable tuna resources of the region motivated many of the cooperative activities which occurred in this period (see below).

Recurring themes. There are two central themes which are evident in most if not all of these challenges facing the region. First is the importance of what Herr has termed "asymmetry" in the region's relationships with the outside world.[8] Given the smallness and economic vulnerability of these states, their dealings with external actors are almost always characterized by a significant imbalance of power, whether military, economic or diplomatic. This has in turn conditioned the strategic approaches of the island states, most strikingly in the direction of cooperation at the regional level, with the objective of increasing their leverage and influence wherever possible.[9] The problem of asymmetry has also led in the past to the adoption of balancing strategies, whereby outside interests were played off against one another in pursuit of maximum advantage for the island countries of the region.[10]

The second theme has been the centrality of international law, and in particular the law of the sea, in defining both the opportunities and challenges facing the region throughout this period. The progressive development of international law with respect to the 200 nm. EEZ, reflected in its ultimate acceptance in the *1982 UN Law of the Sea (LOS) Convention*,[11] formed the basis for the huge expansion of the potential resource base available to the island countries (as well as imposing significant management obligations). At the same time, however, unresolved issues remained which hampered the ability of the island states to take advantage of these gains. Most dramatically, the US refusal to accept coastal state jurisdiction over tuna led to vessel seizures by the Solomon Islands and Papua New Guinea, and retaliatory embargoes imposed by the US.[12] Similarly, problems remained with respect to the extent of management control exercised beyond 200 nm., where over-exploitation or allegedly destructive techniques such as driftnetting could have impacts on coastal state interests in the resource.

There has been great progress in dealing with some of these matters. The US and the island states resolved their main differences over tuna with a 1987 agreement regulating access, fees and other aspects of the fishery.[13] High-seas issues have been addressed by the recent *UN Agreement on Straddling Stocks and Highly Migratory Fish Stocks*,[14] and by actions on high seas driftnetting.[15] What is clear from the post-1982 experience, however, is the 1982 LOS Convention itself provided only the jurisdictional umbrella within which states might exploit their new opportunities and assume their management obligations. The *implementation* of the Convention at the national level would require substantial work and the sometimes aggressive defence of national interests. For the small island states of the South Pacific, lacking capacity and in desperate need of the new resource base, these requirements provided a powerful motivation to cooperate in solidifying what was, in the early 1980s, a largely theoretical jurisdictional entitlement.

Patterns of Cooperation

Given the regional context set out above, including both the potential elements of cooperation and the challenges requiring attention, what has been done in the past 15 to 20 years to advance the interests of the island states through multinational maritime cooperation?

Formal naval or quasi-naval cooperation among the island states has not been a widespread phenomenon, not surprisingly given the lack of long-range capacity. There has been some history of joint "naval" exercises involving island states using patrol boats provided under the Australian Pacific Patrol Boat Programme, and Papua New Guinea did assist Vanuatu in putting down the 1980s rebellion referred to above. There has also been some more recent work to develop regional approaches to transboundary criminal activity, as well as long-standing cooperation on shipping policy (coordinated through the Forum Secretariat) and efforts to improve regional oil spill contingency planning through the South Pacific Regional Environment Programme. But clearly the most significant degree of cooperation has been in the area of marine resource management, specifically the control of DWFN activities.

It is not possible here to deal in detail with all the phases of development involved in the island countries' almost 20 year effort to take control of the lucrative tuna fishery within the region. With the acceptance of 200 nm. fishery and exclusive economic zones through the 1970s, the island states were presented with an enormous potential increase in their limited national resource bases.[16] Serious obstacles remained, however. First, the US continued its opposition to coastal state control of tuna, as noted above. Second, and of broader concern, the island nations in most cases lacked any serious capacity for Monitoring, Control and Surveillance (MCS) of the EEZ, with the result that foreign fishing fleets faced little threat of effective enforcement.

By the early 1990s, the legal position of the island nations, had markedly improved with the negotiation of the US multilateral agreement (see above). Furthermore, important MCS initiatives, many of a cooperative nature, had been put in place. It is useful to consider some of the highlights of this largely successful effort at regional cooperation.

Regional MCS Programme

In 1979 the South Pacific Forum agreed to the creation of the Forum Fisheries Agency, an intergovernmental agency with a mandate to assist island nations in securing the benefits derived from the living resources of the EEZ.[17] The island countries, both through the FFA and separately,[18] eventually developed or supported a wide range of technical programmes in support of its overall objective,[19] with one of the key areas being cooperation in the development of MCS capabilities in the region. The regional MCS programme has been described as having two broad areas of concentration, legal and institutional.[20]

The following are some examples of the multinational cooperative efforts which have taken place under these headings since 1979.

Legal Areas of Cooperation

Minimum Terms and Conditions (MTCs). In 1982, member countries of the FFA first negotiated a set of MTCs, intended as "non-negotiable minimum terms for access" to be incorporated in all bilateral fishery access agreements. The MTCs, revised and updated in 1990-91, include such conditions as uniform identification of fishing vessels, catch reporting requirements and logsheets, terms for placement of on-board observers and agreement to flag state responsibility for fleet activities.[21] Overall, MTCs prevent DWFNs from playing one state off against another in order to minimize the effect of access agreements.

Regional Register. The FFA maintains a Regional Register of fishing vessels, containing data on vessel ownership, operators, masters and past history. Registration of vessels on the Register is imposed as a requirement of fishing access by all member countries of FFA, and a vessel must be in "good standing" on the Register to be allowed to fish in the region. Good standing can be revoked in the event of a "serious fisheries offence" anywhere in the region, which would effectively lead to the blacklisting of the vessel throughout the region until the matter is resolved (i.e., submission to legal process of the island state in question, or reciprocal enforcement in a flag state). The Register has functioned as an important compliance mechanism, as demonstrated by the fact that as of 1993 it had never proved necessary to revoke good standing, as the threat has always been enough.[22]

Cooperative and Combined MCS. The FFA countries have been moving towards a higher level of cooperation in MCS beyond limited regional functions, opening up the possibility for bilateral and sub-regional activities extending to *shared* surveillance and enforcement functions. The 1993 *Niue Treaty on Cooperation in Fisheries Surveillance and Law Enforcement in the South Pacific Region* is an umbrella agreement that "defines the general principles upon which parties may enter into more detailed subsidiary agreements", which are envisaged as including "physical sharing of surveillance and enforcement equipment, the empowerment of [other parties'] officers to perform enforcement duties [in another EEZ], enhancement of extradition procedures and evidentiary provisions".[23] In addition, parties could agree to allow another state's own surveillance and enforcement activities to operate on a transboundary basis, allowing for more effective tracking and apprehension of offenders, and to provide for reciprocal enforcement of penalties. If fully seized upon by member countries, the Niue Treaty opens up a range and level of multinational cooperative activities in this sector which would probably be the most extensive in the world.

Institutional Areas of Cooperation

Physical Capacity. The actual development of physical assets for MCS in the region has not, in most cases, been undertaken on a truly multinational basis, but rather as a series of bilateral exercises planned on a regional basis (as with the Australian Pacific Patrol Boat Programme). There have, however, been at least two examples of a regional role in the provision and management of surveillance assets. With respect to the Patrol Boat Programme, although it has been managed as an Australian initiative, FFA has assisted at the regional level through "provision of surveillance and enforcement training, legal and computer expertise, liaison between defence institutions and fisheries administrations and the development of standard operating procedures".[24] A second regional programme has involved the coordination of aerial surveillance patrols of the region conducted by the New Zealand and Australian armed forces, with planning information supplied by FFA and member countries, and photographic evidence provided to relevant countries for enforcement follow-up.

Training. In addition to training associated with the Patrol Boat Programme (provided by both Australia and New Zealand), the FFA has provided work attachments and formal training in areas such as surveillance systems, boarding and inspection, prosecution procedures and on-board observer skills.

Data Collection and Analysis. A central strategy adopted in the region has been to enhance the information base on which MCS activities are conducted, thereby minimizing the use of expensive physical assets, and improving the effectiveness of those that are deployed. FFA and its member countries have been extremely active in this regard. Programmes in this area have included: establishment of a regional Maritime Surveillance Communications Network; testing and development for a satellite-based vessel monitoring system to allow real time tracking of vessels and immediate submission of catch reports;

development of national fisheries surveillance centres, linked to a regional centre to allow transfer of and access to data on a wider basis.[25] These cooperative efforts, have been built in large part on legal and diplomatic initiatives (MTCs, access agreements, joint surveillance agreements), improved technical coordination, human capacity development and improved use of information technology (communications, transponders, computer databases). Improvements in the availability of physical assets have been important, especially with respect to the Patrol Boat Programme, but the focus of *cooperation* has been more on the intelligent use and effective deployment of the physical assets that do exist.

Basis of Past Cooperation

If it is accepted that these cooperative efforts have been remarkably successful, particularly when one considers the management capabilities of some of the smaller countries involved, then the island countries of the South Pacific would appear to provide a model for cooperation elsewhere. It is important, however, to go further and ask how and why these patterns of cooperation evolved in the Pacific, whether they are transferable to other situations, and whether they will be as successful in the future in the Pacific itself.

The first and most important reason for the extent of willingness to cooperate in fisheries resource management and MCS in the South Pacific was simple necessity. Given the population bases of many of the countries, the limited human, financial and physical capabilities available and the sheer size of the geographic area to be controlled, the island countries had little choice but to pool their resources to achieve the desired result. In the end, despite periodic splits and disagreements over strategy and national interests, what was most remarkable was the extent to which some countries were willing to subordinate direct national interest to important regional goals, as for example in the willingness of the most tuna-rich states to share revenues with others under the multilateral treaty with the US. Without the overwhelming influence of necessity, it is doubtful that this common front could have survived as well as it did.

Second, multinational maritime cooperation was made easier because of the patterns of cooperation built up over many years through intergovernmental activities in a wide range of maritime and non-maritime sectors. There was no need to develop new habits of cooperation unique to marine issues, for the South Pacific has had perhaps the most extensive pattern of regional cooperation in the developing world, as evidenced by the scope of the agencies referred to above.

The third point to note is that the high level of fisheries-related cooperation occurred partly because of unique opportunities; unique in the sense of the regional context and the period in which the major developments took place. With respect to the regional context, the presence of two interested, active developed states (Australia and New Zealand) within the regional agencies provided a base of funding and expertise upon which broader initiatives, supported by outside funding, could be built. The time period was important in that, during key periods in the 1980s, increased Soviet political and economic interest in the region (including a larger fishing presence) made it possible for island states to make a larger claim on external financial resources and goodwill than might otherwise have been the case. The desire to "block" expansion of Soviet influence probably led to greater diplomatic leverage in negotiations with the US, and to the higher than average development assistance budgets accorded to the region.

Prospects and Lessons

Looking back at experience of the South Pacific, both the pattern of cooperation and the factors upon which it was built, two questions remain. First, will this pattern continue with the same degree of success in the future for the Pacific and, second, does it serve as a practical model for other regions?

With respect to future prospects in the Pacific, it does seem clear that cooperation in this sector will continue to be an important part of the regional structure for the foreseeable future. Nonetheless, it is also possible that the nature and extent of that cooperation may change significantly in coming years. It is essential to remember that past levels of cooperation, as argued above, were built on responses to particular challenges and opportunities, and that these formed the underlying conditions upon which cooperation was predicated. Major changes in the underlying conditions could be expected to lead to similar shifts in the nature of multinational cooperation.

It is beyond the scope of this chapter to canvass the future of the region in detail, but it is possible to note some potential areas of change which may prove significant. At the national level, domestic instability remains a problem, (at least in Papua New Guinea), and may be exacerbated elsewhere by stagnating economies coupled with rising population. In some cases (such as Fiji and Western Samoa) there has been continuing concern over challenges to cultural norms and social stability through pervasive outside influences and resultant rising economic expectations. Any or all of these factors, if sufficiently disruptive, could negatively affect a country's ability to participate fully and effectively in the work of regional organizations.

On the regional front, it may be difficult to maintain sustained regional cohesion over the long run, particularly in the absence of immediate outside threats such as US actions on tuna in the 1980s. Consideration must be given to the future roles of Australia and New Zealand, both critical to past accomplishments. Will they maintain the same commitment, or will their own concerns force them to look more to the relationship with Southeast Asia in coming years? What will be the effect of Japan's increased interest and economic dominance in the region? How these questions are answered in the future could dramatically affect the possibilities for, and effectiveness of, regional cooperation in maritime issues.

Finally, the global picture is also a new and potentially difficult one, when compared to the early 1980s. The end (or suspension) of the Cold War removes some of the possibilities for acquiring leverage with outside powers interested in blocking the influence of others. A related, though distinct, problem is the continued decline in real levels of development assistance, assistance which was critical to the expansion of regional agency mandates and programmes. This factor has already led to a review of roles and reorganization of the work of the regional organizations, and more pressure to streamline might be expected in the future.[26] On the other hand, new global opportunities have arisen in the multifaceted (and apparently interminable) negotiations arising out of the 1992 United Nations Conference on Environment and Development (UNCED). The South Pacific island countries used their cohesion to great effect in fora such as the Conference on Straddling Stocks and Highly Migratory Species, and it is possible that global multilateral negotiations of this type may become an even more important avenue for pursuit of regional goals.[27]

In sum, it is possible that future changes in the domestic, regional and global conditions will render existing institutional structures unsustainable in the future, and it cannot be assumed that previously successful modes of cooperation will continue to succeed over time. With respect to the major outside influences, it is unlikely that there will be any change in the fundamental interest of the US, Australia and New Zealand in maintaining stability in this region, nor is there any real doubt of their capability to do so. It is, however, important to question whether that interest will go beyond the minimal requirements of preserving stability and extend to promoting the region's collective interest in further cooperative ventures.

Similarly, with respect to the question of replicability of the "Pacific model" in other regions, great caution must be used in recommending adoption of such approaches elsewhere. It is essential that multinational maritime cooperation at the regional level be tailored to the needs, capabilities and challenges of the *specific* region in question. Simple replication of models from other regions, no matter how successful they may have been, will lead to difficulties if the necessary objective conditions are not present.

Archipelagic States

The *1982 LOS Convention* established a specific regime for "archipelagic waters", which can be claimed or established only by "archipelagic states". These waters have a special status with respect to navigation and other matters that may have an impact on future requirements for multinational naval cooperation. This section briefly reviews the following: the nature of the archipelagic waters regime (extent and legal status); the possible areas of conflict which may arise from application of the regime; the relevance of multinational cooperation; and the prospects for the future.

The Regime of Archipelagic Waters

The right to declare archipelagic waters under Article 46 of the *1982 LOS Convention* is restricted to "archipelagic states", meaning a "State constituted wholly by one or more archipelagos", but possibly including other islands. The main impact of Article 46 is to restrict the application of the regime to states consisting entirely of archipelagos and islands. Thus, mainland states with coastal archipelagos, no matter how extensive they may be, are excluded from making such a claim.[28]

The second restriction relates to the areas of water and land which might be enclosed by an archipelagic claim. The Convention requires that a number of conditions be met in drawing archipelagic baselines around an archipelago. First, the "main islands" of an archipelago must be included. Second, and more precisely, the ratio of land to water within the baselines must be between one to one and nine to one, which has the effect of preventing claims based either on large islands without significant water space, or on large amounts of water with only small island land-masses. Third, baseline segments are to be under 100 nm. in length, except that up to 3 per cent can be as long as 125 nm. Again, this is intended to prevent claims which are simply too expansive. Finally, the baselines must reflect the "general configuration" of the archipelago.[29] Once the baselines are drawn, they are used as the basis for measurement of other zones such as the Territorial Sea and EEZ,[30] while waters inside the baselines acquire the status of archipelagic waters.[31]

Assuming they are validly declared, archipelagic waters, including the airspace above and the seabed below, are defined by Article 49(1) as coming within the "sovereignty" of the state. This is not, however, *full* sovereignty as it would be exercised over internal waters, for Article 49(3) makes it clear that sovereignty is to be exercised "subject to" the other relevant provisions of the Convention, which place a number of limitations on the archipelagic state's exercise of jurisdiction. First, Article 51 requires respect for existing agreements with other states, recognition of traditional fishing rights and other rights of adjacent states, and respect for existing submarine cables. It is, however, the set of provisions respecting navigational rights in Articles 52-54 which are of the most direct relevance to naval cooperation issues.

The Convention envisages two types of navigational rights through archipelagic waters. First, Article 52 confirms a right of innocent passage through these areas, although the archipelagic state may temporarily suspend this right if "such suspension is essential for the protection of its security". Apart from this limitation, the regime of innocent passage does not extend to overflight, and submarines must transit on the surface (Articles 17, 20). These two gaps, of obvious interest to some states, are dealt with under the second type of passage provided for under the Convention, the right of archipelagic sea lanes passage.

Article 53 provides that archipelagic states "may" designate sea lanes and air routes "suitable for the continuous and expeditious passage of foreign ships and aircraft through or over its archipelagic waters...", and that all ships and aircraft "enjoy the right of archipelagic sea lanes passage" through these routes. Designation of the lanes, by Article 53(9), is to be done in consultation with the competent international organization (presumably the International Maritime Organization—IMO), but it is unclear how disagreements between the state and IMO are to be resolved. The right of passage is non-suspendible, and clearly includes overflight, and by Article 53(3), navigation may be in the "normal mode of navigation", which for submarines may include submerged transit. These routes are to be defined by axis lines, and ships and aircraft are not to deviate more than 25 nm. to either side of the axis lines (53(5)). The archipelagic state may impose traffic separation schemes to regulate passage (53(6)). Finally, if the state does *not* designate archipelagic sea lanes or air routes, Article 53(12) provides that the right of archipelagic passage may be exercised "through the routes normally used for international navigation".

Possible Areas for Conflict

A full discussion of potential conflicts would require a detailed review of the situations of the major archipelagic states, including Indonesia, Malaysia and the Philippines. It is possible, however, to identify some general *types* of conflict which might emerge as a result of this new regime.

First, it is possible that conflict will arise over definition of archipelagic baselines. The delineation of these baselines will be crucial to determining the scope, and the impact on navigational interests, of particular claims to archipelagic waters. If claims are made which maritime powers regard as inadmissible, they could challenge the claim by asserting what they contend are normal high seas navigational rights, and this may lead to conflict with the claiming state. Second, the designation of sea lanes or air routes which are regarded as inadequate or inappropriate by other states may lead to disputes. As noted, the routes are to be referred to IMO, and Article 53(9) seems to require adoption by IMO before the state "may designate", but this still leaves ample room for debate as to placement and other aspects.

Third, states may make claims to substantive rights within archipelagic waters beyond what is allowed by the Convention, as is the case with the Declaration made by the Philippines upon signing the Convention, stating that it considers its archipelagic waters to be fully sovereign territory, similar to internal waters. Finally, there is substantial room for conflict in the residual right to exercise sea lanes passage over "routes normally used for international navigation", where no sea lanes have been declared. This is an ambiguous definition, subject to endless debate, and it is conceivable that disputes may arise over efforts by maritime powers to press the right to passage in waters disputed by the archipelagic state.

Relevance of Cooperation

The first and most important avenue for potential cooperation will be through IMO, in the designation of routes and traffic separation schemes. This will obviously involve the affected state and the IMO, but should also provide an opportunity for other interested parties to make representations before an issue reaches the point of open conflict. A second, and related, requirement will be cooperation in further legal development to clarify some elements of this regime, particularly with respect to where and how lanes are designated and managed, and the acceptable level of regulation to be imposed. As with the problem of straddling stocks and highly migratory species, there are gaps or ambiguities in the 1982 regime which would benefit from further negotiations, perhaps using the forum provided by the IMO.

Neither of these approaches to cooperation on archipelagic issues relates directly to multinational naval cooperation, except that they may avoid the necessity for it. However, in the event that an archipelagic state "pushes the limits" of the regime to an unacceptable degree, it may be decided that an open challenge is required. Such action should be a last resort undertaken only after the failure of other avenues of dispute resolution, but if required it would be desirable to pursue any assertion of rights through cooperative multinational naval presence. This would lend such a challenge a higher degree of legitimacy and make it more difficult for the "offending" state to characterize the action as unilateralism.

Prospects

It is entirely possible that the worst-case scenario of open conflict is nothing more than speculation at this time, and that there is no real or pressing problem to be addressed. While this may be true, there are factors present which at least give cause for concern. This is a relatively new and untested legal regime, and the unclear status of some elements could easily lead to disputes, if not confrontation. Furthermore, the geographic circumstances of some of the key states, at the crossroads of trade in Asia, means that the stakes would be high if indeed the limits of the regime were tested. The issue of archipelagic states and their jurisdictional claims is one in which the risk of conflict may be low in terms of *probability* but high in terms of potential severity of *consequences*. As such, it will require careful monitoring if not active responses in the future.

Conclusions

This brief examination of the situations with respect to small island states and archipelagic states suggests a number of conclusions with respect to multinational naval cooperation. First, we must be prepared to look beyond *naval* cooperation to *maritime* cooperation in a broader sense. For many countries, especially small island and archipelagic states, the main maritime security concerns will be tied up in resource management and environmental protection. Accordingly, their involvement in multinational cooperation is likely to focus on activities of relevance to these issues, such as enforcement of the management regime in the EEZ. It is of course possible that such cooperation could be pursued with naval forces acting in the constabulary role, but it is by no means necessary, and in some cases cooperation may concentrate almost entirely on coordination and information dissemination.

Second, it is apparent that legal regimes can be critical to determining the need for and nature of multinational cooperation in the maritime sphere. Much of the law of the sea is an exercise in conflict avoidance; the jurisdictional entitlements of coastal states and the corresponding rights of other states are set out so that activities such as fishing, navigation and naval operations can proceed according to a known set of rules. When new or incomplete legal regimes are involved, or when important players do not accede to the rules, the opportunity for conflict increases, along with the need for cooperative responses. In the South Pacific, regional cooperation came about in response to the refusal of some states to work within the new jurisdictional regime, and to the need to fill in perceived gaps in that regime. Similarly, if conflict does arise with respect to archipelagic states in the future, it is likely to come from similar sources; parties refusing to abide by the rules, or ambiguity and room for dispute in the rules themselves.

Finally, it is clear that modes of cooperation must be closely tailored to the objectives and capabilities of the parties involved. The South Pacific experienced success with a certain model, but this was based on the presence of certain important conditions which may not be replicated elsewhere. Multinational cooperation, whether naval or not, cannot be reproduced from region to region based on one template. Lessons may be learned from prior experience and other geographic areas, but the unique characteristics of each case must be the primary basis on which such efforts are structured.

Notes

1.   This chapter is based on the discussions of the Small Island States/Archipelagic States Workshop Group at the Halifax Symposium on Multinational Naval Cooperation and Foreign Policy into the 21st Century, 21-23 May 1996. Those discussions were assisted by a background paper, "Multinational Naval Cooperation and Foreign Policy: The Situation of Small Island and Archipelagic States", prepared by Mr. Hugh R. Williamson. Mr. Glen Herbert and Commander R.H. Edwards assisted in the compilation and reporting of the workshop session results.

2. This list is roughly equivalent to the scope of the South Pacific Commission (SPC), with the exception of the US territories of Guam and the Northern Marianas, which are members of SPC but are not really as integrated in the region as some other territories.

3. These states and territories are: Cook Islands, Federated States of Micronesia, Fiji, Kiribati, Marshall Islands, Nauru, Niue, Palau, Papua New Guinea, Solomon Islands, Tonga, Tuvalu, Vanuatu, Western Samoa. Australia and New Zealand are also members of the Forum. Tokelau is not a member, as it is a territory of New Zealand.

4. For a more complete discussion of regional institutions in the South Pacific, see R. Herr and P. Saunders, "The Management of South Pacific Marine Resources: Regional Institutions and Canadian Development Assistance," in L. Kriwoken, M. Haward, D. VanderZwaag and Bruce Davis (eds), *Oceans Law and Policy in the Post-UNCED Era: Australian and Canadian Perspectives* (Kluwer: London, 1996), 259-262.

5. *Ibid.*, 258.

6. See the *Declaration of Law Enforcement Cooperation*, issued by the 23rd Meeting of the South Pacific Forum, Honiara (1992).

7. The South Pacific island countries were quite active on marine issues at the United Nations Conference on Environment and Development (UNCED) in Rio in 1992, but their concerns extended to issues of global warming with a particular emphasis on sea-level rise through the Alliance of Small Island States. For obvious reasons, this issue was of particular interest to very low-lying atoll countries such as Tuvalu and Kiribati.

8. Herr and Saunders, "The Management of South Pacific Marine Resources," note 5.

9. "A major response toward moderating the constraints of microstate status has been the development of a system of inter-governmental organisations"; *Ibid.*, note 4.

10. On this issue, see R. Herr, "South Pacific Microstate Sovereignty In the Post-Cold War Order: The Day After Waterloo?", in D.H. Rubenstein (ed), *Pacific History: Papers from the 8th Pacific History Association Conference 249* (Guam: University of Guam Press, 1992).

11. UN Doc. A/Conf.62/122, Dec. 6, 1982; in force Nov. 16, 1994; reprinted at (1982) 21 *I.L.M.* 1261, Arts. 55-58 [Hereinafter, *1982 LOS Convention*].

12. See W. T. Burke, "The Law of the Sea Convention and Fishing Practices of Non-signatories, With Special reference to the United States", in J. Van Dyke (ed), *Consensus and Confrontation: The United States and the Law of the Sea Convention* (Honolulu: Law of the Sea Institute, 1985), 314-337.

13. *Treaty on Fisheries Between The Governments of Certain Pacific Island States And the United States*, Done at Port Moresby April 2, 1987, in force June 15, 1988 (renegotiated and extended in 1993).

14. *Agreement For The Implementation Of The Provisions Of The United Nations Convention On The Law Of The Sea Of 10 December 1982 Relating To The Conservation And Management Of Straddling Fish Stocks and Highly Migratory Fish Stocks*, A/CONF.164/37, September 8, 1995; adopted August 4, 1995; opened for signature December 4, 1995; not in force.
15. This includes the regional *Convention for the Prohibition of Fishing With Long Driftnets In The South Pacific* (Wellington Convention), Nov. 24, 1989, and the General Assembly *Resolution Large Scale Pealagic Driftnet Fishing and its impact on the living marine resources of the world's oceans and seas*, A/RES/44/225, December 22, 1989.
16. The value (unprocessed) of the DWFN catch in the region in 1987 was estimated at US$ 1.3 billion. In addition, by 1990 access fees to island countries were estimated at US$ 25 million. D. Doulman and P. Terawasi, "The South Pacific Regional Register of Foreign Fishing Vessels", *Marine Policy* July 1990, 325.
17. South Pacific Forum Fisheries Agency Convention, 10 July 1978, In force 9 August 1979.
18. The SPC, for example, remained extremely active in monitoring and database development with respect to tuna stocks. In addition, the Australian Pacific Patrol Boat Programme, though it involved FFA in a coordinating role, proceeded largely on a bilateral basis.
19. The "Regional Research and Development Programme", which was to guide FFA's work through much of the 1980s, was adopted by the member countries in 1981. F. Bugotu, P. Sitan, and T. Tekai, "A Review of the Achievements of the Forum Fisheries Agency In Its First Decade of Operations", in Herr, (ed), *The Forum Fisheries Agency: Achievements, Challenges and Prospects* (Suva: Institute of Pacific Studies, 1990), 5-7.
20. FFA, "Overview of The Forum Fisheries Agency Regional Surveillance Programme and Vessel Monitoring System", Paper presented to *FFA Regional Legal Consultation on Fisheries Surveillance and Law Enforcement* (Rabaul, Papua new Guinea, Oct. 1993), 2. See also FFA, "Fisheries Surveillance" in Herr (ed), *The Forum Fisheries Agency*, 387-395.
21. FFA, "Overview of The Forum Fisheries Agency Regional Surveillance Programme", 2-3.
22. *Ibid.*, p. 3. As of 1993, 721 vessels were included in the Register. See generally Doulman and Terawasi, "The South Pacific Regional Register of Foreign Fishing Vessels".
23. FFA, "Overview of The Forum Fisheries Agency Regional Surveillance Programme", 3.
24. *Ibid.*, 4.
25. *Ibid.*, 7.
26. On this point, the SPOCC commissioned a Review of Regional Institutional Arrangements in the Marine Sector in 1994 to assist in aid coordination and

rationalization of mandates; Herr & Saunders, "The Management of South Pacific Marine Resources", 268-269.

27. The Pacific island countries were also very active at the UN Global Conference on Sustainable Development of Small Island Developing States, Barbados, 25 April-6 May 6, 1994.

28. Article 46 (b) also goes on to define an archipelago, albeit vaguely, as follows:

> For the purposes of this Convention.... "archipelago" means a group of islands, including parts of islands, interconnecting waters and other natural features which are so closely interrelated that such islands, waters and other natural features form an intrinsic geographical, economic and political entity, or which historically have been regarded as such.

29. 1982 LOS Convention, Art. 47.

30. *Ibid.*, Art. 48.

31. With the exception of any areas closed off as internal waters in accordance with the normal rules, in areas such as bays, harbours and river mouths. *Ibid*, Art. 50.

PART III
THE EURO-ATLANTIC

10 Multinational Naval Cooperation in the Middle East and Mediterranean: Problems and Prospects

MILAN VEGO

The Middle East and the Mediterranean have enormous importance for the United States and for the West in general. The Middle East has about 75 per cent of the world's oil reserves; in 1996 it produced about 25 per cent of the world's oil. Some 21 nation states, encompassing 8.5 million square kilometres and populations of more than 400 million, line the shores of the Mediterranean. Almost every riparian state in the Mediterranean is dependent for its economic well-being on maritime trade. However, the region is beset with the problems of economic imbalance, resulting in demographic and migratory pressures toward the northern shore of the Mediterranean Sea. Several countries in the area want to obtain weapons of mass destruction and ballistic missiles.

Since the fall of the Berlin Wall in 1989, new hotbeds of crisis have emerged in the Mediterranean, while the existing crises remain unresolved or only partially settled. The perennial Arab-Israeli conflict is unresolved. The Cyprus crisis goes on, and Greek-Turkish relations are, despite some recent positive developments, beset with problems. A new scene of crisis and war has emerged: the Balkans, and throughout the Transcaucasus, ethnic violence is rampant. The problems of the Mediterranean primarily concern the riparian states. However, all these and other potential trouble spots threaten to spill over into NATO territory in the Mediterranean. Though East-West confrontation seems to be a thing of the past, in the Middle East and Mediterranean area there is a growing possibility of conflict between the richer European countries and the poorer countries along the southern rim.

While this century has been dominated by wars of ideology, the next century might well be a time of wars between civilizations. The Middle East and Mediterranean, together, seems a prime locale for such conflicts. The influence of traditional great powers in the region will probably diminish in the years ahead, while that of smaller and relatively poorer, but more aggressive, regional nation-states will correspondingly increase. The importance of military factors in peacetime competition will probably be reduced, while economic, social, and even religious dimensions will gain in importance.

Figure 10.1 The Middle East and Mediterranean

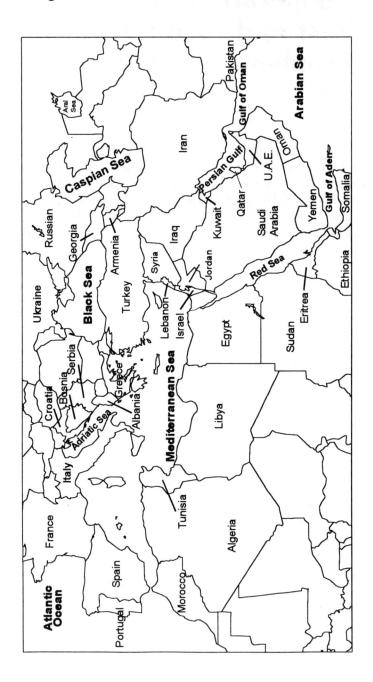

Threats to Regional Security

The security challenges in the Middle East and the Mediterranean vary from ethnic conflicts, terrorism, territorial and border disputes and wars of aggression to such problems as economic underdevelopment, uncontrolled immigration, drug trafficking and proliferation both of weapons of mass destruction and of conventional armaments.

Inter-State Relations

In the Western Mediterranean, the four Maghreb countries (Morocco, Algeria, Tunisia, Libya) represent a strategic link between Northern Africa and Europe. In the recent crises and conflicts in the Mediterranean, the Arabian Gulf and Central Africa these countries played a crucial role in Western military and naval movements. Libya is generally hostile to the West and no change in the policies can be expected unless there is a change of the regime in Tripoli. Further to the East, Egypt occupies a critical position between the Mediterranean and the Red Sea by virtue of its control of the Suez Canal. Egypt is vitally interested in the stability of the Arabian Peninsula and the Horn of Africa.

In the Aegean, Greece occupies a strategic location for the command of shipping lanes in the Eastern Mediterranean. Turkey controls the Turkish Straits and the exit to and from the Black Sea. Russia, like the former USSR, finds it hard to acquiesce to Turkish sovereignty over the Straits. It has never accepted wartime control of the Straits by Turkey and is now seeking to revise the Montreaux Convention of 1936.

The situation in the Eastern Mediterranean is complicated by the still unresolved problem of Cyprus and the problem of the Aegean islands. Cyprus is a key issue in relations between Greece and Turkey. The invasion of Cyprus by the Turkish army in 1974 led to the occupation of a large part of the island which continues to the present day. No solution of that problem is in sight. Turkey and Greece are also involved in a long-standing dispute over the status of restrictions imposed on the islands in the Aegean Sea. This multiple problem deals with status of certain islands, the width of territorial sea and continental shelf, air space and flight information regimes. A solution to all these problems is not in sight.[1]

Turkey is also beset with the seemingly perennial Kurdish problem and the growing influence of the Islamic fundamentalists in the country's political life. The Kurdistan Workers' Party (PKK) wages a vicious guerrilla war against the Turkish government forces focused mostly in the southeastern part of Turkey. Turkey and Syria have an unresolved territorial dispute over the province of Hatay on the Mediterranean coast. Turkey and Iraq have a latent dispute over control of the oil rich province of Mossul which belonged to Turkey until 1929.

Turkey is suspicious of Russia's motives in the Caucasus and Balkans. Both countries want to control exploitation of Azerbeijani oilfields. They have competing pipeline proposals to transport oil from the Caspian Sea area to external markets. The Russians want oil to be transported to their port of Novorossiysk and then by Russian ships to the Mediterranean. Turkey, in contrast, wants to build a pipeline through its territory, thereby bypassing the Russian route. Turkey on its part depends mainly on Russia for its natural gas needs.

There is also growing rivalry between Turkey and Iran in Central Asia; an area that was formerly the exclusive zone of control and influence of the former USSR. Turkey is currently pushing the creation of the Black Sea economic cooperation area as the means of creating an area of regional political stability. Iran actively tries to win the markets and influence in Central Asia and the Caucasus. However, the Kurdish problem tends to bring Iran and Turkey together because both countries are staunchly opposed to the creation of an autonomous Kurdish area that might one day seek to obtain full independence.

Intra-State Conflict

The single greatest crisis that has involved almost all the European countries since 1991 was the conflict in the former Yugoslavia. The US-brokered Dayton Peace Agreement, signed in November, 1995 stopped the conflict at least for now. However, the agreement is deeply flawed, because it does not provide the means to force compliance with some of its key parts. It is almost certain, that after the NATO-led Stabilization Force (SFOR) troops are withdrawn in August 1998 (as currently planned), the entire agreement will start to unravel. Ultimately, Croatia and the Former Republic of Yugoslavia (FRY) will most likely *de facto* annex parts of Bosnia leaving the Bosniaks (Bosnian Muslims) with a steadily shrinking mini-state in their midst. The Bosniaks will be increasingly radicalized and thereby provide additional reason to their opponents to eliminate the Bosniak-dominated part of Bosnia and Herzegovina. Another potential flashpoint in the former Yugoslavia is the Albanian-populated province of Kosovo. The situation there is very tense and can lead to a full-scale conflict between the Serbs and the Albanian native population. Such a conflict is bound to destabilize neighbouring Macedonia where a significant Albanian population lives. The Macedonian question involves all the neighbouring countries plus Turkey. Any attempt by FRY or Greece to carve up Macedonia is almost certain to result in a regional conflict. The current chaotic situation in Albania is another source of the instability in the Balkans. The growing unrest in that country threatens to spread into Kosovo and neighbouring Macedonia. Unless, the United States and its NATO allies step in to stabilize the situation, there is grave danger that some neighbouring countries might exploit the current chaos for their own ends.

A number of states have deep interests in this conflict. Turkey is deeply involved in the Balkan crisis. It is one the strongest supporters of the besieged Bosniaks. Turkey also has growing and close relationship with Albania. It is also deeply interested in the fate of the Turkish minority living in Bulgaria and Macedonia. Albania deeply mistrusts the Serbian policies and resents the treatment of the Albanian population in Kosovo. Greece is generally a strong supporter of the Serbs. It considers the current situation in the Balkans as a threat to its security.

A serious threat to peace and stability in the Middle East and the Mediterranean is steadily-growing violence in the domestic life of many countries in the area. Many of the Islamic parties in several Arab countries have turned to violence as the means to seize power. The Islamic fundamentalists pose the strongest challenge to the governments in Algeria and Egypt. The ultimate aim of the Islamic fundamentalists in Algeria is to unify the entire Maghreb in an Islamic state.[2] Tunisia and Morocco have been successful so far in curbing the appeal of the Islamic extremists, but in the process political freedoms and human rights have been violated. The threat of the Islamic fundamentalists in Egypt remains acute, but apparently less of an immediate threat to the survival of the regime than it was several years ago. They are also a growing threat to the stability of several Arab countries in the Gulf, specifically Saudi Arabia and Bahrain.

The Islamic groups are actively supported by several radical regimes in the area. For example, Sudan provides training facilities for Egyptian and Algerian insurgents, while Iran provides financial and military aid to Hezbollah and Hamas; the two organizations dedicated to obstructing the Arab-Israeli peace process. Syria, although ruled by a secular regime, provides support and protection to a number of the Islamic groups operating in the Bekaa Valley, Lebanon.

Several Middle Eastern and Mediterranean countries, specifically Spain, France, Israel and Turkey are faced with the problem of homegrown terrorism. Most of these groups are directly or indirectly supported by some radical regimes. Syria provides PKK with its headquarters in Damascus, while the Hezbollah and Hamas group in Lebanon and Israel are actively supported by the regimes in Iran, Sudan and Syria.

Population Growth

A growing threat to Mediterranean security is the population explosion in most of the countries along the southern rim. Demographic pressure alone presents a grave challenge to the European countries. The population of Egypt will increase from the current 55 to 100 million within the next 25 years, while the population of the Maghreb countries will grow from 65 to 114 million by the year 2025. The population of the Muslim countries in the Mediterranean is expected to rise from 200 million today to about 365 million in 2025. In contrast to the Muslim countries of the area, France, Italy and Spain all have declining birth rates.[3] These demographic trends are potentially a significant cause of instability not only for the countries concerned but for European security as well.

Regional demographic growth, especially in Turkey and the Maghreb countries will worsen the economic situation and result in emigration pressures to the northern shores. Additionally, major conflict or civil war in North Africa could result in a massive flow of refugees; some estimates cite a figure of 500,000 to 1,000.000, to Europe, primarily to France, Italy and Spain.[4]

Water Resources

A specific feature of the Middle East is the seriousness of disputes on water-sharing or water development plans. Water will be a source of conflict in the 21st century unless a system of rational and balanced management is established between the countries in the area. Several countries will have generous supplies of water for decades to come (Albania, France, Greece, Italy, Lebanon, Turkey and the successor states of the former Yugoslavia). There are also countries in which water supplies will decline, but they probably will be able to balance demand with resources (Algeria, Cyprus, Spain, Morocco). The countries with meagre water resources will be probably involved in a conflict over these resources with the neighbouring countries (Egypt, Israel, Libya, Syria, Tunisia). Currently, the most disputed water system in the world is Euphrates/Tigris shared by Turkey, Iraq and Syria. Dispute over water sharing came into the open in 1990 when Turkey reduced the water supplies, presumably for political reasons, for a month during the Gulf War.[5]

Weapons Proliferation

Proliferation of nuclear, biological, chemical and conventional weapons of all kinds in the Middle East and the Mediterranean is a growing threat to peace and stability in the area. Regimes hostile to the West increasingly see weapons of mass destruction (WMD) as uniquely suited for support of their policies. The proliferation of WMD and modern conventional weapons is facilitated by uncontrolled exports of armaments, illicit dealing with nuclear materials, illegal transfer of armaments and weapons manufacturing, technology and know-how. An excessive arms build-up poses a threat to security, particularly in regions of tension. Also, the introduction of high-technology weaponry in such a volatile region of the world is bound to exacerbate existing tensions.

Israel and several Arab countries have acquired in recent years sophisticated combat aircraft with in-flight refuelling capabilities and stand-off weapons. Egypt, Israel, Syria and Turkey are in the process of modernizing their armies. European navies are also increasingly concerned with proliferation of submarines and missile-armed surface combatants by the North African navies. Land-based aircraft of several potentially hostile countries in the area is also a matter of some concern for Western navies operating in the Mediterranean.

Proliferation of ballistic missile technology and WMD could pose a long-term threat for the European countries bordering the Mediterranean. Several radical Arab countries currently possess or actively seek to obtain ballistic missiles. Israel and Saudi Arabia possess longer range ballistic missiles. But even the shorter range and less sophisticated missiles such as ex-Soviet Scuds can be used as both deterrent and the terror weapons against large urban areas. These missiles can be very effective against an opponent that lacks a retaliatory capacity or is politically restrained, as for example was Israel during the Gulf War of 1991. Libya and Syria possess missiles with sufficient range to hit the targets in the countries of the northern rim.

Iraqi and Iranian arsenals of ballistic missiles also pose a growing threat to countries along the Northern rim of the Mediterranean. Iraq's program to acquire longer-range missiles suffered a setback during the Gulf War of

1991. However, little of the Iraqi WMD infrastructure was destroyed.[6] The UN cease fire terms allows Iraq to develop, test and produce, missiles of ranges up to 150 kilometres. Iraq also has the propellent and missile support equipment that can be used for longer-range missiles. Reportedly, Iraqi agents have successfully acquired critical missile components from abroad in violation of the UN sanctions.[7]

The situation in the Mediterranean is especially acute with regard to the proliferation of WMD. These weapons are perceived by a number of anti-Western regimes in the area as affordable alternatives to conventional weapons. Iran, Iraq and Libya apparently consider them as valuable instruments for pursuing their regional political and military ambitions.[8]

A number of countries in the region possess or have the ambition to acquire nuclear weapons. Israel is an undeclared nuclear power, but is believed to possess large number of nuclear weapons, including a hydrogen bomb. Algeria and more recently Egypt are also believed to have nuclear programs for military purposes. Syria has developed a chemical weapons program with European assistance. Libya is actively trying to acquire both ballistic missiles and chemical weapons, and is possibly pursuing biological and nuclear weapons. The chemical plant built at Rabta is estimated to have at least 100 tons of agents including mustard and nerve gas.[9] According to the recent intelligence reports, Libya is building a chemical plant near Tarhunah, some 40 miles southeast of Tripoli, to be completed within a year's time. It will produce the ingredients for tons of poison gas a day. Libya operates a small nuclear research facility and is alleged to be recruiting Russian scientists to help establish a nuclear weapons program.[10] Clearly, several Arab countries in the Mediterranean might be ultimately successful in obtaining chemical or nuclear warheads for their ballistic missiles. Even the mere existence of nuclear devices could clearly have a decisive impact on a future crisis in the Mediterranean.

In the Arabian Gulf area, Iraq and Iran pose the greatest threat to the stability of the region because of their extensive efforts to acquire WMD. Iraq avoided detection and destruction of critical elements of its WMD infrastructure and the existing stockpiles of chemical and biological weapons and missiles during the Gulf War of 1991. Iran might find the pursuit of nuclear weapons to be an attractive alternative to a higher cost acquisition of large numbers of modern conventional weapons.[11]

Maritime Character and Importance

What will not change is the maritime character of the region, particularly the Mediterranean. The importance of naval forces on the events ashore will remain as strong as it was in the past. The present trend toward using multinational naval forces for a wide range of tasks, ranging from forward presence in peacetime to full hostilities, can be expected to deepen.

What tasks are assigned to multinational naval forces primarily depends on the security threats in a given maritime region. This is particularly true in the Mediterranean region, because of its geographical configuration. The Mediterranean Sea encompasses about 2.9 million square kilometres, and it extends more than 2,300 miles from the Strait of Gibraltar in the west to the coast of Syria and Lebanon in the east. Its average width, however, is only about five hundred miles. No point anywhere in the Mediterranean is farther from shore than some 230 miles. The total length of all the Mediterranean coastlines is about 13,770 miles.

The security of the United States and other Western democracies heavily depends on uninterrupted trade. Thus, anything that threatens the security and stability of the selected regions of the world endangers essential US and Western interests. All the NATO members remain heavily dependent on world seaborne trade, and the Mediterranean is an area important for the economic well-being of Europe. Almost every riparian state in the Mediterranean is dependent for its economic well being on maritime trade. Western Europe dominates intra-regional trade because it is the largest market for raw materials and the principal supplier of manufactured goods. In the late 1980s, about 1,500 ocean-going ships and 5,000 smaller ships plied its waters on any given day.

Roles, Missions and Tasks of Maritime Forces

Because of its predominantly maritime character, the region is well suited to the employment of naval forces across the range of military operations. The down-sizing of armed forces, including the navies, of most of the European countries will make it imperative in a major crisis to pool resources to accomplish the necessary tasks. The passing of the bipolar world in 1991 also made it possible to consider seriously combined employment of NATO and Western European Union (WEU) navies, and the navies of the Partnership for Peace (PFP) countries. Also, the navies of the Arab countries in the Middle

East and the Mediterranean might conceivably be employed jointly with European navies in conflict prevention and peace operations.

Maritime forces are politically attractive, because they offer an extensive range of options to policymakers. They are inherently highly mobile and suited for carrying out a wide variety of tasks. Maritime forces offer considerable deterrent, attack and retaliatory capabilities. They possess organic logistics, and their command and control is highly flexible. They can be deployed first as a symbol of resolve, then to secure and maintain control of the sea and finally, if necessary, to intervene on land.

Maritime forces can operate jointly at short notice for certain simple contingencies, such as forward presence, humanitarian assistance or disaster relief and search and rescue. Cooperation between surface ships, submarines, amphibious forces and naval aircraft has occurred extensively among the European navies over the past fifty years; for example, Great Britain's Royal Marines exercise regularly in Portugal. Exercises with a large amphibious component are conducted every year by France, Spain and Italy. France and Germany also conducted a series of bilateral naval exercises, alternating annually between the Mediterranean and the Baltic.

The scope and intensity of the Western navies' activities in the 1990s have been very impressive. Multinational naval activity in the 1980s included mine clearance in the Red Sea, naval presence and defense of neutral shipping in the Persian Gulf during the Iran-Iraq war and in the recent Gulf war, the Aden rescue, the Beirut operation and the efforts in the Adriatic.

General Missions and Tasks

The diversity of possible threats presents both opportunities and liabilities for the employment of multinational naval forces in the Mediterranean and Middle East regions. On one hand, not every problem can be successfully addressed by multinational naval forces. This is especially true of strikes or raids, where swiftness of action and overwhelming force is the key ingredient of success (some non-combatant evacuation operations are also of the same nature). Multinational naval forces are better suited to crisis prevention and peace operations and also for such less complicated tasks as humanitarian assistance, disaster relief, and search and rescue. In general, they can be employed for the following tasks:

- Humanitarian Assistance
- Disaster Relief

- Search and Rescue
- Counter-terrorism
- Conflict Prevention
- Protection of Shipping
- Freedom of Navigation and Overflight
- Non-combatant Evacuation

Humanitarian Assistance encompasses actions aimed at assisting or safeguarding the delivery of food and medical supplies, and at protecting civilian populations. Sometimes humanitarian assistance is combined with peace enforcement or peacekeeping; the UN Protection Force (UNPROFOR) in Bosnia was involved in such tasks. Humanitarian action may involve a wide range of missions designed to produce an environment that allows humanitarian efforts to proceed. These actions can be conducted by individual countries, one country in concert with others, or under United Nations auspices.

Disaster relief takes in measures carried out prior to, during, or after hostilities or disasters, whether natural (floods, earthquakes, etc.) or man-made (fires, explosions, etc.). Disaster relief attempts to reduce the probability of damage, minimize its effect, and start recovery. This is a task well suited to multinational naval forces.

Counter-Terrorist Actions. Multinational naval forces can also be employed against a terrorist group or a country harbouring terrorists or supporting terrorist actions against its neighbours or another state in the area. Counter-terrorism in general encompasses pre-emptive and retaliatory strikes, and rescue operations.

Conflict prevention includes diverse military activities conducted under Chapter VI of the UN Charter. They range from diplomatic initiatives to preventive deployment of multinational forces, and they aim at preventing the escalation of disputes into armed conflict or at facilitating resolution of armed violence. Ideally, these actions should be conducted with strict impartiality, and normally all sides in a dispute agree to involve other countries as mediators. Multinational naval forces can be deployed in the proximity of the coast of a Mediterranean country where hostilities threaten to break out. However, deployment of naval forces, especially aircraft carriers and amphibious forces, has more chance for success in a dispute between nation-states than in ethnic conflict or civil war. Also, to be effective, such an action must be accompanied by a clear willingness on the part of international community to use overwhelming force if necessary. Otherwise, preventive deployment of multinational naval forces alone, regardless of their size and capability, will rarely result in the desired effect.

The Protection of Shipping encompasses a variety of tasks designed to protect merchant vessels from unlawful attack in international waters, to which multinational naval forces can be assigned. This broad task is accomplished through, among other things, escort of merchant ships (sometimes of individual ships, for a specific purpose), coastal sea control, harbour defence and mine countermeasures (MCM). MCM is an essential element of escort operations, as in Operation *Earnest Will* in the Arabian Gulf in 1987-1988. Radical states in the area, especially if situated close to maritime trade chokepoints, might conceivably attempt to harass Western or neutral shipping, requiring the response of multinational naval forces. Protection of shipping requires coordinated employment of surface, air and sub-surface forces, as well as a suitable command and control structure both ashore and afloat. Protection of shipping is not limited to deterrent or defensive actions but may include pre-emptive or retaliatory strikes or raids against selected targets at sea or ashore.

Freedom of navigation and overflight operations are meant to assert rights to navigate sea or air routes. Normally, a riparian state may exercise jurisdiction and control within its territorial sea; international law, however, establishes the right of "innocent passage" by ships of other nations through a state's territorial waters. Passage is considered "innocent" as long as it is not prejudicial to the peace, good order, or security of the coastal nation. Freedom of navigation by aircraft through international airspace is a well established principle of international law. Threats to aircraft through the extension, by nations or groups, of airspace control zones beyond the international norms may result in counter-measures, acceptable under international law, to rectify the situation.[12]

Evacuation of non-combatants (or NEO, in US terms) can also be conducted by multinational naval forces. These operations are aimed at bringing civilians to safety out of a country in which there is an acute danger of serious violence or hostage-taking. It also involves selected individuals from the host-nation as well as citizens of countries other than that (or those) carrying out the evacuation. The timing and method of these operations are significantly affected by diplomatic considerations, and they may take place in either a permissive or non-permissive environment. Swift insertion of force is followed by temporary occupation of a small piece of territory and then a planned withdrawal. Forces assigned for this task should be carefully selected and limited in size.

Peace Operations

Multinational naval forces will be probably most extensively used in various peace operations: military operations meant to support diplomatic efforts to reach a long-term political settlement. These actions are conducted in conjunction with diplomacy as necessary to negotiate a truce and resolve a conflict. Peace operations are tailored to each situation and may be initiated in support of diplomatic activities either before, during, or after the conflict.[13]

Categories of Peace Operations

Peacekeeping operations (PKO) are intended to contain, moderate, or terminate hostilities between or within states, using international or impartial military forces and civilians to complement political conflict-resolution efforts and to restore and maintain peace. These actions take place after the sides in a conflict agree to cease hostilities; the impartial observers are normally sent to verify implementation of the cease-fire or monitor the separation of forces. A NATO contribution to peacekeeping operations can take a variety of forms: provision of non-material support (e.g., information, expertise, techniques, education and training, coordination, etc.) or of material resources (alliance infrastructure, transportation, telecommunications, logistics); and formal military participation (e.g., the Standing Naval Forces Atlantic or Mediterranean, Rapid Reaction Forces, the NATO Airborne Early Warning assets, or forces from individual NATO countries).[14]

Peace-enforcement operations (PEO) by multinational naval forces involve diverse tasks as authorized by Chapter VII of the UN Charter. The objective here is to compel compliance with resolutions or sanctions that have been adopted to maintain or restore peace or order. Specifically, the tasks of peace enforcement include implementation of sanctions, establishment and supervision of exclusion zones, intervention to restore order, and forcible separation of belligerents. The aim is to establish an environment for a truce or cease-fire. In contrast to peacekeeping, peace-enforcement operations do not require the consent of the sides or warring factions in a conflict.[15] Maritime forces, when used for peace enforcement, must possess at least limited power projection capabilities and be ready to engage in combat if necessary.

Exclusion zones, in the air, at sea, or on land, are often required in peacekeeping operations.[16] The aim would be to persuade a nation or group to change its behaviour so as to meet the desires of the sanctioning body, rather than face continued sanctions or the use of force. The sanctions are meant to create certain economic, political, military, or other conditions to that end. An exclusion zone is usually imposed by the UN or some other international body, but it may be applied even by individual countries.

Maritime intercept operations (MIO) for sanction enforcement often employ multinational naval forces, as was the case in the *Desert Shield/Desert Storm* operation in 1990-91. These actions normally use coercive measures to interdict the movement of designated items into or out of a nation or a specific sea or ocean area. The political objective is to compel a country or group of countries to conform to the objectives of the initiating body. The military aim is to establish a barrier that is selective, i.e., allows only those goods to pass that are authorized to enter or exit. Enforcement of sanctions normally requires action by some combination of surface and air forces.[17]

Expanded peacekeeping and peace enforcement operations are larger in size than peacekeeping, involving perhaps twenty thousand men or more, and may involve multinational naval forces. The consent of the sides in conflict is usually nominal, incomplete, or simply does not exist. These operations include more assertive mandates and ROE, including the use of force under Chapter VIII of UN Charter.[18]

Expanded PKO and PEO are conducted with strictly limited objectives, such as the protection of safe-flight or no-fly zones, or of relief deliveries. If too intrusive, they are highly likely to draw multinational forces into open hostilities; the multinational forces would then either have to be pulled out or be committed to full-scale combat.[19]

The Case of Bosnia and the Adriatic

The involvement of NATO or WEU forces in support of UN forces in Bosnia was a mix of both peacekeeping and peace-enforcement, and subsequently expanded PKO/PEO by NATO to implement the Dayton Agreement. NATO and WEU representatives agreed at a meeting in Helsinki on 10 July 1992 to initiate naval actions to enforce UN Security Council Resolutions (UNSCRs) 713 and 757. These resolutions directed the establishment of a naval blockade to monitor the arms embargo against all the republics of the former Yugoslavia and to ensure the arrival of humanitarian aid to Sarajevo.[20] This required the conduct of MIO. The activities of NATO ships in the Adriatic were referred to as Operation *Maritime Guard*, and those controlled by the WEU were Operation *Sharp Fence*. Italy was entrusted with the task of coordinating the activities of WEU and NATO forces.[21]

The WEU force operated south of a line between Bari, in Italy, and Bar, in Montenegro, while STANAVFORMED (formally established on 30 April 1992) operated north of it. Each force received intelligence and surveillance data from maritime patrol aircraft. In late August 1992 the NATO Headquarters in Brussels sent STANAVFORLANT to relieve STANAVFORMED in monitoring duties in the Adriatic.[22] In late November of that year, both operations *Maritime Monitor* and *Sharp Vigilance* were extended to include the enforcement of UN resolutions and were incorporated into *Maritime Guard* and *Sharp Fence*, respectively.

On 8 June 1993 both NATO and the WEU adopted a combined concept of operations for the implementation of UNSCR 820. This agreement established a unified command, under the name Operation *Sharp Guard*. Cooperation was ensured via a joint *ad hoc* headquarters, known as "MilCom Adriatic". Four days later, the allied commander of Southern European Naval Forces (COMNAVSOUTH) took over operational control of *Sharp Guard*;[23] his staff was complemented by a WEU element. Hence, de facto, the WEU became subordinate to COMNAVSOUTH for decision making and planning.

As part of peacekeeping operations, NATO navies took part in the enforcement of the "no-fly zone" over Bosnia ordered by the UN Security Council. This operation, *Deny Flight*, started on 12 April 1993 and ended on 20 December 1995. The Supreme Allied Commander Europe (SACEUR) delegated authority to execute Operation *Deny Flight* to the Commander in Chief Southern Europe (CINCSOUTH), who in turn assigned the operation to the Commander, Allied Air Forces Southern Europe (COMAIRSOUTH), with headquarters in Naples. Tactical, day-to-day control of all flights was exercised by the Fifth Allied Tactical Air Force, in Vicenza, Italy. About 4,500 personnel from twelve NATO countries took part in this operation. They operated from fourteen air bases in Italy, France and Germany. Also, a US aircraft carrier was deployed in the Adriatic and took part in the operation, and sometimes a French or British one as well.

NATO forces, including maritime elements were heavily involved in expanded PKO/PEO in Bosnia starting in December 1995. Then, SACEUR tasked CINCSOUTH to assume control of NATO land, air and maritime forces, as the commander of the "Implementation Forces" (IFOR) stipulated under the terms of the Dayton Agreement. Transfer of authority from the commander of UNPROFOR to the commander of the Implementation Force (IFOR) took place on 20 December 1995. The IFOR was under the NATO operational chain of command, and operated under clear NATO rules of engagement. This NATO-led operation, *Joint Endeavour*, is NATO's first-ever "out-of-area" employment and its first-ever joint operation with Partnership For Peace (PfP) and other non-NATO countries. The mandate of that force officially ended in December 1996.

Political Authorization and Planning

The employment of multinational naval forces in the Mediterranean will be normally authorized by a regional security organization, specifically NATO, the WEU, or the UN. Also, the Organization for Security and Cooperation in Europe (OSCE, formerly the Council for Security and Cooperation in Europe, CSCE) can authorize their employment for crisis-prevention or peace operations. In crisis prevention and management, NATO can provide alliance assets to a UN or OSCE peacekeeping operation. The North Atlantic Council agreed in December 1992 that peacekeeping should be carried out under the authority of the UN or OSCE, at the request of one or the other. NATO also can conduct and coordinate a peacekeeping operation on behalf of either organization or in support of individual allies carrying out a peacekeeping operation.[24]

Cooperation between WEU and NATO is becoming increasingly important in cases where the two treaties follow different objectives and directions. An example of this is peacekeeping and crisis management. Article VIII of the modified Brussels Treaty obliges all WEU member states, at the request of any of them, to consult "in regard to any situation which may constitute a threat to peace, in whatever area this threat should arise, or a danger to economic stability". This statement was used as the legal basis for WEU's involvement in the Gulf War of 1991 and for the St. Petersburg decisions to make military units answerable to the WEU for peacekeeping, crisis-management and peace-making tasks in accordance with the provisions of the UN Charter. The Washington Treaty, in contrast, did not provide NATO with a similar legal basis. However, in 1991 NATO also agreed to extend its activities to peacekeeping and crisis management. The enlarged interpretation of Article IV of the Washington Treaty says that "the parties will consult together, whenever, in the opinion of any of them the territorial integrity, political independence or security of any of the parties is threatened." This in effect means that the term "out-of-area operations" is no longer valid.

Because both NATO and the WEU have responsibilities in peace operations and crisis-management, the division of tasks in practice can be a problem. The WEU will progressively develop capabilities for peacekeeping and more robust crisis management, drawing on the "Forces Answerable to the WEU" (FAWEUs).[25] Closer cooperation, complementary to the alliance, specifically in the fields of logistics, transport, training and strategic surveillance, is required.

The NATO alliance has a fully developed structure for planning the employment of multinational naval forces in crisis-prevention and peace operations. The WEU, in contrast, did not start to develop joint planning procedures until October 1992, when a "Planning Cell" was created in Brussels. Among other things, this cell became responsible for preparing contingency plans for the employment of forces under WEU auspices, for making recommendations for command and control and communications, for standing operating procedures at headquarters that might be selected, and maintaining an updated list of units and force packages that might be allocated to the WEU for specific operations. The planning cell was tasked in 1994 with joint task force planning, command and control for naval operations (including naval intelligence gathering), logistics (including transport by sea), and coherent naval exercises policy and programs. The planning cell also deals with WEU Operation Plan *Combined Endeavour*, approved by the Ministerial Council in May 1994 on the initiative of France, Italy and Spain.[26]

Multinational Maritime Force Organizational Options

NATO's current strategy requires its naval forces to maintain adequate presence throughout the NATO area of operations in order to safeguard the freedom of the seas and promote stability by demonstrating alliance solidarity and preparedness. A new naval force structure was developed to meet these demands and provide a graduated response to any developing crisis.[27] The new structure includes rapid reaction forces, composed of two regionally based, multinational, standing naval forces: one deployed in the Atlantic (STANAVFORLANT) and one in the Mediterranean (STANAVFORMED). In peacetime, each of these forces provides routine forward presence and surveillance, becoming an immediate reaction force during the early phase of a crisis. A naval rapid reaction force must be of such size as to be able to deal with a crisis that exceeds the capability of the immediate reaction force.[28]

WEU and the European Maritime Force

Normally, a multinational naval force will be organized either as a standing or an ad hoc (provisional) task force. The WEU started to develop this type of organization in 1990, on the recommendation of its Assembly to consider the establishment of a naval on-call force, together with a possible pooling of appropriate national air-mobile assets into a European rapid action force. The St. Petersburg Declaration stipulated that the objective of the *Combined Endeavour* plan was to evaluate predominantly maritime FAWEUs to be employed in response to any mission assigned by the Council. In September 1992, Spain, France and Italy proposed the establishment of aero-maritime forces to ensure more efficient employment of aero-maritime forces of the three navies. With only two fixed-wing carriers and two short-takeoff-and-landing decks (one each for the Spanish and Italian navies), it was necessary to stagger their longer maintenance periods to optimize their availability.

In May 1995 the WEU decided to create, beside the ten thousand-man combined army corps (EUROFOR), a provisional naval task force called the European Maritime Force (EURMARFOR), to be employed primarily in the Mediterranean.[29] Naval units of France, Italy, Portugal and Spain were to be part of EURMARFOR; the United Kingdom also expressed interest. Both EUROFOR and EURMARFOR will be tasked to conduct humanitarian assistance, search and rescue, peacekeeping and crisis management, including peace-making. The new WEU forces are to be employed under either WEU or NATO command.

EUROMARFOR will be a non-permanent, multinational, maritime task force, capable of acting on its own or together with EUROFOR. Its composition and organization will depend on the mission to be accomplished. A typical composition might be an aircraft carrier with four to six escorts, a landing force and a supply ship. Command of EURMARFOR will rotate among senior officers on the scene. This force was originally planned to be fully established by the fall of 1995.

NATO's Combined Joint Task Force

Another initiative currently under development is the concept of the Combined Joint Task Force (CJTF), adopted at the NATO Summit in January 1994. At the same meeting, NATO leaders gave full support to the development of a European Security and Defence Identity (ESDI). NATO has also agreed to make its collective assets available, on the basis of consultation in the North Atlantic Council, for WEU operations undertaken by the European allies under the rubric of a Common Foreign and Security Policy. The CJTF concept envisages "separable" but not "separate" military capabilities that could be employed by NATO or the WEU, even in situations affecting European security in which NATO itself is not involved. This provision is meant to avoid waste and expensive duplication of efforts and assets in responding to security threats both inside and outside the scope of NATO collective defense.

The CJTF concept will provide a credible operational role for the WEU and NATO; it will be also a test case for NATO-WEU relations.[30] The Combined Joint Task Force will provide NATO for the first time with deployable and mobile commands trained to respond to a range of contingencies. It will also allow NATO assets to be used by WEU in cases where NATO itself decides not to act.[31] The initiative is based on the NATO Strategic Concept for more flexible and mobile forces. The CJTF is expected to facilitate cooperation with non-NATO members, such as the Partnership for Peace countries. It will also allow the use of NATO infrastructure and forces to support the evolution of a European Security and Defence Identity.[32]

The CJTF will be capable of rapid deployment for crisis management or peace operations of limited duration under the control of either the NATO military structure or the WEU.[33] Command and control of the CJTF will allow timely response, ensure smooth coordination between NATO and WEU, and accommodate staff liaison from participating non-NATO members. These operations will require a high integration of intelligence, communications, combat employment and logistical support and sustainment. The WEU or a coalition of European countries will be able to draw on the support of NATO infrastructure and NATO officers. In conducting peace operations, non-NATO and non-WEU countries will be allowed to assign their officers to NATO commands; their task will be to facilitate joint operations by conducting regular staff exercises. The United States will provide space reconnaissance and logistics to such forces.[34] The United States, in addition, insists on having staff officers at the headquarters even if American forces are not taking part in a given military action.

Once activated, the CJTF could be deployed in a variety of configurations and operate either under Article V contingencies (defense of NATO territory) or in others, such as crisis management, peacekeeping and peace enforcement, or humanitarian assistance. WEU can use the CJTF for humanitarian and rescue tasks, peacekeeping and the tasks of combat forces in crisis management, including peace-making, as outlined in the St. Petersburg Declaration. In any configuration NATO insists that the CJTF line of command always lead to a major NATO command.

As noted, the CJTF concept was initially to be completed by the end of 1995. However, progress has not been as fast as had been expected. The main unresolved questions center on three areas: CJTF planning for non-Article V operations; interface and guidance from the political authority to the CJTF commander; and the source of the CJTF nucleus. A Capabilities Planning Cell directly subordinate to the Military Committee is planned. Its main responsibility will be to maintain a data bank of nuclei and other contributions proposed by the NATO commands and member states. It will also make recommendations to the Military Committee as to the nucleus of the staff for the CJTF in a given operation.

Another unresolved issue is the question of political control. The French argue that in a WEU-led mission, NATO officers should be subordinate to a WEU command. France is also reportedly unhappy that there will be US element (SACEUR) in the command chain in cases where the United States is not an active participant. NATO foreign ministers are expected to approve the operational plans for the CJTF at their next planned meeting in Berlin in June 1996.[35]

However, the thorniest issue remains to be resolved, i.e., command and political control of operations outside the NATO area. Systematic cooperation between NATO and the WEU in assembling and deploying CJTFs will be crucial in preserving the trans-atlantic nature of the alliance.

Conclusions

The Middle East and the Mediterranean region will undergo significant political, economic and military changes in the next decade. Traditional security threats will steadily emerge. The gap between the richer North and poorer South will widen. Besides the great European powers, a number of smaller powers possessing WMD and ballistic missiles will arise. Several countries bordering the eastern Mediterranean will probably be involved in conflict over the sharing of ever-scarcer water resources.

By the turn of the next century, the Arab-Israeli conflict will be partially resolved, though the Arabs' acceptance of Israel will be incomplete. Russia will re-establish some part of its previous influence in the area. The Cyprus problem will remain contentious, as will be the Greek-Turkish dispute in the Aegean. Turkey, Iran and Russia will most likely be involved in intensified struggle for influence in the Trans-caucasus and Central Asia. The Balkans will continue to be an area of crisis. A new and bloody conflict will probably erupt over Kosovo or Macedonia, and that might involve a number of the countries in the region, even some great European powers. Several large countries in the Middle East and Mediterranean region will most likely be ruled by Islamic fundamentalists or other anti-Western extremists. Hence, there is likely to be a much higher level of hostility toward the West, and the United States in particular, than is the case today.

The lessons of the 1991 Gulf War and the conflict in the Balkans showed clearly both the advantages and disadvantages of multinational naval cooperation. The conflict in the former Yugoslavia revealed that the United Nations is unable to handle by itself the ever-increasing demands of crisis and conflict resolution. Without NATO's involvement and support, the UN could not have enforced the Adriatic embargo or the no-fly zone over Bosnia; UNPROFOR personnel would not have had the protection of NATO air power in carrying out humanitarian and other peacekeeping tasks in Bosnia.

The involvement of the UN and the European Community (European Union today) in that conflict was a dismal failure. Even the humanitarian-assistance side of its performance is open to criticism: it did nothing to moderate Serbian behavior. There is little excuse, if any, for the blunders committed by many members of EC/EU in trying to resolve the crisis. This failure was primarily due to an abysmal lack of leadership and political will. The Dayton Agreement is a flawed treaty, but it is certainly much better than anything that was tried before; without firm commitment, however, on the part of the United States and its NATO allies to enforce strict compliance by all the parties, this promising start is bound to fail. After NATO forces leave the country in August 1998 (as current plans envisage)—conflict in Bosnia will most likely be resumed.

In the Mediterranean, NATO forces must be able first to deter and then react across a broad spectrum of contingency and crisis. Deterrence, to be successful, must be based upon sufficient force, deployed well forward in the potential conflict area to act until the main US forces can arrive. Down-sizing of the US Navy means increased relative importance for a European quick-reaction force. Both the United States and its European allies should display their capabilities from time to time to achieve the necessary deterrent effect on potential aggressors.

NATO and the WEU should field rapidly deployable forces capable of deterring the outbreak of conflicts than might seriously affect the security of the region. If deterrence fails, these forces should be capable of conducting the full range of peace operations and peace-building (or post-hostilities) operations. It is unrealistic, however, to expect such forces to be effective in full-scale hostilities between two or more countries in the region; NATO's main forces are much better suited for such tasks.

NATO and the WEU should never again operate without a clear objective or under so-called "dual key" command and control. Also, for them to act as a "sub-contractor" to the UN or the OSCE is not a viable option. The UN and the OSCE can do many good things, but crisis prevention and peace operations are not among them, as the examples from Africa to the Middle East and Southeast Asia clearly show. Any failure on the part of UN also undermines the credibility of NATO alliance and, by implication, that of its members. The tasks related to crisis prevention and peace operations should be handled by regional security organizations that have a permanent military structure in place, as NATO does.

The CJTF concept seems to have many advantages, but it also has serious flaws. The idea of a WEU-led force made sense at a time when the NATO alliance was restricted from out-of-area operations; this is not the case now. The CJTF should be an entirely NATO-led force, or unnecessary duplication of effort and waste of assets will surely follow. The provision that the CJTF might be led by either NATO or WEU, on a case basis, does not look like a very good solution to the problem. In either instance, NATO assets must be used; the WEU cannot employ the CJTF without NATO's full support. Also, the United States is a part of NATO, and it is not readily apparent what situations affecting the WEU and other members of NATO would not also require US involvement. If one were in fact to arise, the leading American role in the alliance and its commitment to defend its European allies would be seriously undermined. In that case, the day would not be far off when the United States would disengage from Europe.

Participation in the CJTF of naval units from the PfP countries does not seem very practical for the Mediterranean. The normal operating area of the Ukrainian, Bulgarian and the Rumanian navies is the Black Sea. They might possibly take part in a contingency in that area, but the employment of the CJTF in the Black Sea would probably be strongly objected to by Russia, and perhaps even Ukraine as well. Even if the employment of the CJTF there were politically acceptable to Russia, there would still be serious problems to be resolved in regard to common techniques and procedures, communications, logistics and interoperability of equipment. The navies of some Arab countries in the Mediterranean, specifically the Egyptian Navy or possibly the Tunisian and the Moroccan Navy could possible participate as part of the CJTF in some peace operations conducted off the North African shore or in Eastern Mediterranean. However, there are serious problems in interoperability to be resolved before such employment becomes a practical reality.

The EURMARFOR is another multinational naval force that can be employed for crisis prevention, peace operations and humanitarian assistance or disaster relief in the Middle East and the Mediterranean. However, both EUROFOR and EURMARFOR must have clear and unambiguous direction from the political leadership of WEU. The WEU's performance in the former Yugoslavia offers small hope for that in the near term.

As long as the EU lacks a common and coherent foreign and security policy, it is unrealistic to expect the WEU to carry out its tasks successfully. The WEU has still to prove that it is the appropriate organization for strengthening the European pillar of the Atlantic Alliance. Neither EUROFOR, EURMARFOR, or a WEU-led CJTF can be successful in the absence of common foreign and security policies on the part of the European Union. Also, if NATO is to be established as a principal actor in peacekeeping without provision for the participation of US ground troops, the whole CJTF concept might be jeopardized.

The most serious error, however, would be to replace NATO entirely by the WEU with respect to military functions. The United States must and should stay in Europe, not because of the Europeans, but in defense of its own national interests. Consequently, the US Navy (and the Canadian navy as well) should remain firmly linked to Europe, by taking part in any NATO Standing Force deployed in both the Atlantic and the Mediterranean.

Notes

1. Jed C. Snyder, "Turkey's Role in the Greater Middle East", *Joint Force Quarterly* Autumn 1995, 61.
2. Gregor M. Manousakis, "Die Islamisten und der Maghreb", *Europaeische Sicherheit* 1, January 1996, 50.

3. Johnson, *NATO's New Front Line: The Growing Importance of the Southern Tier*, 8; "Die Europaeer fuerchten die Zuwanderung aus Nordafrika", *Frankfurter Allgemeine Zeitung* 27 April 1993, 8; Adriano Sarto, Captain, It. Navy, "Italy's Navy Ready in the Med", *Proceedings* March 1993, 58; Laipson, "Thinking about the Mediterranean," 52.

4. Institute for National Strategic Studies, National Defense University, *Strategic Assessment 1995: U.S. Security Challenges in Transition* (Washington D.C.: Government Printing Office, 1996), 40.

5. "Konfliktstoff Wasser", *Europaeische Sicherheit* 1, January 1996, 8.

6. *Strategic Assessment 1995: U.S. Security Challenges in Transition*, 68.

7. Robert G. Joseph, "Regional Implications of NBC Proliferation", *Joint Force Quarterly* Autumn 1995, 67.

8. *Strategic Assessment 1995: U.S. Security Challenges in Transition*, 68.

9. Jed C. Snyder, "Proliferation Threats to Security in NATO's Southern Region", *The Mediterranean Quarterly* 2:4, 1993, 116; "Impenetrable Libyan CW plant progresses .. and Iran poses threat with missile boats", *Jane's Defence Weekly* 17 April 1996, 3.

10. "Perry, in Egypt, Warns Libya to Halt Chemical Weapons Plant", *The New York Times* 4 April 1996, A6. *Jane's Defence Weekly* 17 April 1996, 3; Robert G. Joseph, "Regional Implications of NBC Proliferation", *Joint Force Quarterly* Autumn 1995, 67.

11. *Ibid.*, 67; Institute for National Strategic Studies, Fort Lesley J. McNair, Washington D.C. *Strategic Assessment 1995: U.S. Security Challenges in Transition*, (Washington D.C.: Government Printing Office, 1995), 69.

12. *Joint Pub 3-07, Joint Doctrine for Military Operations Other Than War*, 16 June 1995, III-4.

13. *Ibid.*, III-12.

14. John Kriendler, "NATO's Changing Role: Opportunities and Constraints for Peacekeeping", *NATO Review* 3, June 1993, 16-21.

15. *Joint Pub 3-07*, III-13.

16. *Ibid.*, III-4.

17. *Ibid.*, III-3 and III-4.

18. Hans Binnendejk, ed., *Strategic Assessment 1996*, (Washington, D.C.: National Defense University, Institute For National Strategic Studies, 1996), 135.

19. *Joint Pub 3-07*, 138.

20. "Kohl on WEU Naval Operation", *Daily Report East Europe* (FBIS-EEUR), 13 July 1992, 4.

21. "Further on Arrangements", *Daily Report East Europe* (FBIS-EEUR), 13 July 1992, 2-3; "French Vessel Joins Operation", *Daily Report East Europe* (FBIS-EEUR-92-135), 14 July 1992, 2; "Stapske vjezbe ili blokada obale" [Staff's Exercises of Blockade of the Coast], *Novi Vjesnik* (Zagreb), 15 July 1992, 25A; "WEU Chief on NATO Coordination", *Daily Report East Europe* FBIS-EEUR,

14 July 1992, 2-3; "WEU Head on Ships' Duties", *Daily Report* (FBIS-EEUR-92-135), 14 July 1992, 2; and Michael Chichester, "Maastricht, the Adriatic and the Future of European Defence", *Navy International* November-December 1992, 361.

22. Michael, Chichester, "Maastricht. The Adriatic and The Future of European Defence", 362.

23. "Die Uneinigkeit der NATO belasted das Treffen der Aussenminister in Athen", *Frankfurter Allgemeine Zeitung*, 9 June 1993, 4; "USS Kauffman sails in Adriatic Operation", *Newport Navalog* 9 July 1993, 4; and "NATO, WEU Combine Navies in Blockade against Ex-FRY", *Daily Report West Europe* (FBIS-WEU-93-109), 9 June 1993, 1.

24. Kriendler, "NATO's Changing Role", 16-21.

25. Hans van Mierlo, "The WEU and NATO: Prospects for a More Balanced Relationship", *NATO Review* 2, March 1995, 7-10.

26. J. Poesze, E. Vad, and H.-B. Weisserth, "Aus dem Schlaf erwacht", *Truppenpraxis/Wehrausbildung* 5, May 1995, 295.

27. Peter Abbott, Rear Admiral, "A Rationale for Maritime Forces in the New Strategic Environment", *R.U.S.I. Journal* April 1993, 36.

28. Leon Edney, Admiral, "The Maritime Foundation of the NATO Alliance", in Bruce George, ed., *Jane's NATO Handbook 1991-92*, 97.

29. "Jetzt auch Europforce und Europmarforce", *FAZ*, 16 May 1995, 11.

30. Van Mierlo, "The WEU and NATO", 7-10.

31. Willy Claes, "NATO and the Evolving Euro-Atlantic Security Architecture", *NATO Review* 1, January 1995, 3-7.

32. *Strategic Assessment 1995: U.S. Security Challenges in Transition*, 46.

33. *Ibid.*, 46.

34. "Ganz normal", *Der Spiegel* 17, 22 April 1996, 56.

35. "Burying the General", *The Economist* 20 April 1996, 39.

11 Security in Northern Waters: A New Nordic Balance?

JAN S. BREEMER

This chapter considers the implications of the end of the Cold War for maritime security in northern European waters. It sets forth as a general proposition that the demise of the Soviet menace and the absence for the foreseeable future of a major military challenge to the security of the northeast Atlantic Ocean and Baltic Sea will compel Nordic security planners to re-examine the political uses and usefulness of military and maritime power.

The Revolution at Sea

In sharp contrast with a decade ago, then the heyday of the American navy's "Maritime Strategy", there is a sense in some quarters that navies, or at least "proper" navies, may become an endangered species. For example, a few years ago, *The Economist* published a lengthy feature article on the future of military forces after the Cold War. For a variety of reasons, it said, navies would probably be the "losers" in the competition for declining defence budgets. For one, the article explained, the demise of the Soviet naval menace meant that the fleets of the NATO partners in particular had lost their primary *raison d'etre*. For another, it went on, the recently concluded war in the Gulf portended the emergence of "peacekeeping" operations in the name of UN collective security as the wave of the future for military operations. War with the UN's "seal of approval" and without the overhanging threat of a crisis between the two superpowers, the article said, meant that nations would be far less reluctant to choose sides and offer a peacekeeping coalition much needed land-based facilities, thus obviating the need for aircraft carriers in particular. Ken Booth, a long-time respected commentator on maritime security, has similarly noted that navies "do not have a great future", at least not as envisaged by Alfred Thayer Mahan and his navalist confrères one century ago. Citing broad systemic changes in international relations (e.g., a trend towards interdependence and security *with* instead of *against* others), he has proposed that navies will become more like coastguards, and some coastguards more like minor navies.[1]

Figure 11.1 North European Waters

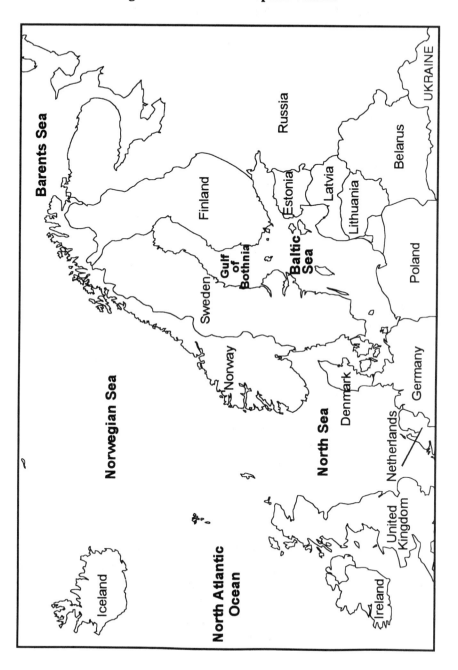

Rapid technological change has been claimed as another reason why navies as traditionally understood may become a thing of the past. For the past 500 years or so, navies, that is to say "fleets", were created primarily for what British Admiral Philip Colomb called one hundred years ago "true naval war".[2] The latter, he said, was about the competition for "command of the sea", or if you prefer, "sea control". As long as navies were the only fighting machines capable of contesting the ability to use the seas, their "independence" was guaranteed. By the same token, of course, as long as navies could not, in the words of Winston Churchill in 1911, threaten a "single continental hamlet", armies were assured of a monopoly over "land control".[3]

Since those words were spoken, the old natural divide between land and sea warfare became progressively blurred, first as the result of the invention of the aircraft, and later the long-range missile. As a consequence, today's land-based forces can compete for sea control at "blue water" distances, and sea-based forces can devastate continental cities thousands of miles inland. This is not a new phenomenon *per se*—"strategic" bombardment across the old land-sea divide has been possible since the Second World War. What *is* new is that the end of the Cold War has created an oceanic security regime—certainly so as far as the NATO area is concerned—that will compel ocean-going navies in particular to re-tool and invest in *land-oriented* missions and technologies. Ocean-going navies are singled out for the simple reason that so-called "coastal navies" are for all intents and purposes already in the business of "land control", albeit "land denial".

It takes little effort to discover that the revolution from-the-sea is well underway already. It is implied in the US Navy's "...From the Sea" concept, the British navy's new emphasis on land attack-capable "core capabilities" (aircraft carriers, amphibious ships, Tomahawk-armed submarines), and the call by French Admiral Francais Caron that, "from now on it is close to shore and not on the high seas that the primary navy role will be carried out".[4] In sum, the centre of gravity for naval operations in an era in which traditional naval strategy has essentially come to an end, must be *on and over land!*

Some, not all, of these revolutionary changes in the traditional meaning of maritime security in general and of naval power in particular are particularly germane to the Euro-Atlantic region, most notably the region's northern waters. Those waters include for the purpose of this chapter the Atlantic north of the Greenland-Iceland-United Kingdom (GIUK) Gap and the Baltic Sea. Perhaps the most basic question to be asked, however, concerns the very purpose of the region's military, including naval, forces at a time when no obvious, "plan-able" threat is on the horizon.

After the Maritime Strategy

The seesaw change in international maritime security conditions since the collapse of the Warsaw Pact and the Soviet Union has had a particularly telling effect on Europe's northern waters. It was here that, until very recent years, the opposing alliance planners expected the main campaign for control of Atlantic waters to be fought. In the North, it was a long-agreed NATO assessment that, come war, the Soviet Union's most powerful, Northern, Fleet would sally forth to support an overland operation against Norway, defend the waters north of the GIUK Gap against a Western anti-submarine campaign against the "bastioned" SSBN fleet, and attack NATO's transatlantic "sea bridge". Further south, in the Baltic, Western planners anticipated a concerted Soviet and Warsaw Pact campaign to seize Denmark, control the Danish Straits and break out into the Atlantic. For their part, NATO maritime planning was built around the sea and airborne reinforcement of Norway, early forward deployment of US Navy striking forces, and in the Baltic, the defensive mining of the Danish approaches. By the mid-1980s, at the height of the US Navy's "Maritime Strategy", US Navy Secretary John Lehman predicted that the Norwegian Sea and the adjacent landmass would be "the principal battleground" of a future war between the superpowers.[5]

Today, seven years after the collapse of the Berlin Wall, Europe's northern waters are a "sea of peace"—or at least so in military terms. It is true that Russia's most powerful fleet remains ensconced on the Kola Peninsula. It is also true that, if one is persuaded of the dominance of geography in strategic relationships, Russia, merely by virtue of its proximity and size, remains a potential menace. And indeed, despite the spirit of cooperation that has generally marked Russian-Norwegian relations, President Yeltsin has not missed the opportunity to remind the Norwegians that, though the Cold War is over, their "special" geography still incurs special obligations. Thus, on the eve of his visit to Oslo in March 1996, Yeltsin expressed his displeasure over recent NATO exercises in northern Norway. Since, he said, Norway was the only NATO country sharing a border with Russia, it should not permit foreign troops on its soil.[6] Nevertheless, and in spite of the "cold peace" language that has marked Moscow's rhetoric since the Communist victory in Russia's parliamentary elections in December 1995, few, if any, NATO planners believe that "chilly superpower politics" will again mark

Europe's northern region in the foreseeable future.[7] If so, the implication at the "practical", i.e. roughly five-year, level of maritime security planning is this: those concerned with maritime security in Europe's northern region (and this includes NATO as a whole) will need to base their planning on a set of roles and missions that will be radically different from those that have traditionally shaped maritime forces in this part of the world. No one knows yet what exactly those roles and missions will be; is seems a near-certainty however, that a key driving force will be the changing nature of the relationship between force and politics.

Politics and War after Clausewitz

Everyone is familiar with Clauswitz's dictum that war is the extension of politics by other, violent, means. The logical corollary is that the ultimate *raison d'etre* of the tools of war, for example, navies, is political. In other words, the kinds of ships, submarines, aircraft, etc. a naval service creates, mans and supports, must ultimately bear a relationship to the kinds of political purposes the national leadership has in mind for the service. In the case of the nations that border on Northern Europe's waters, those political purposes have had to do, first and foremost, with the deterrence and, if necessary, fighting a superpower war at sea, from the sea and *against* the sea. Those objectives were entirely consistent with the traditional Clausewitzian explanation of the existence of military force.

A couple of things have happened to upset this familiar relationship. The first and immediate development has already been touched on, namely the demise of the Cold War military-political rationale for NATO's and the former Warsaw Pact's naval forces. The second development is more complex, and concerns the changing "political" nature of war and, by inference, of its instruments. It is to be recalled that when Clausewitz defined the political essence of war, he wrote in an era when politics and the decision to make war were still largely the prerogative of the sovereign and a small *coterie* of trusted advisors. War during most of the 19th century was still the "sport of kings".

Just as the instruments of war have changed since Clausewitz, so have the "instruments" of politics. No leader of a democratic country today can afford to go to war, stay in a war, or get out if its fortunes turn against him, without popular participation in the decision. The combination of the end of the Cold War, the explosion in global communications, and most important, the new prominence of human rights-without-borders, have served to place the "revolution" in the politics-war continuum front and centre of the present debate over the uses and usefulness of military force. During the Cold War, the spectre of sudden nuclear attack with the very survival of society at stake, a decision to go to war without the "advice and consent" of the people could still be justified; national command authorities of the democratic nations will not have this "freedom" when less-than-survival interests are at stake. Even more important perhaps will be the impact of the revolution in media coverage on the politics of *intra-war* decision-making. In past wars, public opinion could—and did—at times influence decisions on major strategic directions (for example, the American decision in 1942 to go on the offensive in the Pacific at the expense of the "Europe first" build-up was a response, in part, to public insistence that the United States strike back against the enemy who had started the war to begin with), but already decisions on *current* military operations are becoming increasingly dictated by the "CNN factor". One suspects that, as a result, "tough" military decisions will become very difficult.

What are the implications for maritime security planners in Europe's northern region? If the region's post-Cold War political purposes are essentially different from those that dominated the politics of the "Nordic Balance" during the Cold War, if would seem that the purpose of military, including naval, forces should be transformed as well.

The Nordic Balance—Then and Now

The term "Nordic Balance" used to be a short-hand label for an implicit understanding (sometimes called a "theory") among the Scandinavian nations that security changes by one might trigger corresponding changes by the others.[8] The resulting system of self-imposed restraints on defense measures had less to do with regional relations *per se*, than the desire to minimize the competitive penetration by the two superpowers in the region.[9] In short, the Balance sought to ensure a regional equilibrium based on non-provocative deterrence. In the maritime sphere, this found expression in, for example, Norway's wish for regular NATO naval exercises in the Norwegian Sea but an objection to a permanent naval presence.[10] On the eve of the collapse of the Warsaw Pact, the confidence-building essence of the Balance had expanded to include a series of bilateral agreements between the Baltic seafaring nations aimed at the prevention of incidents at sea.

If the Nordic Balance was a mechanism for blunting the sharp edge of superpower rivalry, then what are the implications of the end of this rivalry?

Has the necessity for a Nordic Balance therefore ceased to exist? In other words, have regional security policies been set free from the ties that bound the area's well-being to the two superpowers? Mr. Yelstin evidently believes not; Norway, because of its special location, is still expected to take Russia's interests into account, Cold War or not. The truth is, of course, that the kinds of measured, non-provocative policies that marked the Nordic Balance were symptomatic of a much older Nordic security tradition, a "strategic culture", if you will. That strategic culture has long been characterized—at least since the Napoleonic wars—by a rejection of war other than in self-defense, a reliance on international law and order instead of "power politics", and on cooperation and consultation instead of competition, and the recognition that the nations that make up Scandinavia are strategic "pawns". That is to say, Nordic security planners, be they Swedish, Danish, or Finnish, have long believed that, should war come to their country, it will have less to do with their country's intrinsic strategic value than as the consequence of a war or crisis elsewhere. The Nordic Balance was arguably the "operational code" that translated this strategic culture into policy action during the years of the Cold War. Its essential characteristics—cooperative internationalism, non-provocative defence and a preoccupation with regional security and prosperity, will persist as the guiding principles of maritime security in the region.

How those principles may be translated into practice at sea is touched on elsewhere in this chapter. It can be said, however, that much will depend on the possible emergence of what one Norwegian government official has suggested will be a distinct "northern European dimension" to Europe's evolving security architecture.[11] It is not clear what the security component of such a northern dimension might look like, but it is at least conceivable that the "old" Nordic Balance will evolve to become a northern *balancer*, a counterweight, as it were, to a possibly Franco-German-dominated and *Mitteleuropa*-focused common European security and defense policy. A "new" Nordic Balance of this sort would serve two main purposes: first, ensure the security and stability of the regional "neighbourhood", and secondly, ensure that future steps toward European defence collaboration will not be dictated by the continent's two principal powers—France and Germany.

It is expected that the nature of the post-Clausewitzian relationship between war and politics will reinforce the region's strategic predilection toward the "civil" or "civilizing" use of military power.[12] In Europe generally, but for the Nordic countries in particular, the threat or use of military force have ceased to be seen as part of the "normal" arsenal of foreign policy tools nations use to pursue their "narrow" interests. The result is that, with the end of the Cold War as the only conceivable source of military conflict in the Scandinavian region (the situation is somewhat different for the new Baltic states), the region's military planners are faced with a difficult professional dilemma: how to justify their profession? If there are no enemies, real or perceived, how can the military persuade their political masters that they have a legitimate claim on the nation's scarce resources? A Great Power, for example, the United States, can resort to the argument that its status incurs "special responsibilities" on behalf of the international system as a whole. But what about the smaller nations?

Traditionally, of course, the possession of standing military forces by even the smallest nation was justified if for no other reason that it was the penultimate symbol of national sovereignty. The defining features of the sovereign nation-state have traditionally been twofold: the control of territory and the maintenance of internal order. Both have historically turned on the possession of a centrally-controlled, standing armed force.[13] As far as the maintenance of internal sovereignty is concerned, armed forces have become largely irrelevant—certainly so in most of Western Europe. In most of the region, in Scandinavia in particular, armies are no longer a tool of internal sovereignty. One reason why this is so for the Scandinavian nation-states is the absence of potentially nation-dividing ethnic strife. The situation is somewhat different in two of the three Baltic states—Estonia and Latvia. Here, between 40 and 50 per cent of the population is Russian, which some observers fear is a potential threat to the countries' internal sovereignty, especially if dissidents receive encouragement from Moscow. In both countries, the newly-created armed forces are arguably more important as symbols of independence and national identity, than as territorial defenders against outside aggression.[14]

If maintaining internal order has outlived its usefulness as a source of legitimacy for most of the region's national militaries, do they still have a national role as guarantors of territorial integrity? None of Northern Europe's nations owns the military wherewithal—or expects—to defend the sanctity of its territory by national means alone. The Swedish armed forces during the 1950s and early 1960s—the height of the country's armed neutrality—were perhaps the only ones in the region that might have had a fair chance of successful unilateral defense against outside attack. Since then, the defense of Swedish territorial integrity against a regional aggressor has become as dependent on outside support as has been that of its Nordic neighbours since 1945.

The decline of armed power as the essential symbol of national sovereignty is arguably symptomatic of a broader phenomenon that has been commented upon by a number of astute observers in recent years, namely the "withering away" of the nation-state's monopoly on territorial sovereignty. Norway's former defense minister, Johan Jorgen Holst, spoke of this at the 1992 "Sea Link" gathering of NATO political and military planners. He said:

> The territorial state no longer wields exclusive authority within its borders. It is no longer sovereign. It has been penetrated by the internationalization of finance, production, distribution, communication, learning, environmental impact technology and the power to destroy. The territorial state has lost its exclusive authority and the power to protect. Functional integration has torn it asunder.[15]

Does this mean that national military forces have outlived their usefulness? Have they ceased to be the potent (and practical) symbol of national sovereignty they once were? Was Belgium's defense minister, Leo Delcroix, right when he predicted in the spring of 1995 that, "The time is not far off when it will be utopian, especially for small nations, to maintain independent armies, navies and air forces?"[16] The answer, particularly in the North, seems to be both "yes" and "no". Escalating costs, manpower and equipment cuts, and most of all, the widespread perception in the northern region that a major war is unlikely and that, even were it to occur, defense will require allies, will likely propel the region's military toward *de facto*, if not *de jure*, integration. To be sure, this development will not be unique to Europe's northern nations; "creeping integration" by way of a patchwork of bilateral and multilateral cooperative pacts, ranging from joint research, development and procurement, to shared maintenance, repair, exercises and operational planning, has slowly but surely set Europe on a path towards the "de-nationalization" of military power. Which prompts a provocative thought: if Porter and others are correct that the nation-state was born of military power, does the reverse process hold true as well? In other words, will the functional integration of Europe's national militaries spell the *death* of the territorial nation-state, thus completing the process of the continent's political integration from-the-bottom-up?

It is arguable that the progressive integration of Europe's military forces need not automatically condemn the nation-state to death; individual governments could still reserve the right to *not* use force, the so-called right to "opt-out". But end of the nation-state or not, the ability to *use* force, will be the monopoly of *coalitions*.

A Certain Eventuality

The northern seas are secure! While it is perhaps premature to label the Baltic and Norwegian Seas "seas of peace", the practical situation from the perspective of the Western maritime security planner is that neither body of water ranks high as a plausible theatre of military operations. This is not to say that planners should not think about less pleasant scenarios. Russia's future circumstances remain fraught with uncertainty; as a corollary, so are those of the newly emancipated Baltic republics. It is therefore entirely reasonable for Western planners generally and regional military planners in particular to hedge and undertake contingency planning. The latter has been defined (in a different regional context) as "uncertainty-based planning" based on the perceived necessity to guard against all eventualities.[17] It is impossible to plan for "all eventualities" if for no other reason than that the future holds too many uncertainties. It is realistic that the planner limit his/her imagination to only "certain eventualities", perhaps not very likely, but not quite implausible.[18]

Perhaps the most ominous—ominous because it is plausible—contingency that comes to mind is an outbreak of fighting with the involvement of Russian forces in one of the Baltic republics. A few years ago, a scenario along these lines received notoriety in the Swedish press when it reported an alleged "Pentagon war scenario" in which six aircraft carriers were sent into the Baltic to support Lithuanian and Polish forces against a Russian landgrab. In the event, the Russians reportedly lost after three months of "intensive fighting".[19]

It is not necessary to conjure up combat between American and Russian forces to recognize that hostilities of whatever form on the Baltic littoral would present the region with a grave crisis that almost certainly would entail the involvement of maritime forces. For example, how will the "Nordic Balance" respond to a situation which demands the evacuation of foreign nationals from a strife-torn Baltic republic? The classic maritime response would be an over-the-beach, non-combatant evacuation operation (NEO). Are, or perhaps better put, *should* the Baltic nations, say, Sweden, Poland, Denmark, be prepared to make this a *regional* endeavour and thereby avert the possibly provocative involvement of NATO and the United States in particular? Can the Partnership for Peace (PfP) program be the vehicle for stimulating a degree of regional maritime cohesion that does not quite amount to a formal collective defence undertaking, yet signals that hostilities against any one of the Nordic nations will be seen as a threat to the region as a whole?

NATO's Partnership for Peace (PfP) program has become the framework for a series of bilateral agreements among the Baltic nations aimed at enhancing regional military cooperation.[20] The immediate purpose of PfP combined training and exercises is practical: boost the interoperability of NATO and non-NATO military structures, particularly in the areas of peacekeeping and humanitarian missions. Maritime exercises in particular have centred on search and rescue scenarios, fisheries enforcement, disaster relief, etc. More important than these very practical concerns, however, is the program's overarching political aim of fostering regional security and stability in general. Many of the former Soviet bloc nations, including the Baltic states, believe that PfP is a stepping stone toward the ultimate vehicle for providing such security and stability, namely full NATO membership.

This is not the place to enter into the debate over NATO enlargement, but it may be worth considering how "regionalization", as opposed to "NATO-ization" of security and stability in and about the Baltic, through programs like PfP, might possibly de-fuse a "certain eventuality". The eventuality envisaged in this case is a Russian imperialist reaction against the Baltic states in retaliation for NATO's decision to expand eastward and embrace the "Visegrad Four" (Poland, the Czech Republic, Slovakia and Hungary). In a sense, such a Russian move would be pre-emptive so as to forestall NATO's next step and admission of the Baltic states. If this is not an implausible scenario, then the existence of a Nordic Balance that acts as an intra-European balancer, i.e. as a part of Europe but also slightly *apart from* Europe, could help allay a Russian pre-emptive incentive. The price to be paid—yet one that may be in everyone's interest—would be a tacit undertaking on the part of the West that NATO would not expand to include the Baltic states, that Baltic security will be embedded instead in *regional* forms of security cooperation.

Conclusion

There are sound practical and political reasons why maritime forces should be the instrument of choice for stimulating the regionalization of Baltic security. If national military, including naval, forces were once the penultimate symbol of national sovereignty, so their multilateralization on the eve of the 21st century can be a potent signal of *regional* interdependence and independence. Is it time perhaps for a Standing Maritime Force Baltic?

Notes

1. Ken Booth, "The Role of Navies in Peacetime: The Influence of Future History on Sea Power", in Hugh Smith and Anthony Bergin, eds, *Naval Power in the Pacific: Toward the Year 2000* (Boulder: Lynne Rieder, 1993), 161.
2. Vice Adm. P.H. Colomb, *Naval Warfare: Its Ruling Principles and Practice Theoretically Treated* 2nd edition, (London: W.H. Allen & Co., 1895), 1-24.
3. Winston S. Churchill, *The World Crisis, 1911-1918*, Vol. I. (London: Odhams Press, 1938), 76.
4. Cited in Capitan de Vaisseau (C.R.) Bernard Dujardin, "Toward a New French Strategy", U.S. Naval Institute *Proceedings* March 1996, 72.
5. Cited in Ola Tunander, *Cold War Politics: The Maritime Strategy and Geopolitics of the Northern Front* (London: Sage Publications, 1989), 1. Tunander gives Joseph H. Alexander in "The Role of the US Marines in the Defense of Norway" (U.S. Naval Institute *Proceedings*, May 1984) as his source for this quotation.
6. *Telegraaf* (Amsterdam), 25 March 1996.
7. The phrase "chilly superpower politics" is borrowed from Tunander, *Cold War Politics*, 155.
8. Arne Olav Brundtland, "Norwegian Security Policy: Defense and Nonprovocation in a Changing Context", in Gregory Flynn, ed., *NATO's Northern Allies* (Towota: Rowman & Allanheld, 1985), 178.
9. See Johan Jorgen Holst, "Five Roads to Nordic Security", in Holst, ed., *Five Roads to Nordic Security* (Oslo: Universitetsforlaget, 1973), 1-2.
10. See, for example, Johan Jorgen Holst, "NATO and Northern Security". Speech at Oslo International Symposium, 1986. Cited in Tunander, *Cold War Politics*, 162.
11. See, Bjorn Tore Godal, "Regional cooperation in the European High North", *NATO Review* June 1994, 11. The author was Norway's minister of defence.
12. Francois Duchene introduced the label "civil power" in 1972 to describe the then-European Economic Community as a power that is respected not for its military muscle but because of its economic strength. The civil power's foreign policies give priority to issues like economic reform, social betterment and political consolidation as opposed to traditional concerns like power and influence. See Curt Gasteyger, *An Ambiguous Power: The European Union in a Changing World* (Guetersloh: Bertelsmann Foundation, 1996), 127.
13. Bruce Porter is one recent historian who has argued an even stronger symbiotic relationship between the state and the military. The state, he has written, is the "creature of war". Bruce D. Porter, *War and the Rise of the State: The Military Foundations of Modern Politics* (New York: The Macmillan Press, 1994), 299.
14. See, for example, Colonel Juris Dalbins, "Baltic cooperation—the key to wider security", *NATO Review* January 1996, 7. The author was the commander of the National Armed Forces of Latvia.

15. Johan Jorgen Holst, "The European Pillar of NATO: Dimensions and Limitations of Maritime Applications". Address at the Sea Link conference, Annapolis, MD, 19 June 1992, 15.

16. Peter de Graaf and Wio Joustra, "Nederland en Belgie voegen marines samen" ("The Netherlands and Belgium Join Navies"), *Volkskrant* 27 April 1995. The minister made his remark on the occasion of the operational merger of the Belgian and Dutch fleets into a combined "Benelux" fleet.

17. J.N. Mak, "The ASEAN Military Build-Up: Contingency Planning in an Uncertain World". Paper presented at the Sea Power Conference, London, 5-6 May 1994.

18. The words "A certain eventuality" are paraphrased from the British Chiefs of Staff paper, entitled "British Strategy in a Certain Eventuality", in May 1940 which laid out British chances of continuing the fight against Germany should, as was expected, French resistance collapse. See Eleanor M. Gates, *The End of the Affair: The Collapse of the Anglo-French Alliance, 1939-40* (Berkeley: University of California Press, 1981), 127-28.

19. "Bildt Military Adviser on Navy's Baltic Role", *Svenska Dagbladet* 23 March 1992, 8. Cited in *Federal Broadcast Information Service (Western Europe)*, 13 April 1992, 45-46.

20. See, for example, Hans Haekkerup, "Cooperation around the Baltic Sea: Danish perspectives and initiatives", *NATO Review* May 1995, 14-18.

PART IV
THE AMERICAS

12 Canada-US Naval Cooperation in the 21st Century

PETER T. HAYDON AND PAUL T. MITCHELL[1]

For many North Americans, their borders seemingly secure from foreign threats, the need for a complex bilateral continental defence structure is now questionable. On first inspection, such a concern is not unreasonable: the absence of an immediate threat to North America leads to perfectly valid questions on the size and character of any related defence plans or expenditures. But this simplistic perspective misses the point that international defence plans should not be discarded lightly, especially because they often serve functions beyond the immediate and narrow realm of collective defence. Hence, it may not be wise to discard the existing continental defence structure without being quite clear on the benefits Canada and the United States receive from that structure.

There are those who wonder exactly what purpose the present Canada-US defence structure serves today, particularly some of the agreements intended to address specific Soviet threats. For instance, is there still a need to maintain the fabric of naval plans and agreements assembled long ago to deal with the threat posed to North America by Soviet submarines and special forces? Similar questions are being asked of the future of the North American Air Defence (NORAD) system and other parts of the wide ranging defence structure put in place in the late 1940s. From another perspective, what is at issue, in fact, is the shape of the Canada-US security relationship in the post-Cold War era.

This chapter concerns only the maritime dimension of the relationship and is not intended to dismiss the very real concerns over other aspects. One of the ways this matter can be addressed is through a series of interrelated strategic questions each with its own political, geographic and military dimensions.

- Is there a continuing need for naval cooperation in the Arctic?
- Should Canada-US continental defence arrangements continue to be linked to NATO through the Canada-US Regional Planning Group (CUSRPG)?

- Will the North American Free Trade Agreement eventually change the structure under which both continental and hemispheric security is presently configured?
- Will changes in the Asian balance of power, particularly the evolution of China into a true superpower, lead to a different approach to collective North American security?

These four questions are themselves laden with assumptions about the future nature of the international system, about the place of North America in that system, and about the future of Canada-United States relations. One cannot begin to examine those complex issues without having a clear understanding of the nature of the bilateral continental defence structure. In this, we must not only understand the nature of that structure and what it represents, we must also understand what it is not. One of the main problems in dealing with continental defence issues is that far too few people actually understand the nature of the overarching agreement, the Basic Security Plan (BSP), and the family of subordinate operational plans and cooperation agreements. Understanding how the naval dimension of those plans came into being and how the two navies worked together so closely over the years since 1946 is fundamental to examining the future of the relationship.

The Canada-US Security Relationship[2]

The idea of a joint[3] North American security arrangement dates back to the late 1930s when the storm clouds of war first started gathering over Europe. The actual process of formalizing those arrangements began with President Roosevelt's assurances, made in Kingston, Ontario, on 18 August 1938, that "...the people of the United States will not stand idly by if domination of Canadian soil is threatened...".[4] Those sentiments, which were as much Roosevelt's own as those of his advisors, were acknowledged two days later by the Canadian prime minister, Mackenzie King, with a clear statement of the strategic indivisibility of the two countries:

> We, too, have our obligations as a good friendly neighbour, and one of these is to see that, at our own instance, our country is made immune from attack, or possible invasion as we can reasonably be expected to make it, and that, should the occasion ever arise, enemy forces should not be able to pursue their way, either by land, sea or air, to the United States across Canadian territory.[5]

This tacit agreement on the need for joint continental defence was formalized later by the signing of the Ogdensburg Agreement on 18 August 1940.

Figure 12.1 North America

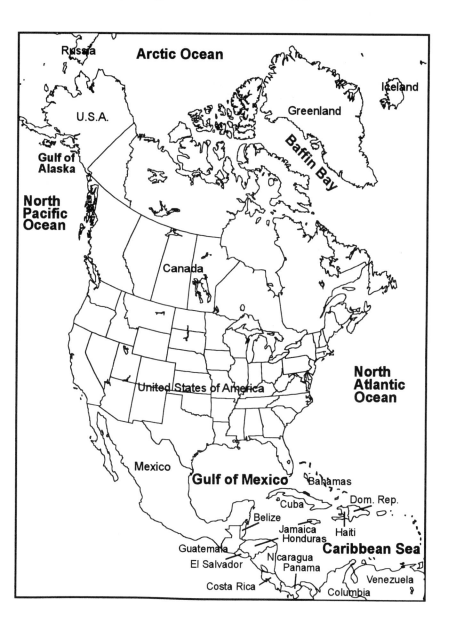

Although a sense of true neighbourliness existed in Roosevelt's opening move, the Americans were largely motivated by self-interest, sentiments that might perhaps be better expressed as natural concerns for self-preservation. King acted more out of desperation than strategic foresight. The fall of France and the bleak British prospects deeply concerned King and forced him to accept that accommodation with the Americans was necessary.[6] There was little doubt that Canada found itself between a strategic rock and a hard place and, as it would be again during the early days of the Cold War, in a strategic relationship with the Americans. A paper written in July 1940 summarizes the reality of Canada's uncomfortable strategic position.

> Above all we are confronted with a startling new possibility: war on our own shores. This we have never seriously contemplated, and for it our defence strategy is woefully unprepared. When Canada's first line of defence was the Maginot Line, her second was the English Channel, and the Atlantic coast was an unlikely third line. Now the Atlantic is the second line, and the first line on the Channel is threatened as never before.
>
> The new situation gives to Canada's relations with the United States a greatly increased importance. Thus far these relations have been most friendly and co-operation has been close. Now passport and exchange restrictions have destroyed that easy intercourse on which a great deal of the good-neighbourliness depended. Meanwhile the need for closer co-operation becomes more pressing every day. The United States is preparing for continental defence on a gigantic scale.
>
> Unless Canada faces the implications of this new continental plan she risks losing her national identity. Geography makes Canada an integral part of any North American defence system. Co-operation with Washington is going to be either voluntary on Canada's part, or else compulsory; in any event it is inevitable. And since the United States seems determined to integrate her policies with those of other American states, Canada's attitude to the Pan-American system needs to be thought out afresh.
>
> Coupled with these new problems of defence and external policy are new problems of economic adjustment. These involve not only the immediate outlook for Canadian wheat and other produce deprived of former markets, They raise graver questions. Defence and economic policy are today inseparable; if our defence is to fit a continental plan, there will have to be corresponding changes in our industrial and financial organization.[7]

In light of that assessment, what options did Canada really have?

In retrospect, though, both the August 1940 Ogdensburg Agreement and the Atlantic Charter that emerged a year later can be seen as instruments intended primarily to further American security requirements. At a time when the collapse of Britain seemed likely, it was only natural that the Americans take steps to ensure that Canada remain free of Nazi influence.[8] The inescapable fact was, and remains to this day, that Canadian security (and thus its internal stability) is fundamental to US security. This is one of the ironies of North American defence: Canadian security invariably seems to be of greater importance to Americans than to Canadians.

In the early years of the Cold War this strategic linkage became more important through the perception that the vast and virtually empty Canadian north could easily become a vulnerability in terms of US security. Initially, a condition of near paranoia existed that the Soviets might invade the Arctic and establish lodgements from which they could launch attacks on the US industrial heartland and on major ports. This was essentially a return of the spectre of Pearl Harbor. At the same time, Canadian politicians came to realize that the Americans were quite capable of mounting independent operations in the Canadian north should they perceive themselves under threat, and not necessarily under an immediate threat. Under such circumstances, Canadian sovereignty would be completely subordinate to US security concerns and there was very little Canada could do about it.

Canadian politicians thus wisely decided that it was better to quell their inherent anti-Americanism, particularly Mackenzie King's paranoia that the Americans would eventually annex Canada,[9] and pursue a concept of joint continental defence as the means of preserving Canadian sovereignty. Nevertheless, the bilateral relationship was always held to be a political necessity rather than a whole-hearted commitment to collective security. Predictably, the Canadians, ever circumspect in their relations with the Americans and ever wary of being drawn too deeply into US foreign policy initiatives, sought ways to protect themselves against American "enthusiasms" and, worse, domination. This "cloud of suspicion" has always hung over the political dimension of the bilateral defence plans. As such, it demands a certain finesse on the part of military planners to ensure that the planning process did not become politicized to the point of producing unworkable solutions and options.

The Fundamentals of Cold War Joint Plans

The military dimension of the Cold War bilateral planning process began in earnest at the December 1945 meeting of the Permanent Joint Board on Defence (PJBD) in New York where the conversion of the wartime Basic

Security Plan (ABC-22) into a bilateral plan for continental defence was first discussed. The Canadian government agreed to revise the plan and informed the Americans of this at the January 1946 meeting of the PJBD in Quebec City.[10] As a result, the basis for future military cooperation was established on the basis of six activities:

- An exchange of military personnel in operational formations, training establishments, schools, etc.;
- Standardization of equipment and organizations;
- The conduct of joint testing, which would later focus on the Arctic;
- Mapping and charting requirements in Canada, essentially to allow US forces to operate safely in northern Canada;
- Exchange of information on military organizations; and
- An exchange of war planning information.

Although this list might seem to have a broader scope than strictly necessary for a peacetime situation, it was logical because the future military relationship had to be founded on a basis of mutual trust and understanding despite any political qualms. This far-ranging perspective was to become an enduring feature of the bilateral defence relationship at sea, on land, in the air and in matters of defence equipment procurement.

Re-writing the BSP was made easier by the selection of experienced staffs to develop the underlying strategic assessment and draft the new plan. The US Joint War Plans Committee (JWPC) quickly produced and circulated a draft concept for the "collaborative" defence of the continent called, simply, *Matchpoint*. Without actually specifying the Soviet Union as the most likely adversary and referring instead to the principal "European" or "Eurasian" power (which was a matter of US policy)[11] the paper summarized the international situation in stating that:

> It is impossible to estimate firmly the likelihood of a major war or when it might occur. It is reasonably certain that no nation desires to become involved in a war now, but the possibility exists that one or more European powers might blunder into war by extension of their policies to a point which Canada and the United States, in their own vital security interest, could no longer tolerate.[12]

This assessment reflected many internal US military concerns, not least of which was the fact that while American, British and Canadian forces were being pulled back from Europe, there was no corresponding demobilization of the Red Army. With communism widespread in many liberated European countries, the risk that Europe would fall under Soviet domination was high. Under such circumstances, the resulting war would have been between unspecified "European powers" and Great Britain in which the enemy's objective would be to overrun Britain before the United States, Canada and the other British Dominions came to its assistance.

The heart of *Matchpoint* was a call for a wide range of military capabilities to counter the potential threat, including:

- A comprehensive air defence system that included a long-range warning system, a network of fighter bases located to ensure interception of enemy aircraft well clear of population centres and air defence systems for strategic locations;
- Air and surface reconnaissance to provide early warning of attack;
- Anti-submarine forces;
- Forces to defend bases and installations and for counter-lodgement operations;
- Naval forces to exercise control of sea approaches; and
- A quick-reaction command structure.

This assessment, which obviously still reflected the ignominy of Pearl Harbor, led to more specific statements of joint defence requirements in the various parts of the continent. Naval tasks provided for local and off-shore defences for key coastal areas and ports (with Hudson Strait singled out as a strategic zone) and the protection of shipping in coastal zones, with US forces being additionally tasked to control the continental sea approaches. US bases in Iceland and Greenland were included in the areas of responsibility. In all, it was a far sighted and realistic plan under the assumed threat. The American problem was to get Canadian concurrence, and this was not easily obtained.[13]

In the summer of 1946, however, joint planning was well underway as *Matchpoint* and the Canadian inputs were melded into a draft Basic Security Plan with an accompanying appreciation of the international situation. But there were delays in the process, most of which were functions of Canadian uncertainty over the political implications of the commitment to such plans.[14] By the end of November 1946, however, it was agreed that bilateral planning would not proceed beyond the completion of the appendices to the BSP. Also, the process by which the plans would be developed in Canada was clarified.

This hinged on making a clear distinction between the BSP and its appendices on the one hand, and any implementation of those plans on the other hand. The BSP was considered a war plan and as such only its implementation required political approval. The plans and any subsequent revisions could therefore be "agreed" by the respective Chiefs of Staff organizations. In making the process correspond to the American system, the way was technically clear to complete the planning. As an additional planning requirement, though, there was a need to come to terms with the costs of implementation, particularly in the near-term, and this was to be the means of exercising political control.[15]

The deteriorating situation in Europe became an impetus for finishing the planning process as quickly as possible. By the beginning of 1947, much of Eastern Europe had fallen under Soviet domination, and it was becoming ever more clear that the rest of Europe, including Britain, Greece and perhaps the Middle East might also be at risk. The situation was greatly compounded by Britain's painful decision in February that it could no longer support Greece or Turkey in their fight against communism. President Truman's historic message to Congress on 12 March 1947 declaring that the United States would in future "support free peoples who are resisting attempted subjugation by armed minorities or by outside pressures" established beyond doubt that the United States was not about to see the whole of Europe turned into a Soviet satellite.

The decision to continue joint continental defence cooperation was made public by statements issued simultaneously in Washington and Ottawa, on 12 February, 1947. *Matchpoint* soon became the new Canada-US Basic Security Plan and was approved in both Ottawa and Washington in early 1948.

Refining the Naval Plans

It was into this rather complicated planning process that the "Sea Lines of Communication" and "Mobile Striking Forces" Appendices to the BSP emerged at the beginning of 1948. Although there was some maritime content in other appendices, such as the mapping and charting and communications, it was the two dedicated naval plans that initially spelled out the maritime dimension of continental defence and this formed the basis for subsequent cooperation.

The operational aims in protecting the sea lines of communications envisaged a highly sophisticated joint operation ranging from surveillance, to centralized command and control to the production of new ASW vessels.

What it all added up to was that the Canadian and US forces would essentially re-fight the Second World War but with Russians operating the U-boats. For the RCN, this represented a significant policy shift, or at least a proposal to change policy, because the Navy would have to abandon its traditional ties with the RN and adopt USN doctrine and procedures.[16]

The aim of the "Mobile Striking Forces" Appendix was to "provide a plan for the employment of air, airborne, amphibious or naval striking forces required to counter possible enemy lodgements in the northern portion of the Western Hemisphere or enemy surface raids against North-West Atlantic or Northern Pacific objectives".[17] This appendix, which later became part of the rationale for the formation of the Canadian Airborne Regiment, was essentially a reflection of the strategic concern for the "empty and vulnerable" Arctic and was based on the premise that enemy objectives would be the destruction of military installations and the establishment of enemy facilities in their place which would serve as bases for sabotage and diversionary attacks.[18]

Although those actual Appendices were to be short lived in their original form, their underlying strategic and tactical concepts would survive throughout the Cold War in other plans. It was this type of developmental work, done by Canadian and American naval staffs as equals, that set the true tone of the future relationship between the two navies. The only criticism that can be levied is that the general weakness of both naval appendices was that they attempted to do too much with too few forces and to create a strategic requirement that would have been unsustainable.[19] At the same time there was a change of heart at the highest levels within the Pentagon over the scope of the BSP.[20] Also, the US Joint Strategic Plans Committee were recommending a change in the concept for the protection of shipping to a concept covering only the North American littoral rather than the entire North Atlantic, which they saw being undertaken collectively by British, Canadian and American forces.[21]

This important change in concept was accepted, and in the final version of the BSP, which was approved in March 1949, the relevant appendix was called "Protection of Coastal Sea Lines of Communication".[22] This Appendix to the BSP would survive in one form or another until 1955 when a major revision of the concept for continental defence was brought in as a result of the change in NATO's overall strategic policy. But the change in continental SLOC protection policy did not mean that the work done in developing comprehensive plans for the protection of ocean shipping was wasted. With the formation of NATO in April 1949, in the face of a clearly deteriorating

European security situation, and the subsequent evolution of the NATO strategic and force planning systems, the early work done under the aegis of continental defence quickly became the basic framework for North Atlantic defence planning.

As NATO evolved into an effective defensive alliance, Canadian and American naval staffs continued to work together in drawing up the necessary plans. At the same time, continental defence plans were refined and practised. Canada and the United States merely accepted that their navies had dual functions: defence of North America and defence of the North Atlantic area. In both commitments, their navies continued to work together. The good working relationship that had been formed during the earlier formative years of continental defence planning continued to provide the framework for cooperation in a very wide range of defence activities.[23]

In hindsight, it may be easy to overlook the importance of the initial planning process to both countries. On one hand, it made the United States aware of the importance of recognizing the idiosyncrasies of a smaller country, especially where that country did not have comparable experience in strategic planning. This became especially important in the evolution of NATO. On the other hand, the process allowed Canada to break free from the "imperial" structure under which its military traditionally functioned. Without this independence, Canada would not have been such an effective member of NATO. Yet Canada also had to realize that collective defence was not a free ride, although it often had to be reminded of this fact in later years.

Although the initial joint plans did not survive in their original form because they were modified to meet the changing circumstances, they provided the basis for future cooperation. Most of that cooperation was mutually beneficial, but it would not be incorrect to surmise that on balance Canada was the greater beneficiary. Not only was the planning process part of the maturing process for the Canadian Navy, it also provided much of the technical base upon which the RCN grew in stature. But this dependence on the US Navy for technical and training support did not mean that Canada was a less than equal partner in continental defence. The relationship between the two navies was always a true partnership.

Yet, the Canadian politicians were never completely happy with the arrangement; they were forever concerned that the American penchant for unilateral action would draw Canada into a strategic situation they could neither afford nor explain politically.[24] The formation of NATO in 1949 was thus a blessing, for it enabled the Canadians to counterbalance US influence through the European link. The management of this rather complicated three-way relationship is a story in itself and beyond the scope of this chapter. Suffice it to say, though, that the Canadian insistence on linking continental defence to NATO was a frequent if not a virtually constant source of frustration to the Americans.

Out of Canadian paranoia was born the Canada-United States Regional Planning Group (CUSRPG). The function of this organization was to ensure that a formal link existed between continental defence (under CANUS) and NATO. In some organizational charts, CUSRPG is shown as having the same status as a Major NATO Commander (such as SACEUR, SACLANT), but this reflects political desire rather than military fact.[25] There is no secret in the fact that at the time NORAD came into being, many Canadian politicians and diplomats wanted to limit the US ability to take unilateral action in the event of an attack (or presumption of an attack) against North America by integrating the NORAD Agreement into the NATO military-political response mechanism. The Americans balked, and rightly so under the circumstances.[26] Moreover, they had grave reservations over the willingness of the Europeans to help in the defence of North America should the need arise. Trans-Atlantic security, many firmly believed, was a one-way agreement. The Europeans never understood the political and military significance of the Pacific Ocean to American security. The view from NATO was that both American and Canadian forces stationed in the Pacific should be made available for European security.

Summation

Several features of the unique relationship stand out which must be taken into account when analyzing the future of the North American security structure. First, is the fact that operational cooperation routinely takes place independently of political factors. As evidence is the 1962 Cuban missile crisis where, despite the impasse between Diefenbaker and Kennedy, the Canadian and US Navies were able to work together in a highly efficient manner that even included Canadian ships assuming responsibility for the security of some US waters.[27] A similar situation occurred during the Vietnam War when Canadian naval and maritime air forces assumed full responsibility for anti-submarine operations in the Gulf of Alaska while US forces were forwardly deployed. Second, even today, ocean surveillance information is shared as a matter of course between Canadian and US maritime headquarters. The SOSUS analysis centre in Halifax is co-manned with USN and Canadian naval personnel, and there are members of both navies in all key headquarters.

Not only do they serve in a liaison capacity, they also carry out staff functions without consideration of nationality. In short, information concerning the security of North American waters knows few political or geographic borders. Third, a mechanism exists, largely through the PJBD and its planning arm the Military Cooperation Committee (MCC), for quick operational and staff coordination. As occasionally happens, misunderstandings arise, mistakes are made and accidents occur that have the potential to cause political concern if mismanaged. Through the well established bilateral cooperation process such incidents can be dealt with quickly and fairly without resort to formal diplomatic procedures. This capability for effective cooperation has been developed and refined over many years and allows both nations to remain sovereign while being able to act as one in matters of continental maritime security.[28]

The Canada-US links remain important. Even in the absence of direct military threat, Canada is still a factor in US security. And as a trading partner, Canada remains a major factor in the US economy. In simple terms, the respective strategic and economic interdependence of the two countries that existed at the outset of the Second World War still exists. In some respects, the relationship is still subject to many of the same perceptions as at the beginning of the Cold War. For the Canadians the problem is still how to manage a security relationship with the Americans in such a way as to ensure that Canadian sovereignty is respected. And for the Americans the issue is one of ensuring Canadian cooperation in those undertakings where North American solidarity is needed.

Future Considerations

To answer the question on the future need for Canada-US naval cooperation we must now come back to the four strategic questions posed at the beginning of this chapter and attempt to draw a conclusion. In simple terms, we need to examine the existing collaborative naval structure from the four cardinal points of the compass and see what the future might hold.

The Northern Dimension: The Arctic

During the long Cold War, the bilateral relationship concerning the waters of the Arctic tended to be overshadowed by political concerns over Canadian claims of sovereignty. The strategic pendulum swung back and forth in tune with the political profile of incidents such as the 1969 voyage of the S.S.

Manhattan, the 1972 Arctic Waters Pollution Prevention Act, the 1985 transit of the USCGS *Polar Sea* and the plan for Canada to obtain nuclear-powered submarines announced in the 1987 Defence White Paper, political support for which subsided considerably following the signing, in January 1988, of the bilateral Agreement regarding Arctic sovereignty.

As far as the navies were concerned, cooperation in the Arctic was a normal function of continental defence planning. From the earliest days when the threat of Soviet lodgements was the driving force behind cooperation to the closing days of the Cold War when it appeared that the Soviets might use the under-ice passages through the Arctic archipelago to introduce cruise missiles into North American waters,[29] bilateral naval cooperation was conducted without political overtones. For instance, the series of under-ice submarine transits (the SUBICEX exercises) were coordinated with Canadian officials and often undertook Canadian research projects, the development of Arctic surveillance systems was also a joint venture, Canadians trained in US nuclear submarines in the 1960s with the intent that they would share in the Arctic deployments, information on Soviet submarine deployments in Arctic waters was shared, and in the mid-1980s planning began for an integrated concept of naval Arctic operations. The logic was simple: because the Soviets had the equipment and the capability to use the Arctic waters for strategic and tactical reasons, a joint North American response capability was needed.

Today, the strategic issues are somewhat different:

- Concern over the preservation of the fragile Arctic environment and its value as an ecological laboratory;
- Canadian sovereignty over the Arctic archipelago and the status of the Northwest Passage; and
- The likely impact of large-scale tourism, perhaps better described as adventurism, especially through the use of Russian nuclear-powered icebreakers.

Although there seems no immediate military threat, the Russians have made it absolutely clear that they intend to retain a sea-launched strategic missile capability for deterrent purposes[30] and have actually fired a ballistic missile from Arctic waters.[31] What does this mean for North American security? The immediate factor is that the presence in Arctic waters of any missile-firing submarine or other platform capable of targeting North America is of concern. That Russia itself poses no threat to North American interests today does not lessen the level of concern because political structures can change quickly and the Russian government is not yet completely safe from a return to a less friendly, perhaps a more independently nationalistic, system.

The point, simply, is that the Arctic remains largely unoccupied, its waters used only occasionally, and, at the moment, kept under only random surveillance. Because the Arctic provides an opportunity for illegal use and because it remains a fragile eco-system as well as being a unique laboratory, there is a need to know what goes on there and to have an ability to respond quickly to challenges to security (in its broadest context) and sovereignty. Moreover, because such challenges have implications for both Canada and the United States, it makes sense that surveillance and presence in Arctic waters be a cooperative undertaking. Much of this can be done as part of scientific operations[32] or activities such as the well-reported joint trip to the Pole made in 1995 by the Canadian and US Coast Guards. But the military also needs to be a part of that process on a regular basis as the symbol of authority.

There is no point at the moment in suggesting that Canada revisit plans to acquire nuclear submarines. Not only is the political climate wrong, but it is also an unaffordable project.[33] It would make sense, though, to return to an old idea and work out an exchange or loan program whereby some Canadian submariners would serve aboard those US submarines engaged in Arctic operations—scientific or tactical. Also, it would make sense to consider some co-manning of icebreakers in the high Arctic. Although this would not meet the narrower requirements of sovereignty assertion, it would send a very clear signal that the Arctic remains a joint security concern.

The existing continental defence structure has the necessary flexibility to let such innovations take place without embarking on enormously complex political agreements. Also, the mere commitment to joint operations and combined manning of vessels engaged in some Arctic undertakings would be symbolic of mutual respect for respective sovereignty and security concerns.

Eastward: The Atlantic

Lord Ismay, the first Secretary-General of NATO, once quipped that the purpose of NATO was to keep the Americans in, the Russians out and the Germans down.[34] In some respects this is hardly applicable or appropriate today, but it contains the essence of the linkage between Europe and the United States—to guarantee the stability of Europe by agreeing to protect it from itself. Without such a guaranteed response and all that it implies in terms of American strategic might, the European Community would not have been able to devote itself to economic development. Moreover, and perhaps more importantly, without the American security guarantee the Western European states would be forced to deal with their own security. Here, the lessons of history speak for themselves.[35] Thus, the American linkage to Europe is strategically important and is likely to remain so.

The military linkage between Canada and Europe has become virtually irrelevant. Canadian troops and combat aircraft have been withdrawn from their European bases and those fighting capabilities have been allowed to wither. Today, the commitment has become far more maritime in its nature and is retained through continuous assignments to the NATO Standing Naval Force Atlantic (SNFL), to the various Supreme Allied Command Atlantic (SACLANT) contingency plans, through participation in the wide range of NATO naval exercises and by occasional deployments with the Standing Naval Force Mediterranean. Simply, the withdrawal of Canadian land and air forces has made SACLANT Canada's strongest link to the Alliance. While Canada actively contributes to Partnership for Peace (PfP) initiatives and NATO's Airborne Early Warning (AEW) program, its most visible and tangible contribution is through its navy.

As NATO continues to re-define itself in the post-Cold War era, North American participation still has the potential to represent a significant political symbol for a European political system poised on the edge of a new century yet still fearful of the legacy of the previous one. While Canadian withdrawal is still controversial and its results have yet to be played out fully, the naval commitments remain an important component of NATO maritime cooperation. This situation, according to Joel Sokolsky, may not accord Canada any great influence over American and Allied policies, but at least it will allow Canada to sit comfortably at the table.[36] Likewise, Canadian expertise, especially at the formation and command levels, continues to be respected through invitations to command the Standing Naval Force Atlantic and to take command of large multinational forces in major NATO exercises. Ironically, although Canadian political leverage in NATO may be slipping, its naval influence remains high.

In some eyes, there is a second, somewhat tenuous linkage through Article 2 of the Treaty, but in reality, any economic commitment is a function of Canada's role in the much larger global economy. Although total Canadian direct investment in Europe is now over $25 billion and European investment in Canada is more than $30 billion, this does not lead to a direct security interest. The dominant factor is that Canada is now one of the largest global trading states and a leading contributor to the resource sector. That over 80 per cent of Canadian trade is with the United States does not detract from the overall position in the world market, for in most respects the Canadian and American economies should be considered as one. Canadian exports and imports directly form part of the much greater North American contribution to the international marketplace. How does this impact on future joint security concerns at sea?

The nature of the Canada-US bilateral relationship in terms of the Atlantic is not widely understood and, in fact, is frequently misinterpreted. One popular misperception, for instance, is that bilateral operations were always synonymous with NATO operations and thus it was always the NATO maritime strategy and contingency plans that would determine the way bilateral operations were conducted. In reality, two completely separate structures existed with their own command and control systems including rules of engagement.

The bilateral defence framework in the Atlantic was intended purely to deal with direct threats to continental North America. In naval terms, this became an almost entirely strategic ASW role directed at Soviet missile-firing submarines. Even before 1960-61, when the first Soviet SSBs deployed into North American waters, the bilateral concept of naval operations was broader and directed at all Soviet submarines (some of which carried torpedoes with nuclear warheads) and the intelligence gathering activities of the Soviet fishing fleet. Bilateral ASW operations, on both coasts in fact, were completely integrated whereby ships, submarines, aircraft and shore stations (SOSUS and HF/DF) operated under a collective command structure.[37] The point that is so often misunderstood is that these strategic ASW operations were never intended to be integrated into NATO. The reason was really very simple, NATO contingency plans or a NATO declaration of war called up a completely new strategic setting. From a Canadian perspective, activation of NATO plans required a shift from strategic ASW to the reinforcement of Europe and the projection of power against the USSR. Canada's problem was that its naval and maritime air forces were co-tasked to bilateral ASW operations and NATO reinforcement. The Americans did not have this problem because they had sufficient forces to undertake both tasks at the same time. NATO contingency planning did not encompass any part of the North American littoral other than with respect to support services. Simply, the protection of North American ports and shipping in local waters, other than reinforcement shipping, was a strictly national responsibility. Hence there was always a need for two defence structures.

However, there have naturally been instances when the bilateral experience paid dividends elsewhere. For instance, the Canadian Navy was invariably able to tap into the American logistic system when deployed with NATO or engaged in NATO naval exercises. But this did not happen because of the link through NATO, it happened because the bilateral was, in fact, the stronger and more flexible structure, as was the case in the 1990-91 Persian Gulf War when a Canadian was the only non-US national to exercise command over US naval forces.[38]

That Canada was never able to tie North American operations to NATO through CUSRPG, with the result that CUSRPG became little more than a token means of coordinating some planning activities, essentially makes that organization redundant today. Without a common threat to NATO and North America there is very little reason to link the two defence structures other than for the traditional Canadian paranoia of being drawn into American initiatives. However, one should ask whether such a linkage has any symbolic value. A related question, and one that may well be beyond answer at the moment, is whether some requirement might emerge in the future for a joint Canada-US commitment to a European security operation undertaken under the aegis of the WEU rather than NATO.

What is clear is that Canada is a sovereign nation within NATO and acts in accordance with what it sees as its national interests in making commitments to ad hoc and contingency operations. This does not require that continental planning be linked to NATO. Canada has the freedom of choice in how it functions within NATO. That said, though, it is fair to add a note of caution over the future of NATO and its inevitable shift in strategic focus to European security. In time, this could well see a change in the nature of the transatlantic link, particularly the naval dimension with changes planned for the command relationships between SACLANT and SACEUR. Thus, it is quite possible that a mechanism such as CUSRPG may be needed to link the two regional security organizations and thereby uphold the traditional transatlantic link.

For these reasons, it is premature to advocate either the retention or the demise of CUSRPG, as the present link between North American and European defence structures. In time, and when the new European security framework takes more concrete form, it may be possible to make recommendations on CUSRPG, but until then it should stay in being because there is little advantage to be gained by abandoning it.

Looking South to the Rest of the Hemisphere

The North American Free Trade Agreement (NAFTA) at the moment functions without a security relationship, and because of the potential to use the security provisions of the Organization of American States (OAS) (the Rio Treaty), should the need arise, there seems little immediate need to contemplate a dedicated NAFTA security structure. But that does not mean that the hemisphere is immune from security problems. Far from it, in fact, several areas of potential instability exists and has led to some security arrangements. But such agreements in themselves do not guarantee security. For instance, even though Mexico has long been integrated into the American economy and bilateral defense arrangements have been in place for some time, that does not mean the relationship will always be stable. Today, potentially divisive issues exist in many parts of the hemisphere over immigration, drugs and environmental protection.

The point here is that inasmuch as Canada is fundamental to US security to the north, Mexico is fundamental to its southern borders, and is perhaps even more critical to American security given the rising Hispanic population within the United States and the latent instability of Mexico. Similarly, much of the Caribbean and Central America has security implications for the United States. Instability in those areas will almost certainly draw an American response. This, as we have seen over the years with Cuba, can set Canada and the United States on different paths. Hence the management of the broader regional relationship as well as good management of the Canada-US relationship will call for both compromise and innovation in regional matters.

As the NAFTA trade structure expands, the potential for regional disputes may increase. One cannot overlook the possibility of instability arising from trade disputes or differing rates of development. There is simply no certainty that the region will always be stable. Likewise, there can be no guarantee that force will never be needed to restore order.[39] The OAS is not, in itself, powerful enough to create a regional security mechanism without the involvement of the Americans. Yet, it may not be in the collective interest to have a regional security system based primarily on the US military. In much the same way that Canada embraced NATO as the means of counter-balancing US foreign policy enthusiasms, it may become necessary for some of the more influential American states, such as Chile, Argentina and Brazil, to press for a more formal regional security relationship. Such a broadening of the present bilateral security relationship may also suit Canada's larger political needs, especially if US unilateralism in the region becomes politically difficult for Canada in the future.

But how would such a security framework function? Would it be necessary to develop a military committee for the OAS or could the requirement be met by ad hoc means much as they have been in conducting the UNITAS series of exercises and to arrange OAS support for the American quarantine of Cuba in October-November 1962? Here one has to consider the nature of any potential threats to hemispheric security. While the United States, or at least US overseas interests, are likely to come under threat from time to time, it is probably fair to assume that direct external military threats to the hemisphere are of the same low order as those to North America. But there will be security challenges from within the hemisphere and some of these will be of wide concern.[40]

Likewise it is fair to assume that the United States will respond to some of those challenges under the concept of the Monroe Doctrine and will not necessarily seek assistance from other members of the OAS. Yet, it could well be that the politics of some such incidents would make a collective response far more palatable. This is not a new concept. Canada helped in Haiti, albeit under a UN mandate, and has contributed to the UN Honduras-Nicaragua operation. It is very possible that in the future, the Americans might prefer that a collective hemispheric task force undertake some of the regional security. The down-sizing of the US Navy could well lead to a situation where they simply did not have the resources to undertake a regional security problem as well as a major operation in another part of the world. Under such a condition, a UNITAS task force might make a considerable difference.

Now that Canada is a member of OAS and a participant in the UNITAS exercises[41] (as well as continuing to be a member of several inter-American naval conferences) it has the opportunity to lend its expertise to the creation of an effective regional multinational naval force. Although much progress has been made through the UNITAS exercises, there is still work to be done in training for more complex operations. In this, Canada could both help the United States in sharing the regional security burden and also serve as counterbalance to what could easily be seen as unwanted US dominance. Many opportunities also exist for Canada to undertake an even greater role in providing training, at several levels, for the navies and coast guards of the region, especially in the Caribbean. The other regional security issue of concern to both Canada and the United States is the flow of drugs into North America. At the moment, the Americans are shouldering the full load of extra-territorial operations. There is absolutely no reason why Canada should not periodically assign a warship or submarine to those operations. Halting the flow of drugs is very much in the Canadian interest.[42]

Overall, there are several reasons why Canada should become more deeply involved in hemispheric security issues. At present, the best means of making that happen lies in greater involvement in existing structures such as UNITAS and by generally becoming a stronger partner to the United States in regional security matters. This may be unacceptable to the present government because it could well mean resolving differences over Cuba. Here again, is one of those situations where broader political differences of opinion need not be reflected into the existing operational concepts of bilateral cooperation. The various Canada-US naval operations plans and specific agreements are sufficiently flexible to allow joint operations outside the immediate North American littoral, they could easily be extended in a larger concept of a maritime security zone. Simply, Canada has everything to gain from a greater commitment to regional maritime security and very little to lose. Similarly, the Americans would stand to benefit from a greater Canadian involvement in the Americas.

Westward: Across the Pacific

The United States has traditionally played a solo hand in matters of Pacific security, and there is no reason to believe this will change. Canada, on the other hand, has largely maintained a European focus in its foreign policy.[43] In the last decade, however, Asia-Pacific issues have come into political prominence. This reflects three factors: the growing Asian population in Canada, the growing level of Asian investment in the country, and the value of transpacific trade.[44] Yet in comparison, the value of the Asian trade is barely 10 per cent of that with the United States. There is good reason to believe that the present Canadian flirtation with Asia is an attempt to reduce the dominance of the US economy through what may be a reincarnation of Mitchell Sharp's "Third Option" foreign policy of the early 1970s.[45]

The new Canadian interest in Asia has, however, expanded into general security matters independently rather than remaining within the traditional approach through the Canada-US naval security framework. But one has to ask whether Canada is able to act autonomously in Asian security issues. In view of US dominance in the region, Canadian efforts to influence events are likely to be of little avail if they differ greatly from US policies. Canadian efforts to address the security issues in the North Pacific through its proposed

North Pacific Cooperative Security Dialogue were ultimately stillborn, largely due to American scepticism.[46] Further, Canada was denied membership in the Western Pacific Naval Symposium because of a perceived lack of relevance in the area.[47] Nevertheless, Canada has been quietly forging ahead on a number of fronts in the effort to cut a larger presence in the region. For instance, deployments of naval ships to the region have been increased since 1994 with warships visiting ports in both northern and southern Asian countries.[48]

The conclusion one is forced into is that Canada's ability to be an autonomous part of the Asia-Pacific region will be strongly affected by the strength of the bilateral relationship with the Americans. This need not require that Canada endorse all American policies, but it does suggest that any "domestic" differences should not be allowed to affect the larger scope of the bilateral agreements. Without the ability to compete independently as a Pacific power, Canada would either have to temper its transpacific ambitions or continue them in such a way that they were more consistent with American policies. In this, Canada may have to reflect on the position it would take if called upon to return to Korea—a situation that is not beyond the bounds of possibility. Also, Canada would be well advised to keep in mind the various benefits that came as a result of involvement in the long series of RIMPAC exercises in which it participated under that auspices of the Canada-US agreement. Essentially, that era was one when Canada acknowledged its relative inability to influence Asian matters on its own and tempered its involvement to reflect its prevailing national interests.

The rush to Asia today has to be put into its correct perspective to be valid. There is more to be gained by continuing to act as a partner of the United States within the framework of the bilateral agreement than trying to be independent in a "helpful fixer" role. However, there are genuine regional issues of concern to Canada and it is correct that it continue to operate independently to address them, but this should not be done at the expense of the long-standing bilateral naval agreement. There is much more to be gained by remaining in that defence framework than by attempting to be totally independent in a manner that causes concern to other major maritime nations, the United States in particular.

Conclusion

What can we draw from these four brief analyses? First, though, a caveat. Of necessity, little has been said about the ways US and Canadian foreign policy diverge and converge on many issues, including respective national maritime interests. In this chapter, we are looking specifically at naval cooperation and at the way it is often able to take place outside the intricacies of higher-level politics. In Canada-US naval relations it has often been the case that cooperation has taken place to a high degree despite temporary disagreement at the political level. It would seem that the bilateral naval relationship typifies the notion that Canadian relations with the United States are forever "interdependent yet independent". Moreover, they typify the other theory that relationships at one level are invariably unaffected by issues at other levels. In this, the relationship has been referred to as one of "complex interdependence".

What is evident from the experience of the 40-year Cold War is that the bilateral maritime defence structure in all its forms has served both countries enormously well. The changed strategic situation has indeed given rise to questions on the need for future cooperation, and before passing judgement it is useful to review the ways in which the new international system could lead to requirements for joint Canada-US response.

- The Arctic, especially because of its vast emptiness and ecological vulnerability, remains a strategic concern to both Canada and the United States. Issues of sovereignty aside, both nations need to know what is happening there and they also need to be able to respond to challenges should the requirement arise. It would be sensible therefore that much of this be done collectively. In this respect, constant monitoring and information sharing are the keys to effective cooperation.

- The Atlantic, long a major strategic focal point, now has a very different strategic meaning for both Canada and the United States. As Europe seeks greater security autonomy, the long-standing transatlantic link maybe weakened and in the process the need to coordinate North American security issues with those of Europe is probably unnecessary Yet, there may be another day when the North Americans will have to return to help the Europeans defend themselves. It thus makes no sense to disband the existing CUSRPG structure.

- In the Americas there appear to be more opportunities for useful cooperation than before the end of the Cold War. The hemisphere is not completely stable and although the likelihood of external military threat is low, collective action to intra-regional challenges makes more sense than the traditional pattern of near-exclusive US unilateral action. Hence, the existing bilateral framework holds the promise of leading to an effective regional maritime security framework.

- Canadian adventurism in Asia, especially attempts to act independently in the security field, have not produced significant results, and in view of local suspicion of Canadian motives, are unlikely to be productive in the future. Hence, it makes more sense for Canada to return to the practice of participating in Asian maritime security matters from within the framework of the bilateral agreement.

In summary, the Canada-US bilateral maritime defence structure, admittedly somewhat unstructured at times yet enormously flexible in providing mechanisms for cooperation, has served both partners well in the past 50 years. Despite calls to do away with this structure, which is maintained at little real or political cost, the sensible conclusion is to maintain it in its existing form. But in saying that, it is also clear that the formal naval relationship must evolve with the changing circumstances that surround it. In several areas, in the Arctic and in the Americas especially, there is much to be gained by an even greater level of cooperation. For Canada, a relatively limited naval power but with considerable experience in multinationalism, continuing the bilateral relationship will provide opportunities to act as a mentor to other nations who have not been as fortunate. Through this process Canada would surely gain stature. On the other hand, ending the formal bilateral naval relational would undoubtedly set Canada on a path of marginalization on the world's oceans. For a major maritime nation, as Canada indeed is, that would be a foolish step to take. As in 1940 and in 1946, Canadian sovereignty and security interests are generally served much better through cooperation with the United States than by adopting an isolationist stance.

Notes

1. The authors would like thank Professors Dan W. Middlemiss of Dalhousie University and Joel J. Sokolsky of the Royal Military College of Canada for invaluable help and suggestions in writing this paper.
2. This section draws on research done by Peter Haydon, Joel Sokolsky, and J.T. Jockel for a manuscript examining Canada-US naval cooperation in the early Cold War period to 1968 which will be published in the near future as *Ocean Approaches: Canada U.S. Naval Cooperation 1945-68.*

3. Throughout this paper *joint* is used to describe the Canada-US defence activities. This reflects original rather than contemporary usage which indicates multi-service activities.
4. Quoted in J.C. Arnell, "The Development of Joint North American Defence" *Queen's Quarterly*, 1970, 191. However, the origins of the joint continental defence structure actually started in August 1936 with a speech by Roosevelt at Chautaugua, New York.
5. *Ibid.*
6. See C.P. Stacey, *Mackenzie King and the Atlantic Triangle (The 1976 Joanne Goodman Lectures)* (Toronto: Macmillan of Canada, 1976), 50-51.
7. Report "A Programme of Immediate Canadian Action drawn up by a Group of Twenty Canadians Meeting at the Chateau Laurier, Ottawa, July 17-18, 1940", 1-2. (PAC, MG30, E159, Vol. 2 - Defence and Foreign Affairs).
8. Wartime Canada-US naval cooperation is beyond the scope of this chapter. The few comments here are merely intended to show that the cooperation has deeper roots than the Cold War period. For more complete discussions of the war-time period see Marc Milner, *The U-Boat Hunters: The Royal Canadian Navy and the Offensive against Germany's Submarines* (Toronto: University of Toronto Press, 1994); W.G.D. Lund, "The Royal Canadian Navy's Quest for Autonomy in the North West Atlantic", in James A. Boutilier, ed., *The RCN in Retrospect, 1910-1968* (Vancouver: University of British Columbia Press, 1982); and Colonel Stanley W. Dziuban, *Military Relations Between the United States and Canada 1939-1945* (Washington: Office of the Chief of Military History, Department of the Army, 1959).
9. Stacey, *Mackenzie King and the Atlantic Triangle*, 66-7.
10. See the memoirs of Lieutenant-General Guy V. Henry, US Army (DND, Directorate of History and Heritage (hereafter DHH) collection File No. 79/316), 89-90. Also, see James Eayrs, *In Defence of Canada: Peacemaking and Deterrence* (Toronto: University of Toronto Press, 1972), especially Chapter 6 "Defending the Continent". At the same time, the scope of future military cooperation between the two countries was discussed. In many respects, the process was unbalanced. The Americans took the lead in pressing for cooperation on a wide range of items and pushed the reluctant Canadians into closer cooperation. (See Christopher Conliffe, "The Permanent Joint Board on Defense, 1940-1988", David G. Haglund and Joel J. Sokolsky, eds, *The U.S.-Canada Security Relationship: The Politics, Strategy, and Technology of Defense* (Boulder: Westview Press, 1989), 153-5).
11. Minutes of Chiefs of Staff Committee (hereafter COSC) meeting No. 360 9 August 1946, para 3.
12. US Joint War Plans Committee document No. 4443/2 "MATCHPOINT" dated 6 May 1946, pp. 6-7. (US National Archives (hereafter NA), JCS Files RG 218, CCS 092 (9-10-45) Ser 3.

13. It was at this stage that the fundamental differences between the two political systems, specifically the way in which civil control was exercised over the military, came to prominence. In the United States, military planning was, by precedent and tradition, a purely military undertaking with little political input. Political considerations entered the process upon implementation of a plan. The Canadian approach to strategic planning was more deeply politicized through a complex process of interdepartmental coordination. The Chiefs of Staff Committee, for instance, was routinely attended by senior members of other departments and secretariats who regularly spoke to items of perceived collective interest. It was necessary to have interdepartmental agreement before any issue was presented to the next level of review—the Cabinet Defence Committee in the case of war or contingency plans. As often happened, principals from key departments, essentially Defence and External Affairs in the case of strategic planning, held different perceptions on the scope and division of responsibility of collective defence plans and commitments. Resolving these differences was not always a simple task; much to the frustration of the joint planning staffs, the PJBD, and its subordinate planning agency, the Military Cooperation Committee.

14. Memorandum to the Canadian Chiefs of Staff Committee from the Canadian Joint Planning Committee (essentially the Canadian members of the Military Cooperation Committee (MCC)) dated 29 October 1946. (PAC, RG24, Acc 83-4/167, Vol. 8067, File NSTS 11270-15-1 (Vol. 1)). As the minutes of COSC meeting No. 366 on 8 October 1946 paras 8-9 show, the Canadian Chiefs of Staff continued to discuss the details of the joint documents through the summer and into the fall of 1946.

15. Minutes of the COSC meeting No. 375 of 7 January, 1947.

16. In fact, the operational policy shift was not as radical as it might appear. There had been several quiet changes in operational policy since the end of the war, mainly in the wider use of USN communications procedures and the adoption of the USN task group structure. Relatively little has been written on this subject but the details are publicly available in the archives of the Department of National Defence's Directorate of History and Heritage, especially the files of the Naval Staff and the minutes of the Naval Board.

17. Minute of COSC meeting No. 417 of 2 March, 1948, para 4.

18. It was assumed that until 1950 enemy capabilities would be confined to the landing of a few hundred men in peripheral areas only, but that by 1950 this capability might be expanded to attacks employing 6,000 men in the North-eastern approaches and somewhat greater numbers in the North-west. If North-west Europe were overrun, airborne or amphibious operations might be mounted from that area. Surface raiding groups might also be employed for harassing attacks.

19. Warning signs that the concept of planning was too rich for the defence budgets of either country can be found in the debate held simultaneously in Ottawa and

Washington in 1948 and 1949. In March 1948, the MCC advised both the American and Canadian Chiefs of Staff that implementation of the Appendices would be a problem. The force requirements were of such magnitude that it was probably necessary to return to the Basic Security Plan itself and review its fundamental concepts. See "Report by the Canada-United States Military Cooperation Committee to the Chiefs of Staff, Canada and the United States on Implementation Measures for the Canada-United States Basic Security".

20. General Bradley, who had just replaced General Eisenhower as Chief of the Army Staff was openly sceptical of the continental defence plans believing that they were out of proportion with the threat and called up more US capabilities than in reality should be devoted to defending North America. (Internal staff memorandum from Captain H. D. Riley USN (Op-30X) dated 8 April 1948. (NA, Records of the Chief of Naval Operations, Box "Strategic Plans—Canada").

21. "Report by the Joint Strategic Plans Committee to the Chiefs of Staff on Protection of Sea Lines of Communication Appendix to Canada-United States Basic Security Plan" (J.C.S. 1541/52 dated 31 July 1948) (NA, Records of the JCS (RG218) CCS 092 (9-10-25) Ser. 11.

22. *Canada-United States Emergency Defense Plan* (MCC 300/1 dated 25 March 1949) (NA, Records of the Chiefs of Staff (RG218), CCS 092 (9-10-45) ser. 16.)

23. Much of the story of the evolution of NATO's maritime structure is told by Sean M. Maloney in *Securing Command of the Sea: NATO Naval Planning 1948-1954* (Annapolis, MD: Naval Institute Press, 1995. The minutes of the Canadian Chiefs of Staff Committee for the 1949-51 period also contain an fairly complete account of the political in-fighting.

24. See R.J. Sutherland, "Canada's Long Term Strategic Situation" *International Journal*, XVIII:3, Summer 1962, 206-8. That preceded the formation of SACLANT and the demise of regional planning groups other than CUSRPG.

25. Canadian requirements for three-way linkages through CUSRPG led to a security model which the late John Holmes referred to as "the Dumbbell" with one end representing political linkages in Europe and the other representing the Ottawa-Washington linkages. The concept, intended more for public relations purposes than as a working model, was intended to show political equality in North America and a parallel political unity in Europe. This, of course, was an illusion, if not a grand act of Canadian self-deception, for political parity never existed between Washington and Ottawa in terms of NATO. The American role in NATO was significant whereas the Canadian was not. Canada did not hold forth the promise of strategic forces or vast armies, merely food and raw materials. However, Canada was a very significant factor in American security, as mentioned earlier, and for that reason the unity implied in the western end of the dumbbell was not unacceptable. Thus, the myth was perpetuated. And thus a unique and perhaps slightly curious three-way relationship came into existence, and it is this which

lies at the heart of the question of whether a continental security structure is still needed.

26. This is discussed in detail by Joseph T. Jockel in *No Boundaries Upstairs* (Vancouver: University of Vancouver Press, 1967) and in his article "The Military Establishments and the Creation of NORAD," *American Review of Canadian Studies* XII:3 Fall 1982.

27. See Peter T. Haydon, *The 1962 Cuban Missile Crisis: Canadian Involvement Reconsidered* (Toronto: Canadian Institute of Strategic Studies, 1993).

28. Albert Legault in his paper "Canada and the United States: The Defense Dimension," in Charles F. Doran and John H. Sigler, eds, *Canada and the United States: Enduring Friendship, Persistent Stress* (Englewood Cliffs, NJ: Prentice-Hall Inc., 1985), 174-182, discusses the maritime dimension of the contemporary relationship.

29. See Peter T. Haydon, *The Strategic Importance of the Arctic: Understanding the Military Issues* Strategic Issues Paper No. 1/87 (Ottawa: Department of National Defence, March 1987).

30. See Arkidy Pauk and Igor Sutyagin *The Russian Navy: Now and in the Future* (Alexandria, VA: Center for Naval Analyses, March 1997).

31. Office of Naval Intelligence *Worldwide Submarine Challenges* (Washington: ONI, 1997) discusses the re-emergence of the Russian fleet and its submarine fleet.

32. For more details on these deployments see David Griffiths "Science Under the Ice," *Maritime Affairs Newsletter* April 1997, 11-13.

33. Present DND plans to acquire the four British *Upholder*-class diesel-electric submarines and eventually retrofit them with an Air Independent Propulsion (AIP) system will give them a limited under-ice capability but not an Arctic capability. To operate under the permanent ice of the high Arctic and transit safely under the keels of the icebergs in the Davis Strait a full nuclear propulsion capability is needed in a submarine able to dive safely to depths in the order of one thousand feet.

34. Cited in Joseph T. Jockel, "Canada in a Twin-Pillared Alliance: The 'Dumbbell' May Just Have to Do", *International Journal* XLVI, Winter 1990-91, 14.

35. John Mearsheimer, "Back to the Future: Instability in Europe after the Cold War", *International Security* 15:1 Summer 1990.

36. In correspondence with Paul Mitchell, 25 June 1997.

37. For a more detailed discussion of continental maritime defence structures, see Haydon, *The 1962 Cuban Missile Crisis: Canadian Involvement Reconsidered*, 78-84.

38. See Commodore Duncan (Dusty) E. Miller and Sharon Hobson, *The Persian Excursion: The Canadian Navy in the Gulf War* (Clemenstport, NS: The Canadian Peacekeeping Press, 1995), 155-180.

39. David Haglund, "Does Canada Have 'Security Interests' in Latin America?," *Canadian Foreign Policy* 2:2, 1994.

40. For a further discussion see Commander Glenn M. Irvine, U.S. Navy, "UNITAS: 'Forward...from the Sea'" *Proceedings* June 1997, 74-75.

41. See Commander Barry Coombs, U.S. Navy, *United States Naval Cooperation with Canada* (Newport, RI: U.S. Naval War College, 1995).

42. This subject is discussed in greater detail, and with careful integration of the views of several other scholars, by Robert H. Thomas, "Regional and Canada-US Considerations of Future Canadian Naval Capabilities," in Ann L. Griffiths and Peter T. Haydon, eds, *Maritime Forces in Global Security* (Halifax: Centre for Foreign Policy Studies, 1995), 293-308.

43. The 1987 Defence White Paper makes no reference whatsoever to Asia Pacific, whereas the 1994 white paper is interspersed with commitments to "reach out" to Asia Pacific, as well as other parts of the world. *Challenge and Commitment: A Defence Policy for Canada* (Ottawa: Department of National Defence, 1987); *1994 Defence White Paper* (Ottawa: Department of National Defence, 1994), 37.

44. Brian L. Job and Frank Langdon, "Canada and the Pacific", in Christopher Maule and Fen Osler Hampson, eds, *Global Jeopardy: Canada Among Nations 1993-1994* (Ottawa: Carleton University Press, 1994), 269, 276.

45. Andrew Purvis, "Super Exporter", *Time*, 38.

46. Job, *Canada and the Pacific,* 289-290.

47. Although it did succeed in gaining observer status and has been an active participant at WPNS workshops and symposia since 1994.

48. HMCS *Vancouver* visited Japan, South Korea, Russia and China in 1994 and HMCS *Regina* and *Vancouver* made tandem visits to ASEAN states, Hong Kong, Australia, New Zealand and the South Pacific in 1995. *Westploy '96* included four ships including two *City*-class frigates, an *Iroquois*-class destroyer and an AOR, although in 1997 the deployment was scaled back to the typical two ship deployment.

13 Latin American Multinational Naval Cooperation: Trends and Prospects

H.P. KLEPAK AND MICHAEL A. MORRIS

We are in a unipolar period of some unknown duration where security matters are concerned. The debate rages as to whether we are living through a unipolar *era* or merely a unipolar *moment,* but unipolar this point in history seems most certainly to be.

This is not to suggest that the international system is altogether unipolar. It is clearly not in trade, investment, fiscal and many other economic senses where the superpower club might not be numerous but would at least include Japan and Europe/Germany as well as the US. But where power projection is concerned, and at least until Russia again finds its way, unipolarity seems to be the order of the day. And neither Germany/Europe nor Japan, for historic and any number of other reasons, seems in the slightest seriously tempted to challenge this unipolar order for the time being or even for the justly infamous "foreseeable future".

The United States is uniquely able to project a serious degree of power internationally and to sustain it abroad for a significant period. Even more striking, only the US seems able to build coalitions which can act to support and legitimize its objectives across a wide spectrum of the world's areas of instability, potential or current. This US prominence in the security sphere is especially important for Latin America, which for decades has been evolving partially but not completely out of a US area of influence (or hegemonial sphere). Latin American multinational naval cooperation (MNCO) at a time of both global and regional transition is therefore distinctive.

This chapter first describes the Latin American security context for multinational naval cooperation including relevant historical antecedents and contemporary trends. Prospects are then assessed for naval cooperation in what appear to be nine promising functional areas. Prospects vary not only by functional area and country but also by ocean basin. These are examined

263

in the South Atlantic, the South Pacific and the Caribbean. In the final section, some guidelines for successful regional multinational naval cooperation are set forth.

Figure 13.1 Latin America

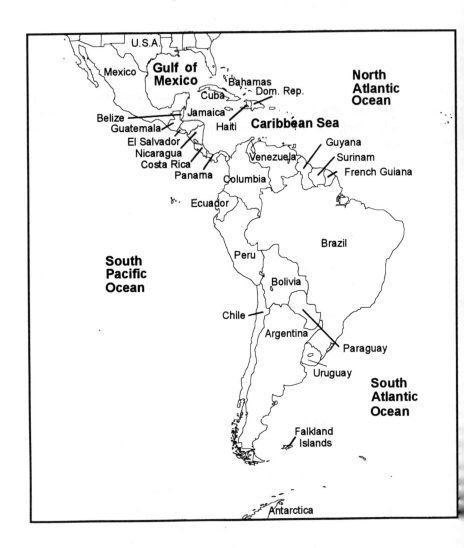

Latin America in the Present Context

The current context is something of a patchwork with many countries doing very well indeed, while others are in the doldrums, to say the least. Democracy flourishes as it has never done before. In many countries a great deal of progress has been achieved and in several others at least some headway has been made. Economic progress is impressive in much of the Southern Cone, parts of Central America and in some of the Andean countries. It is less so in Mexico, Venezuela, other parts of the Caribbean, Central America and other Andean states. Even more troubling, the present wave of prosperity is leaving out huge portions of the population who seem to be ever more marginalized at a time when great riches are being accumulated by some.

Economic integration and drastic measures to confront the challenges of globalization are making for dramatic headlines. The speed of progress in the South American Common Market (MERCOSUR) is in some areas rapid while the need for quick action is understood more widely than at perhaps any time for a century. Trade continues to grow among NAFTA partners, and the North American trade grouping may still be extended to other countries in the hemisphere.

The battle against corruption is having an even more spotted success story, as is that against the illegal drugs trade. The crime wave is skyrocketing almost everywhere with a growing sense of citizen insecurity across virtually the whole region.

In the context of advancing democratization and wide-ranging efforts at improving interstate security relations, armed forces are generally felt to be back in the barracks, at least in the most formal sense and their budgets are more in civilian hands than at any time for many decades. Their future roles are in question and in many cases there is resentment at their treatment over the past few years by a civil society which they often feel misunderstands their role in politics and the state.

At the same time there is a growth in the non-traditional roles of the military in many countries. This is a result of some of the challenges mentioned above, posed by the vast changes sweeping the area and leaving large elements of the population out of the progress being made. The threat of an *estallido social* or widespread social disorder phenomenon is growing in many countries and is doing so in ways which often outstrip the power of the police to cope.

The Inter-American System

In the face of this vastly changed panorama both in the Americas and more globally, the inter-American system seems on the face of it little changed. Formally, there is the Organization of American States, turning fifty in less than two years, the successor to a Pan-American Union dating back in some respects to 1889. Its Charter is still in force, and its membership has gained in numbers steadily since the early 1960s, most recently with the entrance of that perennial sceptic on inter-American affairs: Canada.

Only Cuba of the independent countries of the Americas does not sit in its councils and even this is not Cuba's choice. The current government has of course been expelled from the Organization for several decades now. And even here most members have expressed the wish that Cuba should be reintegrated into the OAS as soon as possible.

The peaceful resolution of disputes provisions of the various accords dealing with this issue are also still formally in force. And the inter-American security system, based on the Rio Pact (Inter-American Treaty of Reciprocal Assistance) as well as a wide-ranging series of mutual assistance pacts, commanders of armed forces conferences, the Inter-American Defense Board and its College, etc. is still there. In addition, exercises of all kinds among the armed forces of the Americas occur on a regular basis, and under the rubric of bilateral and multilateral accords, cooperation in areas as diverse as search and rescue operations and anti-drug activities takes place.

In reality of course the scene is anything but that of a fully functioning regional system as conceived by many a half-century ago or even earlier. This state of affairs results from very different ideas among the members about the role of the system, the terms of reference and limitations to that role, and where indeed the 'system' should be going. The OAS is undergoing reasonably dramatic change under the leadership of its new Secretary-General César Gaviria of Colombia. But no one would suggest that it functions properly or according to the hopes of the drafters of its charter. This does not mean that there is no interest in revising the security system as a whole on the part of Latin Americans, the United States or even Canada. It does mean that the current state of affairs satisfies no one.

US observers tend, on the other hand, to emphasize the positive and suggest that all that is needed is reform to bring the system back to a useful role. It may be unfortunate but it is nonetheless true that these calls as well tend to fall largely on deaf ears. Firstly, for many Latin Americans the system has never had a useful role. Equally, many see those proposals for reform put forward by Washington as much more responsive to the exclusive geopolitical and domestic concerns of the United States than any real attempt to suggest multilateralism as the way of the future in inter-American security relations.

Multinational Naval Cooperation until 1945 in this Context

If this is the context for multinational security cooperation in Latin America, one can now turn to where naval cooperation would find its place. Where would riverine, coastal and open seas operations find roles which would support objectives shared by a number, or perhaps all countries of the hemisphere?

As several naval historians have shown us, naval power has had an enormous impact on the military and diplomatic history of Latin America. It was Spanish and Portuguese sea power which established empires in the Americas, and the pattern of settlement in most of Latin America, where the coastal regions became key almost everywhere, reinforces this perception. Indeed, it was the weakness of Spanish naval strength in the early years of the revolutions for independence that allowed the fledgling states to anchor their political structures and organize their armed forces. And it was the return of at least a degree of Spanish naval power after 1814 which was vital in helping ensure for almost another century that Cuba and Puerto Rico would not join their continental cousins in rebelling against the *madre patria*. Local navies in key newly-independent countries were neither large nor particularly efficient but they were enough to maintain independence and, in several cases, to fight the first wars between Latin American states.

The Monroe Doctrine of 1823 was itself entirely dependent on British naval strength for its effectiveness in deterring Spain, and perhaps the Holy Alliance, from intervening to re-establish Spanish rule in the region. And naval power proved crucial in the major wars of the mid-19th century in ordering what Burr has called the South American "balance of power" of that era.[1] Many of the boundaries one sees today in Latin America are the direct results of the application of sea power in the context of the difficult geography and other factors affecting conflict in the region during this period.

Chile at this time became a significant naval power in the southeastern Pacific context. And Argentina and Brazil, as part of their long rivalry, set up navies which essentially mutually deterred one another. And while the states of the north, the Caribbean, Mexico and the northern Andean countries, developed no such powerful maritime tradition, they also could not ignore naval power, usually its consequences being felt in terms of foreign military interventions from a number of countries but increasingly from the United States. Indeed, such interventions, whether French, British, German, Italian or American, were essentially naval operations usually involving largely marines or similar landing parties.

The origins of inter-American naval cooperation have been romantically placed in the context of resistance to Spain during the revolutions or to the later Spanish naval raids on western South America in the mid-1860s. In fact, the cooperation really only began during the First World War, and even then it is easy to exaggerate the degree of collaboration. Indeed, most naval connections among American states tended to be confrontational, not cooperative, until well into the 20th century. As late as 1914-18, the major naval connection between the Allies and Latin America was a series of joint Brazilian Navy-Royal Navy operations in the South Atlantic rather than any inter-American activity.[2]

In the years immediately preceding the Second World War, the situation began to change with US naval missions, as well as army and air force counterparts, starting to go to Latin America, at first replacing those of the fascist powers but later those of the democracies as well. The immense prestige of the Royal Navy, however, slowed this trend where navies were concerned. In the case of armies the British had never really been in the game of competition among the powers for influence over Latin American land forces. France was supplanted after a century and a half of considerable prestige and activity in the region's armies, and everywhere the new influence was to be distinctly that of the United States.[3]

The war itself was crucial in changing the inter-American system into something much more effective. Successive meetings of foreign ministers, largely in reaction to events in Europe and the Far East, ensured the growth of more Pan-American solidarity and cooperation. Even before war broke out in Europe, the American republics moved to coordinate policy and ensure their neutrality in case it did. Between 1936 and 1940, US policy evolved dramatically in the direction of a need to take Latin America more seriously. This was not only because of the danger of fascism in the region but also, especially after the fall of France in 1940 and the immediate danger that the same fate might be reserved for Britain, the real possibility, viewed from Washington, that the British and French fleets would be added to Nazi Germany's land and air power and present a massive and direct danger to the Americas themselves. In that case, Latin America could provide the Germans with a North American "soft underbelly" for an attack.[4]

During the war the United States made bilateral agreements with a large number of Latin American countries, especially in the Caribbean basin but also farther south. Even ever-reluctant Mexico agreed to US radar cooperation, the recruitment of Mexican nationals working in the United States, emergency arrangements for the engagement of Mexican agricultural workers to replace US citizens called up for military service, a joint defence board, a vast array of special commercial arrangements and the despatch of an air squadron to the Pacific war.[5]

Naval and air forces received priority in many spheres. Most Latin American navies at this time could not provide even coastal operations of a standard required to meet the potential threat of submarines and possible surface raiders posed by the Axis. Only the southern South American states had reasonably serious navies and even these tended to be unbalanced and hardly battle ready.[6] The USN's priority was therefore to gain access to naval and air facilities in key countries aiming at operations in defence of vital points, in particular the Panama Canal, which would essentially be a US affair with Latin Americans in a distinctly auxiliary role.

In general, however, although cooperation at a formal level grew in the Americas during the war, and while US influence displaced the Europeans in all security fields, one can hardly talk of a united hemisphere fighting any kind of war with a common enemy. Canada fought its war as part of the British Commonwealth, starting at the very beginning in 1939. The United States came in only after a direct attack from the Japanese over two years later. Latin America formed a patchwork of countries coming in, some quickly, some slowly, some hardly at all, in the aftermath of the Pearl Harbour attack and later developments.

Naval Cooperation from 1945 until Today

After the war events moved quickly with the Cold War showing clear signs of becoming something permanent by 1947. At that time the inter-American system was being reinforced and restructured in accordance with the new hemispheric and regional realities, which of course included the vastly superior position of the United States in international affairs resulting from the collapse of the fascist powers and the exhaustion of those which had fought them from the beginning. Washington found itself the unquestioned leader of the Western world with the only challenge being the ideological and military one posed by the Soviet Union, the other great victor of the Second World War.

The reflection of this struggle in Latin America was not likely to be great. After all, the region was Catholic, traditionalist, with powerful established elites in charge of affairs and a US position of immense influence. Also Moscow was under-represented diplomatically and economically in the area and showed little sign of changing this state of affairs. Nonetheless, the US desire to secure its southern flank so that it could be free to act with decisiveness elsewhere on the planet meant that Washington would move to revamp the Pan-American Union and anchor the inter-American security system which had served Washington so well during wartime.

The result was the series of negotiations leading to the signing of the Rio Pact in 1947. In return for what they hoped would be something of a Marshall Plan for Latin America, the region's countries accepted that they should consider the Soviet Union as a potential enemy against whom they would collaborate in partnership with the United States. The treaty is formally a system of collective security wherein an attack on one signatory is considered an attack on all and where the states party agree to coordinate a military response to defeat the aggression jointly.

In addition, over the years the inter-American cooperative system in security grew in depth through the Commanders Conferences. Each year or two, the Commanders of each of the services of most hemispheric countries meet to discuss common problems and seek cooperative initiatives to meet common goals. While not all countries attend as fully accredited delegations, most do and several of those who do not can choose to attend as observers.

Navies have been especially active in this area and meetings are usually warm and well received. It should be pointed out that these meetings also spawned a series of annual and other meetings of the Commandants of naval colleges and superior naval academic centres over some thirty-five years now.[7]

A number of multilateral exercises at the regional and sub-regional levels have been held regularly or on *ad hoc* basis within the context of the inter-American system. Here as well, navies have been especially active. The UNITAS series, for example, is now over 35 years old, and has been well regarded by almost all those involved. They take place in the Caribbean, Atlantic or Pacific and can have any of a number of types of scenarios posed.

At an operational level, there have been some periods of inter-American security cooperation. During the Cuban Missile Crisis, there was an attempt to make the blockading force more inter-American.[8] This was frustrated by understandable US concerns about the nature of the stakes involved and the consequent need to have a firm chain of command, and operational efficiency during the crisis.

The US invasion of the Dominican Republic was given an inter-American flavour as soon as possible thorough the despatch of some Latin American countries' troops to the country in 1965. Exercises meant to send an unmistakable message to Nicaragua after the capture of power by the Sandinistas in 1979 were organized with Central American forces during the 1980s and under a supposed inter-American umbrella. The 1983 invasion of Grenada was mounted with token forces coming from the Eastern Caribbean states.

In addition, "peacekeeping" operations were mounted in a small number of cases under OAS auspices in the case of fighting between member states. They were advocated by the Carter government as late as 1979 as a means of keeping the FSLN from seizing power in Nicaragua and providing a method of easing out the Somoza dictatorship without letting in its often leftist opponents. In virtually all cases where such operations occurred or were put forward during the Cold War, it was because the US wished to give legitimacy to something it wished to see happen and was considering implementing unilaterally. Thus the term "peacekeeping" got something of a bad reputation in Latin America, a view which only now is being attenuated.

Unfortunately, the idea of inter-American military cooperation came to mean the use of the inter-American system to further the foreign and defence policy of the United States. This of course meant that many countries tended to be ill-disposed towards the idea independent of its merits in a particular case. This public image of the system, and especially of the Rio Pact, became even more negative in the 1980s when the inter-American approach brought few positive results over the 1981 fighting between Ecuador and Peru, no results in the 1982 Falklands War, little in the Grenada case, and nothing in the especially tragic case of the widespread conflicts in Central America over the whole decade. In Panama, prior to 1989, the inter-American system tried but failed to produce results, and the US felt completely justified in intervening militarily at the end of that year.

Navies took a very large role, relatively speaking, in those operations and exercises undertaken by the inter-American system during the Cold War. It was naval power which was crucial in the Cuban Missile Crisis, operations against Grenada, intimidating manoeuvres against Nicaragua in the 1980s, as well as the Falklands War. It was equally naval power which ensured the success of the intervention in the Dominican Republic.

The Post-Cold War Context

The above elements constituted the main features of the inter-American security system during the Cold War, at least insofar as military cooperation was concerned. Since the Cold War's end, the system has gone through a phase where it has been deeply criticized as irrelevant to the needs of Latin America and completely out of date.

More recently, perhaps as the realities of the reinforced asymmetries of the post-Cold War Americas have sunk in more completely, there have been fewer calls for abandonment of the system and more for its reform. Even the latter have tended to be much less radical than many heard in the early part of the nineties. Most have been willing to place their hopes in a renewed system, reflecting the improvements in the OAS of recent years, the creation of the organization's first permanent Security Committee to discuss these matters, and the pace of regional and even hemispheric integration.

What Kind of Multilateral Security Cooperation Can be Envisaged?

The OAS and especially its security committee, the Inter-American Defense Board and its College, the defence ministers' summits set in motion by the US after the Miami Summit of December 1994, the Commanders' Conferences, and many individual states have been wrestling to find ideas which can help to move the agenda forward in the area of the reform of the inter-American security system. Seminars have been held from Canada to Chile dealing with these matters and books have proliferated on the subject.

What has become clear is that there is no consensus as to what is the best way ahead. Almost all observers agree, however, that this is a golden moment for the advancement of the security agenda in the Americas. The presence of formal democracies throughout the region, dramatic improvements in civilian control of the armed forces in most countries, a generalized move towards closer economic and to some extent political integration, a desire to transfer funds from security sectors to development, an end to the Central American wars achieved or in sight, reduced tensions in most of the hemisphere and many other factors point to a special moment in the turbulent history of the continent.

There are nonetheless real rivalries and jurisdictional, territorial and resource disputes still flourishing in the region. Distrust of where the US wishes to take the system is real and remains widespread. What many Latin Americans see as US attempts to force the region to adopt Washington's views on the drugs trade, ecological matters of great import, economic and political integration, sustainable development, civil-military relations, confidence-building measures, demilitarization and many other sensitive issues are much resented.

What then may give a basis for further cooperation in military affairs? What issues are seen by decisive majorities as ones requiring addressing? Once these questions are answered one can finally come to discuss where specifically naval cooperation can find its place.

Latin American Perspectives: The Search for Common Ground

Latin American decision-makers generally would agree that they wish to reinforce stability in the region and indeed within their countries. There are few hold-outs on the need to address the drugs trade more seriously although their suspicions that the US is not really serious about the matter have not disappeared. All would agree that the international illegal arms trade has to be brought under control. All feel work can be done better in search and rescue, transportation security, natural disaster relief and prediction and other areas.

On the other hand, few wish to see long-standing traditions of sovereignty and non-intervention impinged upon even though some are tempted to do so for the defence of democracy and humanitarian intervention. Many are thus still reticent about peacekeeping and peace enforcement and cooperation on matters which affect the domestic affairs of members. While many see the need for confidence-building measures to be put in place, some see them as necessary for others but not for themselves. The long-standing Latin American tradition is one of considering the region somehow not like others in that it has fewer violent disputes, and is a sort of Latin Common-wealth. While not without its elements of truth, this view often has the unfortunate effect of making Latin Americans less hurried in finding solutions to outstanding problems. And when open conflict breaks out such as in 1995 between Peru and Ecuador, they are shocked.

Ideas of cooperative security have gained considerable credence in Latin America of late, at least among civilians interested in security matters. However, it must be said that so far in many countries it has had less impact on military thinking, which has tended to stay much more in the traditional mode. It must also be said that Latin American militaries are often more than a little suspicious about reductions in their muscle and influence when they see the results of demilitarization in El Salvador, Haiti, Nicaragua and Panama.

In these countries the treatment of military forces demobilized was shockingly shoddy in many cases. And while this was also true of demobilized guerrillas such as the FMLN in El Salvador and the Contras in Nicaragua, this does not make military officers feel any better. Salaries are very low, re-education programs are few and far between and pensions are small or non-existent. In this context, officers tend to have knee-jerk reactions against confidence-building measures, arms reduction proposals, demilitarization and the whole package of reforms which they are told are in everyone's best interests but for which they feel from past experience they alone will be asked to pay the price.

The range of views as to where to go with inter-American security cooperation is vast. Argentina desires to become ever more active in international and regional peacekeeping, confidence-building measures, and reinforcement of the Security Committee and the whole OAS security structure. Mexico holds deep and abiding suspicions of a process often seen as little more than a thinly-disguised US attempt to replace the communist bogey-man with new ones in order to continue their domination of the inter-American security scene, indeed the inter-American scene *tout court*.[9]

As a recent Inter-American Defense College Symposium on political-military relations and international organizations emphasized, "Discussion of the New World Order and its implications for national security and the roles of the armed forces underscored that the hemisphere community must resist the temptation to 'invent a consensus that does not exist'."[10] That consensus does indeed not exist. However, one should equally eschew the opposite idea that there is absolutely nothing one can do about hemispheric security since there is no consensus.

Mexico does not oppose confidence-building measures in areas outside its own. Indeed, it has called for more in the Southern Cone and also between the US and Cuba. The Chilean armed forces' reluctance over some elements of peacekeeping has not meant that they have been unhappy to see UN successes in several international hot spots. Distrust of long-term US intentions has not stymied all bilateral cooperation to combat the drugs trade. Commanders Conferences have found much scope for cooperation on wide-ranging issues.

It is perhaps a time for "ad hockery", that much maligned but often useful approach to human affairs. It is in this sort of context that inventive arrangements can do more on a case-by-case basis than the grand scheme effectively can attempt. There is a need for evolution in the military and wider thinking by all parties. The United States must show that it is serious about new rules for its relations with Latin America, ones which show it to be interested in a true multilateral approach to problems where the views of all are respected and where unilateralism is visibly a thing of the past.

What Can Navies Do to Help?

Latin American countries are having difficulties keeping their fleets up to standard given the rapidly escalating costs of ship production and the pace of technological advance. This may be an element favouring cooperation but it must be said that the nervousness in threat perceptions caused by such circumstances can just as easily result in tensions between and among states.[11]

These navies will not be anxious to abandon what they see as their main mission, that is, the defence of their countries and their maritime extensions from the hostile intentions of other states and the deterrence of those countries from attempting to impose military solutions on them.[12] This is unlikely to change for some time, although it is to be hoped that growing multilateral cooperation will serve to reduce tensions and build confidence in the region in such a way as to slowly end the rivalries and mutual suspicions which feed these tensions.

The challenge is to see in what ways these navies can cooperate multilaterally in the future given the present and likely future circumstances and context described above. The rhetoric is in place. All the countries of the region have expressed their determination to reduce tensions and move on to an era of true economic integration. All the armed forces of the region have seconded their governments with public statements in the same vein. Thus one should have a context favorable, both within the realm of traditional security concerns and that of non-traditional areas, to the cooperation being discussed here. Several areas which seem to offer some promise are discussed briefly here as an invitation for more specialist opinion to be expressed on this topic.

Peacekeeping. International peacekeeping is a role where navies are more active than ever on the current international scene. Although there was a transport and general support role given them in a number of such operations as early as Suez (1956), fleets tended to see this as very minor indeed compared to their combat roles in traditional national defence and deterrence.

With the explosion of the concept since the late 1980s, all this has of course changed. The navies of several countries of the hemisphere have been involved in such activities. In the traditional roles outside the hemisphere one has seen the participation of some Latin American states and of course Canada. More importantly, however, was the Argentine naval involvement in the UN observor mission in Central America (ONUCA) in the Gulf of Fonseca from 1989 to 1992.

As mentioned, inter-American peacekeeping had acquired something of a bad name during the Cold War with attempts to use the term for all manner of US-inspired operations against leftist governments. Reluctance to become involved in such operations was thus widespread and had its impact on slowing what might have earlier been a more important role for Latin American navies. Thus Buenos Aires' willingness to help in Central America represented something of a break with tradition.

Peace Enforcement. More difficult, of course, has been the question of the evolution of "peacekeeping" in recent years to include actions more in the line of peace enforcement. That is, increasingly one speaks of *imposing* the international community's will rather than merely moving when the agreement of all the parties to a dispute has been obtained. In this context, several Latin American countries have shown considerable reticence about the evolution of these operations. Brazil, Chile and Mexico were especially critical of the trend.

More recently, only the latter has steadfastly opposed the issue while the other two have been converted to the idea that a "case by case" approach to the phenomenon is the best way to proceed. Mexico, on the other hand, feels strongly that the whole drift of intervention in matters which do not really threaten international peace, and which instead are really interference in the domestic affairs of other states, is wrong-headed and should cease. Moreover, Mexico City feels a United States agenda is in play.[13]

Despite these difficulties, other Latin American countries have come to the fore in the current era with offers of assistance to the international community's peace enforcement efforts. And while most of these have still been largely-army dominated, navies (and indeed air forces) have seen their role increase steadily. The Uruguayan Navy assisted in the Cambodia operation despite its highly intrusive nature. Venezuela offered naval support for the blockade of Haiti during the military dictatorship. Argentina has moved to increase its naval support of peacekeeping and its ability to do so through closer connections with NATO.[14] For example, it has sent naval medical officers to El Salvador in that very intrusive operation and has taken a leading role in the development of peacekeeping thinking not only at the UN but also at the OAS in recent years.[15] A major reason for its interest in NATO has been to render the fleet interoperable with the navies of that alliance in order to have it operate more easily with those forces when called upon to do so.

In peacekeeping and peace enforcement, there is scope for cooperation among the navies of the hemisphere. It is difficult to be certain how fast progress will be with peacekeeping in the western hemisphere, because of the nature of the OAS, the history of peacekeeping in the Americas, and the continuing doubts of a number of countries about where all this is leading. There is more potential for such naval collaboration outside the Americas.

Some navies, such as the Canadian and Argentinian, already have a great deal of experience with these fields. Others have begun more recently to obtain some. The USN is in the special situation of having often provided considerable logistic and other support for peacekeeping operations while on several occasions being the lead element in peace enforcement activities. There is much to be shared here in the area of training just as there is much potential for better collaboration on operations.

Search and Rescue. Search and rescue operations are often conducted by the navies of the Americas already. And while some bilateral and even multilateral accords are in place, most activity takes place in a rather *ad hoc* fashion. This is of course quite normal, but there is surely room, in the increasingly interconnected environment in which commerce, tourism and many other activities take place, for more collaboration here.

Air forces have already taken the lead here. The System of Cooperation among American Air Forces (SICOFAA) aims primarily at cooperation in the area of search and rescue. While other aeronautical problems common to members are explored within the system, SAR concerns have so far tended to be the single most important sphere of collaboration. Many issues discussed have major maritime dimensions and navies might be able to profit from better connections of this sort.

Zones of Economic Exclusion and Fisheries Protection. A particularly thorny problem in all the Americas is that of fishery protection and zones of economic exclusion. These abound in the hemisphere. Indeed, much of the new law of the sea and related thought has come out of Latin America. Work in this area could pay large dividends as these zones, and the activities in them, constitute one of the hemisphere's main sources of tension.

As opposed to many other parts of the Third World, Latin American countries with zones of exclusion often have navies of some importance.

Indeed, in the absence of police and coast guard capabilities to patrol these zones adequately, navies have had to consider this role as almost exclusively their own. And while naval resources as well have generally proven insufficient for this duty, the need for such patrolling has generated a continuing role for fleets which are in general more designed for maritime defence than for this sort of duty.[16]

In this context, there should be some scope for sub-regional or regional collaboration. This could go some way to reducing tensions. It must, however, be remembered that there are few issues more sensitive in many parts of the Americas than these.

Environmental Protection. Another area of potential for collaboration but also, it must be admitted, for disagreement, is that of the protection of the environment. Latin American countries can be highly sensitive on this subject. Brazil is the best known case because of its deep concern about sustaining its unrestricted sovereignty over the bulk of the Amazon region. But other Amazon countries are not without their strong reactions where international attempts to limit their jurisdiction over their Amazon territories, supposedly only for the best environmental reasons, take place.[17]

Environmental degradation is taking place at an alarming rate throughout much of Latin America. And much of it is related to maritime phenomena although the bulk of the military debate on how to help in this field has been in the army sphere.[18] Navies, with their capacity for sea lift, for reaching isolated areas, for bringing flexible units of equipment and personnel to key areas, may be able to assist a great deal here. Many Latin American countries already have this role as part of their responsibilities. It is difficult to imagine that there is nothing which could be done on a sub-regional or regional level, rather than simply national, in this sphere.[19]

In this context it is perhaps worth mentioning the special problem of the Antarctic region where so many Latin American countries have a stake. Here the ecological balance is of course especially fragile. Navies have already proven their utility for the projection of a state presence in the region. It is also well known that there is a need for international collaboration on any number of points in this continent, and plenty of room for dispute if that cooperation does not continue. Therefore there seems every reason to think that naval collaboration here, in a field of obvious common interest, might bear fruit in a number of ways.

Illegal Immigration. Some years ago the idea that illegal immigration might be considered a security threat would have been considered far-fetched indeed. But today it is rare to have its inclusion in discussions of international security questioned.

The invasion of Haiti in 1994 was in large part a reaction to illegal immigration pressures felt in the United States. Immigration crises over Cuba have been addressed in large part in a military context. Earlier illegal immigration had a large part to play in the Honduras-El Salvador War of 1969.[20] The phenomenon has often had a souring impact on US-Mexican relations, and has potential for more, with security implications often to the fore.[21]

The navies and coast guards of some American nations have already taken part in the control of illegal immigration, either on a long-term or *ad hoc* basis. Cooperation here, while no doubt difficult to agree upon and organize, could help to reduce tensions on the issue as well as improve the efficiency of the job done.

Anti-Narcotics Operations. The "war on drugs" has of course had a maritime dimension for some time. Maritime forces have both operated themselves directly against the "scourge" or have assisted the police to do so. The breadth of the involvement is great. Latin American riverine patrols intercept precursor chemical shipments coming through the Amazon Basin. US radars discover suspicious aircraft and boats for navies and coast guards to intercept in the Caribbean. There is even limited navy-coast guard cooperation in the maritime zones alongside the US-Mexican border. The list of activities is a long one.

Collaboration in this area is nonetheless fraught with difficulties. There is much disagreement on the key source of the problem, especially in its security dimension, between countries which are often, if improperly, divided into three types: consumers, producers and countries of transit. The rhetoric of inter-American cooperation has often been only that. The desire to be perceived as doing something about the problem seems often to outstrip the reality of action. Blaming one another often appears much more important than helping one another.

As the Caribbean experience shows, however, naval cooperation can be of use here and is easier to coordinate than army or air force initiatives. The vast resources of the *narcotraficantes* are such that only the best use of national and regional resources can hope to begin to match them. Thus the need for collaboration is clear. But the modalities of that cooperation are often still lost in the generalized misunderstandings on this matter, and the deep tradition of *aprés vous*, afflicting the hemisphere's governments in this field.

Disaster Relief. There has developed in recent years an enormous degree of *ad hoc* assistance in the area of disaster relief. For example, Nicaraguan helicopters have brought assistance to Costa Rica, and Canadian, Venezuelan and US vessels have brought help to stricken island communities in the Caribbean.

There is now increasing discussion of making the measures to be taken more clear and the means to bring assistance less cumbersome and *ad hoc*. Air forces and navies have discussed these points at the Conferences of Commanders of the Americas in recent years. There would seem to be every reason for progress in this era of seemingly increased natural disasters.[22]

Reinforcement for an Inter-American Security System. Many of the above areas of cooperation have enormous potential for the most comprehensive issue which should be of concern to the countries and forces of the hemisphere, i.e., the building of a more secure Americas where confidence among countries is great and risk of misunderstanding slight. Such broad cooperation would allow for the navies of the Americas to become better acquainted, to work together more, and thereby to build confidence in one another.

As elsewhere in the world such security collaboration can bring down barriers and create a fund of good will on which one can draw when problems arise. It can reinforce the already proceeding process of economic and political integration in the hemisphere thus helping to remove the tendency for security forces to lag behind in these wider efforts.

Multinational Naval Cooperation and Latin American Ocean Basins

Latin America is an artificial construct. The area is very diverse with few region-wide common interests. Shared situations include: a legacy of Inter-American military collaboration, region-wide democratization and economic liberalization and increasing complexity and number of military/naval tasks with declining resources. These commonalities do not provide a foundation for common approaches to regional maritime security. Nevertheless, there are multiple opportunities to strengthen multilateral naval cooperation in specific contexts. Appropriate MNCO measures must be tailored to specific bilateral or sub-regional situations. For example, there have been numerous bilateral and sub-regional confidence-building measures.

A recent article documented the array of Argentine-Brazilian CBMs including the naval sphere and advocated counterpart CBMs to further improve Argentine-Chilean relations. Current and potential CBMs, it was recognized, build a strong base for MNCOs.[23] Just as CBMs can prepare a framework of cooperation to support MNCOs, so too ongoing cooperation in one ocean basin can influence events positively in an adjacent ocean basin as these examples demonstrate. Unfortunately, the paucity of cooperative naval relationships in each of these two oceans (the South Atlantic and the South Pacific) in previous decades all too often had a negative impact on the other.

Changing Perceptions of the Role of Seapower in Maritime Security

A widely shared conviction is that naval planning must be approached in terms of direct national interests within national ocean zones and adjacent ocean basins. This view is more evident among Latin American states bordering the South Atlantic and South Pacific ocean basins than those along the littoral of the Caribbean basin. The former group of South American countries are generally fairly large states with substantial navies facing open seas, while the latter countries in and around the Caribbean are mostly small mainland and island-states facing an enclosed sea with small navies or coast guards with limited maritime interests. Another relevant contrast between these two areas is the decline of US military presence in South America while it remains substantial in and around the Caribbean basin.

Traditional military missions continue to orient the larger regional navies. The traditional national interest approach is nonetheless complicated by the increasing impact of trans-national forces and developments. New issues on the security agenda (i.e., maritime drug interdiction, migration by sea, maritime pollution, fisheries enforcement, piracy/terrorism) require ongoing collaboration. However, regional countries differ markedly regarding the appropriate kinds and extent of multilateral naval cooperation.

Complex security challenges pose a need for naval modernization. Modernization of the armed forces, including the navies, in nearly all regional states has been deferred over the last decade for reasons of economic austerity. As economic recovery proceeds, pressures are building for new equipment to meet the new security issues mentioned above, as well as for traditional defence missions. When fleet replacement eventually occurs, possible destabilizing effects between countries should be managed within more cooperative frameworks. This will pose new challenges for civil-military relationships in the already fragile democracies.

Currently, a "relatively benign" security environment exists in Latin America. Interpretations of the causes of this environment and the resulting need for multilateral naval cooperation differ. (A case in point is the sharply contrasting enthusiastic Argentine and negative Mexican views on peacekeeping.) Two opinions condition views about the desirability and need for specific multinational naval cooperative measures.

The first opinion is that regional countries nurtured the current benign security environment, therefore a laissez-faire or ad hoc security approach would generally suffice. For example, long-standing restraint in military spending has occurred without any treaties or specific agreements. A corollary to this opinion is that economic integration and progress are the driving forces strengthening regional security—as the region prospers, stability will be reinforced and greater opportunities for multilateral security collaboration will occur.

The second opinion is that at present there are complex, pressing security challenges which require an active agenda of multinational naval cooperative measures. Here, while economic integration and progress are acknowledged to be long-term solutions to regional stability, in the short and medium-term security challenges can undermine development. Cooperation in security and economic issues must increasingly work in tandem.

The US hedges between these two views. While the US continues to promote regional stability in Latin America under US leadership; (Latin Americans perceive this as an embedded hegemonic claim); it tries to limit its regional military interests and involvement when unduly costly or not in its direct national interest. This dichotomy in US policy complicates the current US-Latin American relationship. Latin Americans may perceive the United States as pursuing unilateral interests or legitimizing US preferences when promoting cooperation in hemispheric security issues. Troubled US efforts to coordinate hemispheric drug interdiction illustrate these policy dilemmas.

A related dilemma is that successful multinational naval cooperation may require US participation but may be difficult to dovetail with Latin American interests. Interest in collaboration with the United States exists, but it varies with each nation's individual interests and by ocean basin.

Ocean basins constitute an appropriate focus for examining naval strategy in Latin America. There are three relevant ocean basins: the South Atlantic, the South Pacific and the Caribbean Basin. Each region will be discussed individually below.

South Atlantic

Significant results have been achieved in South Atlantic collaboration and prospects for greater collaboration are good. These include:

* South African incorporation into an expanding web of naval collaboration including naval exercises;
* A series of Anglo-Argentine collaborative measures to manage the Malvinas/Falklands problem; and
* Important developments complementary to naval collaboration including the MERCOSUR common market pact and ongoing collaboration between Southern Cone armed forces within the demilitarized Antarctic Treaty system.

While South American littoral states are concerned with ocean basin stability, national visions differ considerably. Brazil championed the United Nations Resolution on a Zone of Peace and Co-operation in the South Atlantic (ZPCSA), but there has been a lack of regional and extra-regional consensus about its specific military and naval implications. The Argentine approach to South Atlantic collaboration is at once more informal and global in orientation. This global vision has been particularly evident in Argentinean involvement in out-of-area peacekeeping.

While important conflict resolution measures have been applied successfully to the Malvinas/Falklands Islands, the underlying dispute over sovereignty remains. In contrast, there have been more comprehensive South American conflict resolution measures which have helped resolve underlying issues and promote accommodation between participating states. The Argentine-Brazilian rapprochement constitutes the most dramatic example. A counterpart Argentine-Chilean accommodation has included a treaty delimiting land and sea boundaries in the far south, subsequent land-based boundary delimitations, CBMs and joint projects. This raises the question of how comprehensive international collaboration must be to ensure success.

Views differ regarding the permissible extent of national jurisdiction within the Exclusive Economic Zone (EEZ) and beyond into adjacent high seas. The large South American states have tended to territorialize offshore zones, while the maritime powers have viewed national rights therein restrictively. For example, Brazil protested over recent war games conducted by US warships within its national EEZ. While views continue to differ, the impact of contrasting interests has been contained by all parties. The challenge is to reinforce moderation and cooperation on all sides. MNCOs are oriented toward this end, but jointly managed and/or enforced EEZs and adjacent high seas areas do not appear at this time to be politically feasible.

South Pacific

West coast South American maritime collaboration has been limited to fisheries and law of the sea. However, shared concern with resources and their protection in the Pacific has not generated joint enforcement measures. National approaches to South Pacific collaboration vary considerably. For example, Chile's approach is distinctive.

While the Pacific Basin is regarded as representing the future of Chile, this has been driven by economic need without attendant collaborative security measures. Chile is committed to responsible management of adjacent high seas areas which is expressed in part through the *Mar Presencial* (a sizable maritime triangle of national interest extending westwards from the coast to Easter Island and then southeastwards to Antarctica). By proclaiming a vast offshore area of national interest, Chileans hope to mobilize national interest in the sea to encourage public support for future ocean development.

Here as elsewhere the US and many other developed countries are concerned with "creeping jurisdiction" within the EEZ and jurisdictional extension beyond it. Regional measures triggering such concerns include Chile's *Mar Presencial*.

During the Cold War, Chile did try and enlist the support of the United States and some others to help protect the southern passages and adjacent offshore areas from Soviet incursions. Obstacles to collaboration at the time included US reluctance to be closely associated in security matters with the Chilean military government.[24] The post-Cold War context does benefit from the decline of the East-West confrontation and Chile is now democratic. Contrasting US-Chilean views on offshore rights and obligations nonetheless continue to constrain collaboration.

The 1995 United Nations Convention on Straddling Fish Stocks and Highly Migratory Fish Stocks may provide for an institutional framework for regional cooperation in the controversial high seas issue. Regional states view this as a useful precedent for addressing more effective international management of the high seas.

South Pacific and South Atlantic security issues often converge. As mentioned in the South Atlantic section, Argentina and Chile have overlapping Antarctic claims, but have pursued significant collaborations within the demilitarized Antarctic treaty framework including between their armed forces. More broadly, Argentina and Chile have implemented a series of far-reaching collaborative measures including stabilization of the strategically-located land and sea areas at the tip of the continent. Chile's June 1996 association with MERCOSUR reinforces South American economic integration with implications for military cooperation.

A recent arms sales case likewise illustrated the overlap, if in this instance potentially negative, between South Pacific and South Atlantic security issues. In April 1997, the United States lifted a 20-year ban on the sale of sophisticated weapons to Latin America by authorizing a potential sale of fighter jets to Chile. While the Chilean air force regards this acquisition as needed to modernize the country's aging fleet, Argentina has expressed its concern about a potential regional arms race. Chile, for its part, has been influenced by Peru's recent purchase of Russian fighter jets.

A critical issue in the South Pacific is the management of the Ecuadorian-Peruvian boundary dispute. During the 1995 conflict, naval deterrence was pivotal in preventing escalation. Although a cease fire was negotiated through international diplomatic efforts, it did not resolve the basic boundary difference. Similarly, CBMs between Ecuador and Peru, which pre-dated the conflict, did not address this difference.

Boundary disputes are a potential source of instability here and elsewhere in Latin America. Current unresolved boundary disputes include Malvinas/Falklands, Guyana/Venezuela, Belize/Guatemala, El Salvador/Honduras, Nicaragua/Colombia and Colombia/Venezuela. As in the Ecuadorian-Peruvian case, CBMs which don't address basic problems can have a negative impact, and even when properly conceived they must be appropriately implemented at various levels. The CBMs between Chile and Peru are another case in point.

Caribbean Basin

Maritime security problems vary considerably from the islands to the mainland, but the entire area is increasingly interdependent with North America. This growing interdependence increases the need for multinational naval cooperation, but considerable obstacles remain.[25]

Drug traffic and illegal migration have spurred increasing US interest in Caribbean basin stability. Throughout the Caribbean basin, the United States has been promoting multilateral approaches to unregulated migration and interdiction of narcotics traffic. There are even implicit Cuban-American

CBMs, including the mutually-agreed-upon rules of behaviour for the naval base at Guantanamo Bay and the recent bilateral migration accord.

There is a divergence of views on whether Cuba, drug interdiction and illegal migration are solely US or regional problems. Latin Americans generally prefer to leave such intractable problems to the United States but object if US unilateral solutions are imposed. Multilateral approaches offer an alternative to the present impasse.

Haiti in fact represents an attempt to respond multilaterally to interlocking problems of drug traffic, illegal migration and political instability. However, the United States only turned to multinational cooperation after unilateral pressures had failed and a unilateral military intervention became necessary.

In Panama, there has been a legacy of unilateral US and bilateral US-Panamanian approaches to security including the Panama Canal. For example, the United States intervened militarily in the country in 1989, and subsequently both countries were to cooperate in reforming and preparing Panamanian defence forces for complete US military withdrawal by the end of the century as specified in the bilateral 1977 Panama Canal treaties. Since late 1995 bilateral talks as well as political debates have been exploring the possibility of retaining some sort of American military presence after the turnover of control of the Panama Canal in the year 2,000. While multinational naval cooperation might help protect approaches to the Canal as well as the Canal itself, prospects remain limited due to the legacy of unilateralism and bilateralism.

US-Mexican military and paramilitary collaboration has been increasing on both the Pacific and Gulf coasts. In spite of increasingly closer US-Mexican economic, military and political relations, Mexico regards peacekeeping involvement as incompatible with their non-intervention doctrine and therefore does not consider this an appropriate collaborative measure.

Even where sub-regional cooperation exists, strengthening of ties is problematical. The Regional Security System (RSS) of Commonwealth Caribbean islands includes multi-tasked coast guard collaboration, but resource constraints are adversely effecting off-shore police activities of all the islands. While the United States has been scaling back aid and preferential trade commitments to the Caribbean, the area has been re-emerging as a favourite transit route for drug traffickers. Additionally, many maritime boundaries remain unresolved because of overlapping EEZ claims.

Conclusions: Guidelines for Successful Multinational Naval Cooperation

There are mixed prospects for multinational naval cooperation in Latin America which vary by MNCO category and from country to country and ocean basin to ocean basin. There are some important instances of MNCOs, but too often they coexist and compete with unilateral and bilateral measures as well as US-driven multilateral cooperation. Mistrust and bilateral problems continue. Table 1 synthesizes these relationships in indicating prospects for MNCOs by category and ocean basin.

Some guidelines for successful regional multinational naval cooperation are evident:

- US-instigated and directed multinational naval cooperation will not be supported unless they directly support Latin American national interests.
- MNCOs which grow out of specific Latin American interests and practice have better prospects of success.
- Successful MNCOs may still frequently require US support, such as logistics or planning support.
- Relatively modest naval operations tailored to specific circumstances have good prospects for success (i.e., search and rescue and disaster relief as well as MNCOs for illegal immigration and anti-narcotics operations, if targeted, as along the southern border of the USA); more ambitious ones do not.
- Broad diplomatic rapprochements between neighbors including CBMs strengthen prospects for MNCOs. Similarly, carefully crafted CBMs and MNCOs in one ocean basin can complement those in an adjacent ocean basin.
- There will be some possibilities for peace-enforcement multinational naval cooperation within the region but more opportunity for peacekeeping missions. Some South American countries have participated in these kinds of operations within and beyond the region, and are likely to remain active. In contrast, capabilities of Caribbean states to participate will generally remain limited, although there will likely be occasions for them to benefit from MNCOs.
- MNCOs are not likely, at least in the short term, in especially politically sensitive categories (i.e., zones of economic exclusion and fisheries and reinforcement for an inter-American security system). Environmental protection is a similar politically sensitive issue, but

is deemed critical for the many Caribbean basin states often in close proximity to one another. Hence, Caribbean MNCOs in this area are regarded as more likely than elsewhere in Latin America.

- Continuing progress in Latin American economic and political development will help generate and sustain effective MNCOs which can complement this development but must ultimately depend on resolution of larger problems.
- As North America continues to integrate economically, there are increasing pulls towards greater military and political coordination including MNCOs which would include some Caribbean basin states, as well as Canada, US and Mexico as coalition partners.
- The increasing interdependence of numerous Caribbean basin states with North America reinforces the need for multinational naval cooperation. US participation will generally need to be substantial, but even small contributions by a number of Caribbean basin states can be useful. A case in point is maritime drug interdiction. Because of the generally small size of the military establishments (or constabulary forces) of most Caribbean basin states, their contribution to peace enforcement will be very limited.
- MNCOs in South America will be influenced by the nature of economic development and integration in the hemisphere. It is uncertain how far NAFTA or MERCOSUR will be extended or overlap. Either South America will become progressively integrated with the hemisphere politically, militarily, as well as economically or the subregion will become increasingly autonomous from North America. Planning and implementation of MNCOs will be affected accordingly.
- The generally sizable South American countries and armed forces have lent importance to bilateral cooperative measures, which have not required US participation for success. Counterpart multilateral measures have often only involved a few countries. An existing network of cooperative measures among small groups of South American countries can provide a strong base for wider participation in multilateral measures including MNCOs. South American participation in both peacekeeping and peace enforcement demonstrates their potential contribution to MNCOs.

Table 13.1 Prospects for Latin American MNCOs

	Ocean Basin		
	Caribbean basin	South Atlantic	South Pacific
MNCO Categories			
Peacekeeping (in region and out-of-region)	X	X	X
Peace Enforcement (in region and out-of- region)	X	X	X
Search and Rescue	X	X	X
Zones of Economic Exclusion and Fisheries Protection	O	O	O
Environmental Protection	X	O	O
Illegal Immigration	X	O	O
Anti-Narcotics operations	X	O	O
Disaster Relief	X	X	X
Reinforcement for an Inter-American Security System	O	O	O

X = favorable prospects
O = prospects less certain and/or problematic

Notes

1. Robert N. Burr, *By Reason or Force: Chile and the Balance of Power in South America 1830-1910* (Berkeley: University of California Press, 1974).
2. Arthur O. Saldanha da Gama, *A Marinha do Brasil na Primeira Guerra Mundial* (Rio de Janeiro: Capemi, 1982).
3. For the story of this struggle for influence and despatch of military missions, see Frederick Nunn, *Yesterday's Soldiers: European Military Professionalization in South America, 1890-1940* (Lincoln: University of Nebraska Press, 1985); Jürgen Schaefer, *Deutsche Militärhilfe an Südameika: Militär—und Rüstungsinteressen in Argentinien, Bolivien, Chile vor 1914* (Düsseldorf: Bertelsmann

Universitätsverlag, 1974); and H. Klepak, *Military Aspects of French Policy in Spanish America 1871-1914* Unpublished Ph.D. thesis, University of London, 1985.

4. See David Haglund, *Latin America and the Transformation of U.S. Strategic Thought: 1936-1940* (Albuquerque: University of New Mexico Press, 1984).

5. For the Mexican elements of this situation, see Josefina Zoraida Vázquez, *México frente a Estados Unidos: un ensayo histórico 1776-1988* (Mexico: Fondo de Cultura Económica, 1989), 181-190; and Héctor Aguilar Camín and Lorenzo Meyer, *A la Sombra de la revolución mexicana* (Mexico: Cal y arena, 1989), 195-196.

6. See the appropriate national naval sections of Adrian J. English, *Armed Forces of Latin America* (London: Jane's, 1984); and M.A. Morris, *The Expansion of Third World Navies* (London: Macmillan, 1987).

7. Rodolfo Garrie Faget, *Organismos militares interamericanos* (Buenos Aires, Depalma, 1968), 56-57.

8. Hugo Luis Cargnelutti, *Seguridad interamericana ¿Un subsistema del sistema interamericano?* (Buenos Aires: Círculo Militar, 1993), 118-119.

9. See the Argentine chapters of Andrés Fontana, ed., *Argentina-NATO: Perspectives on Global Security* (Buenos Aires: Latinoamericano, 1994); and for Mexico see Sergio Aguayo Quezada and Bruce M. Bagley, eds, *En Busca de la seguridad perdida: aproximaciones a la seguridad nacional mexicana* (Mexico: Siglo XXI, 1990).

10. Margaret Daly Hayes, "Political-Military Relations within International Organizations", Rapporteur's Report, 1996, i.

11. This is repeatedly brought out in a discussion of military expenditures in Latin America provided by Francisco Rojas Aravena, ed., *Gasto militar en América latina: procesos de decisiones y actores claves* (Santiago: FLACSO, 1994).

12. See, for the army, Frederick Nunn, *The Time of the Generals: Latin American Professional Militarism in World Perspective* (Lincoln: University of Nebraska Press, 1992).

13. Juan Manuel Gómez Robledo, "El Debate sobre el uso de la fuerza por parte de las Naciones Unidas", in Olga Pellicer, ed., *Las Naciones unidas hoy: una vision de Mexico* (Mexico: Fondo de Cultura Economica, 1994), 124-149.

14. See the results of the exceptional Argentina-NATO Seminar on Global Security in Fontana, ed., *Argentina-NATO*.

15. See Hernán Patiño Mayer, "Aportes a un nuevo concepto de seguridad hemisférica—seguridad cooperativa", in *Seguridad estratégica regional* IV, September 1993, 84-89.

16. See Michael Morris, "Medidas de confianza en Sudamérica", in Augusto Varas and Isaac Caro, eds, *Medidas de confianza mutua en América Latina* (Santiago, FLACSO, 1994). 101-132, especially 119-124; and the wider- ranging if earlier

study by the same author, this time with Victor Millán, *Controlling Latin American Conflicts: Ten Approaches* (Boulder: Westview, 1986).

17. Magdalena Segre and Héctor E. Bocco, "Brasil: el fin de temporada", in Heraldo Muñoz, ed., *El Desafío de los '90: anuario de políticas exteriores latinoamericanas 1989-1990* (Caracas: Nueva Sociedad, 1990), 30-44, especially 41-43; and in the same volume Fernando Bustamante, "Ecuador: el fin del aislamiento", 163-179, especially 177-178.

18. See, for example, Gabriel Aguilera, ed., *Seguridad, función militar y democracia* (Guatemala: FLACSO, 1994), 28-29.

19. See, for example, "Medidas de confianza mutua en la region", Presentation of the Argentine Navy at the Conference on Confidence-Building Measures, May 1995, from *Seguridad estrategica regional* VIII, October 1995, 86-88.

20. Carlos Lopez Contreras, *Las Negociaciones de paz: mi punto de vista* (Tegucigalpa: Imprenta Lithopress, 1984).

21. Jorge Bustamante, "Mexico-Estados Unidos: migracion indocumentada y seguridad nacional", in Aguayo Quezada and Bagley, eds, *En Busca de la seguridad perdida*, 340-366.

22. Andres Serbin addresses these issues in his edited work, *Medio ambiente, seguridad y cooperacion regional en el Caribe* (Caracas: Nueva Sociedad, 1993).

23. Commander Pedro Luis de la Fuente, "Confidence-Building Measures in the Southern Cone: A Model for Regional Stability", *Naval War College Review* L, Winter 1997, 36-65.

24. Michael A. Morris, *The Strait of Magellan* (The Hague: Martinus Nijhoff, 1989).

25. Michael A. Morris, *Caribbean Maritime Security* (London: Macmillan and New York, St. Martin's Press, 1994).

Leading Marks for the 21st Century - Envoi

JOHN HALSTEAD

Looking at the rich tapestry of multinational naval cooperation, two of the threads that stand out particularly are the twin themes of change and uncertainty. With international affairs, as with the weather, change is the one thing that can be counted on these days, and uncertainty is its handmaiden; they impact every region of the globe. Admiral Sir James Eberle said it best when he remarked that change and uncertainty are the chief features of the 1980s and 1990s.

Old Concepts and New Realities

In Asia, no less than in North America, Europe, the Middle East and Latin America, the end of the Cold War has transformed the security environment. The polarizing effect of the Cold War ideological conflict and its attendant pressures on middle and smaller powers are gone. The superpowers have downscaled their overseas commitments. There is in fact only one superpower with global reach now and the concern is not with dominance by the United States, but with the possibility, if not the probability, that it may reduce its presence abroad still further, and thus tempt others to fill the resulting power vacuum. Indeed there are already signs of a more assertive posture by some of the regional powers, of sharper rivalry among them and of an accompanying arms build-up.

The bipolar ideological conflict has given way to a multipolar pattern of economic competition in which new power centres, particularly in Asia, are challenging the previous pre-eminence of the United States and Europe. Everywhere, centrally-planned economies are being replaced by market-based economies, while national and even multinational production is being replaced by truly global production due to the increased mobility of capital, goods and services. At the same time the explosion of technology has driven the globalization phenomenon, compressing time and space, making national borders porous, and re-shaping national sovereignty. I would rather say this than "fraying the nation state", because I think the nation and the state are

292

seldom co-terminus these days. It is the traditional notion of sovereignty that is being frayed, and the traditional power of governments to control events that is being diminished by non-governmental actors. Interdependence, both of states, and of policy factors is growing by leaps and bounds. Economic integration is proceeding on a regional basis. and the dividing line between foreign and domestic policies is increasingly blurred.

A related theme is the evolution of our definition of security. Forced by circumstances, a broader definition of security needs to be adopted as the "four P's"; population, poverty, pollution and weapons proliferation take on the dimensions of the four horsemen of the apocalypse. As the global gap between rich and poor widens, unconventional security threats arise in the form of terrorism, illicit drug and arms traffic, illegal migration and so on. Clearly the end of the Cold War has not brought peace, and the passing of the bipolar order has not yet produced a new world order. The high risk environment of nuclear confrontation exists no longer, but the relative stability of that era has gone as well. Threats to stability are now multi-faceted, multi-directional, and unpredictable. And because they are unconventional and unpredictable, it is more difficult than ever to provide the right mix of armed forces, or even a convincing rationale for them sometimes.

The New Geopolitics of the 21st Century

These issues play out in different ways in different areas of the globe. Let me suggest that there are in fact two key security regions in the world: what I would call the Euro-Atlantic region, and the Asia-Pacific region, and North America is where these two regions intersect—the bridge between them, or the fulcrum. This is not to downgrade the other regions, particularly the flanks, that have been examined, but only to say that they are likely to influence global security through one or the other of the key areas.

There is no doubt that the centre of economic gravity is shifting towards the Asia-Pacific region, however that is defined. It is also the region of greatest flux in power relationships. The way the principal powers there, including the United States and Russia, and also of course China, manage this adjustment will largely determine the security of this region in the 21st century.

This does not mean that the Euro-Atlantic region is becoming absolutely less important to international stability and security: rather the contrary. If the Asia-Pacific region is in flux, it is in my view all the more important that the Euro-Atlantic region remain stable. In this context NATO has become a key institution. The way it adjusts to the new requirements of collective security in Europe will determine its future role. It is encouraging that cooperation between the WEU and NATO is improving, and that France is participating more closely in NATO affairs. It is also encouraging that NATO is giving the PfP program a successful application in the IFOR and SFOR operations in Bosnia. But I must confess to considerable concern about the long term viability of the Dayton Accord when the parties have given little evidence to date about their serious intention of respecting it once SFOR is withdrawn. I must also emphasize the importance, in my view, of ensuring that the timing and the modalities of NATO expansion be such as to secure the full participation and integration of Russia into a new security regime in Europe.

Implications for Foreign Policy

What about the implications of all this for foreign policy? War was once the normal method of settling international disputes. "War is the continuation of politics by other means", as Clausewitz wrote. International affairs were regarded as a zero-sum game, with winners and losers. Today war has become far more problematic, if for no other reason than we now have nuclear weapons, as well as the invasive power and presence of the media, and the growing influence of public opinion. A more realistic idea is taking hold: that one party's security cannot be purchased at the cost of another party's insecurity. Of course the idea that states should refrain from the threat or use of force in their international dealings is enshrined in the UN Charter, but this is by no means universally respected.

The circumstances of an increasingly interdependent world are beginning to turn Clausewitz's maxim on its head. Foreign policy is becoming the continuation of war by other means. Military force is still essential in the real world, but its purpose is changing. Rather than to fight a war, its primary purpose is moving towards war prevention or containment—that is, deterrence. For this purpose, legitimacy is an important condition for the use of force. Conversely, diplomacy that is not backed by credible force cannot be effective in a situation where the other party or parties are ready to use force.

There are other implications for foreign policy which have been noted in this book. Interdependence is driving multilateral cooperation, which has expanded exponentially in all fields, accompanied by an expansion of international regulation. The Law of the Sea Convention is the most obvious example in the maritime field, where it has transformed relations among coastal states, not always with positive results. It has radically reduced the extent of the high seas, and has encouraged a trend away from freedom of use, to management of the high seas. To cope with this trend the international community will have to pay close attention to institutional arrangements (particularly those under the aegis of the UN), to reliance on emerging marine science and technology, and to changing conditions, such as the prospect of creeping jurisdiction, beyond the 200 nautical mile limit. And there is always the question of who makes these management decisions, and how they are to be enforced.

It is hardly surprising under these circumstances that there are some built-in tensions that are increasingly difficult for foreign policy to resolve. One is the conflicting requirements of the sovereign state— still the basic building block of the international system—and the global village we are living in. Seaborne trade is determined more by international than national considerations now and the notion of seapower ensuring the protection of national trade interests is becoming anachronistic. Yet the protection and regulation of shipping is still largely national. Environmental protection, conservation and management of marine resources can only be ensured by international regulation, but again, who will make the management decisions? This is a particularly difficult problem for the island states, such as those in the South Pacific.

Another inherent tension is between regional and global security arrangements. In circumstances where the United Nations is obviously over-stretched, and doesn't command either the financial or human resources to do everything everywhere, it seems likely that regional security regimes will grow in importance. There are various forms of multilateral arrangements in a number of regions, for example the ASEAN Regional Forum in Asia, the South Pacific Forum Fisheries Agency and the Rio Pact and the OAS in the Americas. But they are all relatively limited and underdeveloped in comparison with the Euro-Atlantic region, where the Organization for Security and Cooperation in Europe is an official regional arrangement under Chapter 8 of the UN Charter, and of course NATO is the only organization in the world with an integrated military command and standing interoperable forces. The need here is for a clearer division of labour, and a better working relationship between these organizations and the United Nations. Here we find different cultures, as was demonstrated in the dual-key arrangement in the former Yugoslavia, which didn't work very well. It takes time to develop mutual understanding and confidence so that NATO can work more effectively with the United Nations, and the United Nations can make more effective use of NATO.

Change and Naval Operations

What are the implications for naval doctrine and practice? If the projection of economic power is no longer dependent on seapower, and if SLOC protection has lost primacy with the end of the Cold War, what can we expect the future role of navies to be? Quite simply what it has always been in one form or another: power projection. Or to put it in terms of the changing relationship between force and politics, the projection of foreign policy.

As deterrence becomes the key to the preservation of peace, and enforcement to its restoration, particularly in an era of growing instability, the power projection potential of navies should come into its own. Indeed I would go so far as to say that the changes we are witnessing in the international system dictate that navies return to their roots as instruments to influence the outcome of events on land. This is in fact in keeping with the progressive blurring of the division between land and sea warfare, and with the new emphasis on *From the Sea* in the British and French as well as the US navies. Power projection. is now needed as never before to deter the unauthorized use of force, and to back up preventive diplomacy, particularly in the early stages of crisis management.

Maritime forces, with their inherent mobility and versatility, their attack and retaliatory capabilities, their organic logistics and their command and information management flexibility offer an extensive range of policy options. They can be deployed first as a symbol of resolve, then to secure control of the sea and finally to intervene on land if necessary. As a symbol of the sovereignty and authority of the home state, they can also give a signal of concern over a potential crisis situation, provide disaster relief, support trade or cultural initiatives, or simply contribute to good relations. Unlike land forces, naval forces do not have to occupy ground to make their presence felt, and unlike air forces, naval forces can remain on station as long as necessary.

In an increasingly multilateral world, this considerable potential can best be realized through multinational cooperation. Even the US Navy, which rules the waves of every ocean now, cannot do everything, everywhere, alone. Those who share the common interest in peace and security should not let it. Navies are well suited to multinational cooperation, and operational cooperation among them is increasing especially where logistic and technological support is shared. Such cooperation should be aimed, as has been mentioned several times in this book, at building confidence, improving communications and preparing for interoperability. In this way, deterrence and confidence-building would become a sort of two-track naval doctrine for the 21st century.

Better prevention than cure, but this is easier said than done. Experience shows that the earlier the call for preventive action, the harder it is to muster the political will. Advance planning for preventive intervention is desirable whenever possible and a concerted effort must be made to bring together suitable political, economic and military measures in an integrated plan of "escalation management". In other words, cooperative exercising of navies is not enough. If navies are really to be the agents of foreign policy projection, the political authorities must also get involved.

In this, as in other aspects of foreign policy, enlightened policy depends upon enlightened public opinion. This must be constantly cultivated, and the themes and issues on navies and foreign policy raised in this book can make a valuable contribution both to public policy and to the public opinion that supports it.

Index